Capitalism
and
Leisure Theory

CAPITALISM AND LEISURE THEORY

Chris Rojek

Tavistock Publications
London and New York

First published in 1985 by
Tavistock Publications Ltd
11 New Fetter Lane, London EC4P 4EE

Published in the USA by
Tavistock Publications
in association with Methuen, Inc.
29 West 35th Street, New York, NY 10001

© 1985 Chris Rojek

Typeset in Great Britain by
Scarborough Typesetting Services
and printed by
Richard Clay (The Chaucer Press) Ltd,
Bungay, Suffolk

British Library Cataloguing in Publication Data
Rojek, Chris
Capitalism and leisure theory. – (Social science
paperback; no. 291)
1. Leisure.   2. Capitalism
I. Title.   II. Series
306'.48   GV15
ISBN 0–422–79060–5
ISBN 0–422–79070–2 Pbk

Library of Congress Cataloging in Publication Data
Rojek, Chris
Capitalism and leisure theory.
Bibliography: p.
Includes index.
1. Leisure – Social aspects.   I. Title
GV14.45.R65   1985   306'.48   85–2869
ISBN 0–422–79060–5
ISBN 0–422–79070–2 (pbk.)

CONTENTS

For Ilya Neustadt
and
Eric Dunning

ACKNOWLEDGEMENTS

There is only one rule to follow in compiling a list of acknowledgements: nothing exceeds like excess. I am grateful to Harvie Ferguson and Eric Dunning for introducing me to some of the ideas developed here, and causing me to produce new ones. Geraldine Peacock talked 'about Libya' with me and helped with the index. Stewart Collins helped 'not to lose sight of this one'. My 'sociological imagination' has benefited immeasurably from the bark (but not the bite) of Ilya Neustadt. The Research and Staff Development unit of The Queen's College, Glasgow, gave me every support and encouragement. Finally, I want to thank Gug, who is, and Dup, who is no more.

INTRODUCTION: LEISURE WITHOUT SOCIETY?

The main proposition of this book is that the sociology of leisure has, to date, been marooned on a narrow reef of theoretical interests. Our thoughts seem to career between two extremes. On one side they pursue the grand ambition of formulating a general theory of leisure. On the other, they are dispersed in numerous microscopic and somewhat inconclusive inquiries into leisure and its 'associated variables'.[1] In both cases forms of theory have grown up which may be described as 'self-referential'. Their object of inquiry is the history and nature of contemporary leisure relations. Their aim is to describe leisure in all of its various forms, and to ascertain its definitive characteristics. Leisure patterns are delineated, and variables like sex, age, race, occupation, status, and class are linked to them.

One is reminded of the torrent of criticism that issued from the Frankfurt Institute for Social Research in the 1950s against the post-war 'pure science of society', the so-called *Realsoziologie* of the positivist tradition. The criticisms were numerous and wide ranging. But they centred on one fundamental point. In the voguish words of the day, *Realsoziologie* was condemned for perpetuating a model of 'sociology without society' (Frankfurt Institute for Social Research 1973: 9). Today, in the sociology of leisure, something similar is warranted. The field is dominated by forms of theory which deal with the extensive critical literature on power, knowledge, signification, interdependency, agency, and the mode of production, by ignoring it. We have, in short, theories of 'leisure without society'.

Leisure and Academic Sociology

This unsatisfactory state of affairs undoubtedly reflects the antecedents of the sociology of leisure as a sub-discipline within academic sociology. According to Parry and Coalter (1982: 222) it emerged as a footnote to the narrowly focused 'plant' sociology of the First World War and inter-war years. For the most part, it was studied as an appendix to questions of workplace productivity and efficiency. The notable exception appears to be in the field of community studies. From the earliest days, writers like Robert Park, Ernest W. Burgess, and Helen and Robert Lynd displayed an interest in exploring life beyond the factory gates (see Park and Burgess 1921; Burgess and Donald 1964; Lynd and Lynd 1929, 1937). The Lynds' discussion of 'backyard culture' and the family barbecue in the social life of 'Middletown' now reads as a precursor of the modern sociology of leisure.

After the Second World War sociologists began to pay more attention to questions of leisure. This was the result of a combination of factors. Chief among them was the rise of the so-called 'affluent societies' in the west. The masses experienced a growth in disposable income and free time which was unparalleled at any point hitherto in the process of industrialization. This applied to all age groups. But it was especially striking among the young. A proliferation of youth subcultures emerged, each espousing a different lifestyle, and each rooted in leisure experience. By the same token, the post-war years experienced an enormous growth in the scale and range of leisure goods and services. By the fifth decade of the century the production and merchandising of leisure commodities had developed into a central dynamic of the capitalist economic system. At the same time, academic sociology underwent a major expansion. One facet of this was a renewed interest in the process of industrialization. Many sociologists argued that the growth of leisure and the levelling of inequality between social strata signalled the dawn of 'the leisure society'.[2] They predicted that the shift from 'work-centred' to 'leisure-centred' life was the 'natural' effect of advanced industrialization. Leisure was studied as an inherently progressive force. It was seen as real evidence of free choice and personal liberty in the western democracies. Much of this work was policy inspired and relied on the survey method to get results. It was also tenaciously a-theoretical. Questions of theory were reduced to general statements about the 'long march of industrial progress' or definitional disputes relating to the nature of leisure. A major paradox in the sociology of leisure was thus established. Writers like Dumazedier (1960), Aron (1962), and Brightbill (1963) became united in regarding leisure as a proper subject for scientific inquiry. Yet their definitions of leisure allowed for latitudes of subjectivism which frustrated their 'scientific' ambitions. For example, it is not easy to see how the following well-known definition propounded by Dumazedier can be used in a *scientific* manner:

> 'Leisure consists of a number of occupations in which the individual may indulge of his own free will – either to rest, to amuse himself, to add to his knowledge or improve his skills disinterestedly or to increase his voluntary participation in the life of the community after discharging his professional, family and social duties.'
>
> (Dumazedier 1960: 527)

This definition is of limited scientific value for at least two reasons. First, it treats leisure as a general property of the social system which can be studied without regard to its precise social context. Second, it refers to vexed concepts in the history of western social thought, such as 'free will', 'disinterestedness', and 'voluntary' action, as if they could be understood and applied in an unproblematic fashion.

The Submerged Tradition in Leisure Theory

I shall argue that the main defects in social formalism, the dominant research tradition in the sociology of leisure, arise from the failure to situate leisure relations in the context of the history and general power structure of capitalist society. Furthermore I shall reassess the antecedents of the sociology of leisure with a view to claiming that the writings of Marx, Durkheim, Weber, and Freud represent a submerged tradition in leisure theory. This is important because these writings do situate leisure relations in a definite historical and structural context. At this point in my argument I shall not attempt to substantiate this claim in detail. This is, after all, the subject matter of the whole of the first part of the book. However, it is necessary to give an outline rationale of what many people will regard to be a controversial point of view.

The main argument against incorporating the work of Marx, Durkheim, Weber, and Freud into the tradition of leisure theory is textual: none of these writers addressed the question of leisure at length in their publications; consequently, their work appears to be of little direct relevance to the sociology of leisure. The apparent consistency in this line of argument is belied by the terms of reference that Marx, Durkheim, Weber, and Freud applied in their social theories. They set out, as Durkheim (1933: 33) puts it, 'primarily to study reality'. What is this if not an *exclusive* venture? When Weber writes of 'the disenchantment of the world', and Freud declares that 'civilization demands the renunciation of instinct', they are presumably referring to processes that cannot be restricted analytically to any section of society such as the world of work, religious belief, or leisure relations. Rather, these processes are located in society as a whole. We cannot think of them in a partial or truncated way without nullifying their original meanings. In addition, these writers were not oblivious to the importance of secularized non-work relations in maintaining and reproducing industrial society. For example, Marx fully appreciated the value of 'disposable time' in personal development, and the significance of 'individual consumption' in capitalist industry. Similarly, Durkheim clearly expressed the recuperative power of leisure in restoring the industrial labourer's energies and in the 'remaking' of collective life. Weber's discussion of lifestyle and rationalization, and Freud's work on repression and social order, are equally pertinent to modern leisure theory. The point to note is that the mere fact that the question of leisure is not systematically examined by these writers is no licence for assuming that their writings have no bearing upon the subject.

Leisure and Multi-Paradigmatic Rivalry

I have alluded to dominant forms of theory in the sociology of leisure and juxtaposed them with a 'submerged' tradition in leisure theory. But it would be an error to suppose that the field of leisure theory is free of ambiguities. The writings of Marx, Durkheim, Weber, and Freud may constitute a submerged tradition in leisure theory, but they have been a seminal influence elsewhere in modern social theory. In particular, Marx's work has been used to generate a variety of important, new approaches in the sociology of culture and industry which have touched upon matters relating to leisure. These contributions will be examined in this book. Connections can also be made between Durkheim's work and social formalism; Freud and post-structuralism; and Weber's thesis of rationalization and Foucault's analysis of power and knowledge. I shall make these connections explicit in the text as and when necessary. The point I wish to emphasize here is that these various approaches are in competition with each other. Indeed, one of the aims of this book is to show that the present condition of leisure theory approximates to a state of multi-paradigmatic rivalry. I mean by this a state in which a number of mutually incompatible theoretical perspectives hold the terrain. This is not inconsistent with my opening remarks that the field is dominated by narrow, self-referential forms of theory. Indeed, what is striking about many of the leading reviews of the state of the sociology of leisure today is the limited precincts of opinion which they represent. For example, neither Roberts (1978) nor Parker (1983) fully conveys the intense paradigmatic rivalry that exists in the field. More specifically, they fail to give adequate coverage to the important theoretical innovations in leisure theory associated with varieties of neo-Marxism, post-structuralism, and figurational sociology.

The problem is no less acute among approaches to leisure which are antithetical to social formalism. For example, it is now almost a ritual among neo-Marxist commentators to rap social formalists on the knuckles for adopting 'functionalist' assumptions and propositions (see Stedman Jones 1977; Rigauer 1981; Hargreaves 1982). But it is by no means the case that contemporary neo-Marxism has transcended functionalist notions. For example, the distribution of leisure resources and opportunities is frequently 'explained' by recourse to the alleged 'needs' of the capitalist state. Similarly, patterns of leisure are often rationalized as a consequence of inequality and the fact of wage labour.

The second part of the book aims to convey the full intensity of multi-paradigmatic rivalry in the field. I shall focus on what I take to be the most important and stimulating approaches to leisure theory, and examine them in critical conjunction with each other. In this way I hope to counter the rather anodyne view that leisure theory is groping towards some ultimate consensus. In many formalist and some (vulgar) Marxist accounts, the impression is conveyed that leisure exists 'out there' in society. All that researchers and theorists need to do is immerse themselves in the richness of leisure forms, and basic, invulnerable truths will emerge. My position in this book rejects such positivist and naïve notions out of hand. In place of them I want to argue that the concept and meaning of leisure occupies contested theoretical space. Writers representing different paradigms disagree fundamentally about what leisure signifies, how it has developed, and why it should be studied. My purpose is to convey fully the sense of working with tangible and emerging paradigmatic contradictions.

Leisure Theory and Scientific Establishments

Central to my overall argument is the thesis that individuals and groups involved in 'scientific' inquiry into leisure comprise a single totality.[3] Within it, a distinctive power hierarchy between competing 'scientific establishments' can be identified. Its precise topography is still in a molten state, for the institutionaliz-ation of 'leisure study' is a relatively recent phenomenon in the development of western social science.[4] Even so, as I have already noted, it is clear enough that the commanding force in the terrain is represented by the formalist tradition. The formalist approach is discussed in Chapter 4 of this book. I do not propose to give a detailed account of its method and theory here. I shall, however, submit that this dominant scientific establishment is disposed to equate 'progress' in leisure study with the attributes that typify its own characteristic forms of practice. It is therefore necessary to note briefly what the essential features of these forms are. My own view is that social formalism looks to natural philosophy and the methods of natural science as exemplary archetypes for theory and practice. Procedurally, it elects to study composites in terms of their consistuent parts. Thus, society is broken down into a series of interconnected elements. Leisure is studied as one of these elements. As regards method, the aim of study is to accumulate 'hard data' on leisure. This is expressed in the relatively high value placed upon quantitative methods (notably the survey method), and the correspondingly low value assigned to interpretive, and especially ethnographic, studies.

I want to make it clear that I am not indulging in a gratuitous attack on social formalism. As it happens, I do believe that its approach to leisure is open to fundamental objections. I shall make them known in Chapter 4. At this point in my argument, however, the putative strengths and weaknesses of social formal-ism are not at issue. Rather, I am concerned to draw attention to the fact that a power hierarchy exists in the sociology of leisure, and that at its head are representatives of social formalism. The point is essential, because I want to contend that the structure and development of leisure theory cannot be satisfactorily understood as dry academic debate on substantive matters. It is not simply that people disagree about the meaning of leisure and its importance as a subject for sociological analysis. The crucial additional fact to bear in mind is that they do so as representatives of competing paradigms. Each of these paradigms exhibits a distinctive pattern of institutional recruitment and integration. And each of them is engaged in a power struggle for hegemony in the field.

This book is intended to be an introduction to theory in the sociology of leisure. Even so, it frequently deals with arguments that are both difficult and involved. The essentially benign intent of most introductions in the field is to aim at simplicity.[5] In so far as this has led to the mistaken idea that the issues involved in leisure theory are intrinsically simple, it has had a negative effect. I have avoided the temptation to oversimplify. Thus, for example, questions of 'being', 'power', and 'methodology', which do not usually figure in introductory texts on leisure, are here addressed directly.

No doubt this partially compromises my claim to have produced an 'introduction' to the field. The book was indeed written in the conviction that the parameters of theory in the sociology of leisure need to be fundamentally revised. To the extent that I have presented a new view of what these parameters are, and also a critical analysis of their limitations, I expect the book to be of interest to the specialist.

Three additional points need to be made in these introductory remarks. First, the use of the term 'capitalism' in the title of this book is designed to emphasize that contemporary leisure relations are produced and reproduced in the context of a historically specific system of power. Capitalism is based on the division of interests, individual competition, and the ideology of acquisition.[6] Throughout the book I shall seek to exploit and develop the proposition that leisure forms both reproduce and undermine these principles. At all events, however, relations of leisure cannot be studied meaningfully in isolation from the power structure of capitalist society.

Second, I make no claim to present a comprehensive survey of the field. Obviously, for reasons of space, it is not possible to give detailed consideration to every approach in social theory which is either directly or indirectly relevant to the sociology of leisure. In this book I have elected to concentrate on *sociological* theories in the *realist* tradition. No attempt has been made to consider theories in the *nominalist* tradition, e.g. phenomenology, symbolic interactionism, and ethnomethodology. By the 'realist tradition', I mean an approach to social study which regards society as irreducible to its constituent parts. I recognize that there are fundamental difficulties with the way in which realist models have formulated the relationship between society and the individual. I shall make my detailed reservations known in the course of examining specific theories in later chapters. However, my general view is that the distinction between the individual and society is invalid, and has been the source of basic errors in sociological analysis. I have no truck with the arguments that society is 'outside' the individual, and that individuals merely fulfil society's will in their thoughts, actions, and feelings. Equally, I cannot take seriously the ideas that individuals are free to act as they please, and that the individual is the ultimate source of reality. Against these polarized views of human behaviour, I want to emphasize the relational aspects of human history and interaction. This means recognizing the dual character of society and human praxis. I agree with Bhaskar's (1979: 43–4) position that 'society is both the ever-present *condition* (material cause) and the continually reproduced *outcome* of human agency. And praxis is both work, that is conscious *production* and (normally unconscious) *reproduction* of the conditions of production, that is society' (his emphasis).[7] I would also want to add that these relations must be considered *processually*, i.e. as occurring in historical time. I should note, parenthetically, that the inclusion of Freud as a 'sociologist' representing the realist tradition is made on the basis of the numerous forays into social theory that occupied him in the later years of his life.[8]

Third, if the field of leisure theory really is beset by multi-paradigmatic rivalry, it is axiomatic that the contrasts between paradigms constitute the basis for conclusions regarding their comparative utility and probity. I decided against devoting a separate chapter to an evaluation of the comparative strengths and weaknesses of the various approaches to leisure theory considered in the book. The question is examined on a chapter-by-chapter basis. Little would be gained by repeating these points in a concluding chapter. However, the final chapter does attempt to set out a position on the essential considerations for an objectively adequate sociological approach to leisure.

PART ONE
LEISURE TODAY AND THE
SUBMERGED TRADITION IN
LEISURE THEORY

1 THE STRUCTURAL CHARACTERISTICS OF MODERN LEISURE PRACTICE

In this chapter I set forth a position on the structural character-istics of modern leisure practice which informs the whole of the remainder of the book. The aim is to provide the historical and structural context for situating the various rival theories of leisure that I shall consider later. The chapter is divided into four sections. In the first section I argue that we need to depart, once and for all, from the convention of associating 'free time' with leisure experience. Indeed I shall submit that the concept of free time has *no* intrinsic meaning. Rather, its meaning always depends on the social context in which it occurs. The case of women and leisure is given as an example of the problems involved in trying to use the concept. In the second section I shall examine the main organizational features of leisure in capitalist society. In the third, I shall consider the importance of a historical dimension in sociological inquiry into leisure practice. Finally, I shall critically evaluate attempts to anchor the sociology of leisure around a single, unified problematic: the problematic of class.

Leisure and Free Time

The saying that work for some is leisure for others is not only a popular truism, it is also a vital analytical insight. In fact, it accounts for the great difficulty that sociologists of leisure have traditionally encountered in trying to define the field. As Van Moorst (1982: 158) notes, the overwhelming majority of socio-logical definitions equate leisure with free time. Thus free-time experience is juxtaposed with time which is functionally obligated in some recognizable sense. Vickerman's definition can serve for illustrative purposes: he obeys the above-mentioned convention by inviting us to 'take leisure time to be roughly equivalent to free time, that time left over after meeting commit-ments to work and such essential human capital maintenance as sleeping, eating and personal hygiene' (Vickerman 1980: 192).

Prima facie, this definition possesses three important virtues: it is precise, it is value free (Vickerman uses not subjective, but apparently 'objective', criteria to distinguish leisure behaviour), and it can be operationalized in research. Vickerman himself uses it to report that:

(1) Between 1950 and 1980 the average working week for UK manual workers declined from between 45 and 50 hours with one or two weeks' annual paid holiday, to between 35 and 40 hours with at least three weeks' annual paid holiday.
(2) Between 1970 and 1977 UK expenditure on leisure rose by 3.6 per cent. Over the same period, expenditure on alcohol went up by 4.3 per cent; on television, radio, and audio equip-ment (the second largest category after alcohol), the increase was 9.5 per cent; and expenditure on sport and recreation went up by 8 per cent. All figures are expressed in real terms.

These findings are far from unique. Using a similar working definition of leisure, Martin and Mason (1982) present a host of detailed statistical correlations in long-term trends in work and leisure which they offer as a guide to public discussion and state policy formation.[1] In particular, they stress the increasing signifi-cance of leisure in the UK economy, and the redistribution of the national time budget away from work to leisure. Thus they report that in 1981 one-third of all UK consumer spending was on 'leisure related' goods and services. In the same year it was esti-mated that work took up 10 per cent of the total of all UK people's time; the time devoted to leisure was three times as great (Martin and Mason 1982: 230, 44).

Trend indicators and social-survey methods play an indispens-able role in social analysis. They produce information about statistical regularities relating to the composition, incidence, and development of social relations which could not be achieved by any other means. In principle, this is not in dispute. What is in dispute is their value as the central plank of theory and policy. Let us consider the enumerated findings in more detail. In particular, I want to focus on their alleged precision, objectivity, and operational research value. To begin with, doubts can be raised about the precision of these findings. The information on the rise in leisure expenditure and the shift in the UK time budget refers to aggregate figures. For example, Martin and Mason (1982: 45) obtain their basic figures on the current UK leisure budget by multiplying the number of hours in a non-leap year (8,760) with the total population of the UK (55.9 million). No convincing attempt is made to relate the distribution of leisure expenditure, or time, to the key variables of capital ownership, occupational status, sex, race, and health. A similar point can be made in respect of the objectivity of the findings. A global picture of leisure which marginalizes the importance of social differences in society is a feeble basis for the development of theory and policy. For example, the finding that the average working week for UK workers declined over the 1950–80 period does not, in itself, support the conclusion that the average amount of leisure time has increased. Thus, Gershuny (1978, 1979) has argued that the contraction of the working week is compatible with the growth in the 'informal economy' (casual labour and the 'black' economy) and the expansion of the 'household production system' (cooking, cleaning, home improvements, etc.).[2] Leisure time is therefore transformed into more work by a dual process. 'Free time' is consumed in paid labour activities in the informal economy as a means of increasing personal income; and as the cost of purchased services rises relative to the declining cost of 'domestic capital goods', domestic labour takes up more time.[3] Gershuny provides evidence that both of these processes have gone hand in hand with the decline in the average working week during the post-war period. My third point relates to the question of operational research value. Findings on leisure trends ultimately depend on how leisure is defined. There are fundamental difficulties here. For example, eating may be defined as an essential item of 'human capital maintenance'; but it is also exploited and developed as a basic leisure activity by at least one major leisure industry: the hotel and catering industry. Similarly, there are insuperable problems involved in applying 'free time' as a coefficient of leisure activity. I want to illustrate these problems by looking more closely at the concept of 'free time'.

THE PROBLEM OF 'FREE TIME': THE CASE OF WOMEN'S LEISURE

One of the recurring themes in this book is that leisure should not be described as free time or freedom, even in metaphorical terms. As Parry and Coalter (1982: 222) point out, there is a good semantic reason for this view. The word *leisure* derives from the Latin word *licere*, meaning to be lawful or to be allowed. This implies that leisure activity is not 'free' but, on the contrary, subject to some form of constraint. The sociological importance of this lies in the following idea: leisure is not free time, but an effect of systems of legitimation.

Since I shall be taking up the theoretical implications of this idea in the final chapter of this book, I shall not attempt to set out a detailed rationale of it here. However, it might be helpful to illustrate the deficiencies of the concept of free time by considering a specific example. I propose to examine the case of leisure patterns among women. I shall follow the precedent typically observed in the field, and distinguish between their available leisure time and leisure space. In respect of both leisure time and space I will argue that women are seriously disadvantaged in comparison with men.

There is no great problem about the calibration of time between the sexes. Sixty minutes for a man is sixty minutes for a woman, a day is a day, a week is a week, a year is a year, etc. But calibration tells us nothing whatsoever about the quality of life experience in leisure time. All of the evidence suggests that women's experience of leisure is significantly different from men's.

Barrett and McIntosh (1982), in their book on the family, show that the adult-life options consecrated for young females in family socialization patterns are hemmed in and curtailed by sexism. Thus, the *sine qua non* of being a fully developed woman in capitalist society is having a family and being a good wife and mother. This is the 'real work' for women. It has devastating effects on the way women relate to men, their future, and their general position on the labour market. As Barrett and McIntosh explain:

> 'For a girl, the need to marry is . . . often the chief thing she looks forward to in the future. It will alter her whole life much

more than it will her husband's life. Realistically, her chances of earning good money are low, and marriage and dependence on a husband to supplement her income offer a better standard of living and more security than she could expect if she was single. So, early in life the girl feels she must regulate her sexual behaviour to serve this goal. The danger of being labelled a slag is the danger of not being taken seriously as a partner.'

(Barrett and McIntosh 1982: 75)

The interest which girls show in make-up, hairstyles, dress, and jewellery is often scorned by their male counterparts as a 'waste of time'. However, viewed in terms of their adult career expectancies it can be interpreted as the essential prerequisite for attracting and keeping 'the right man' (see Griffin *et al.* 1982: 107).

Oakley's (1974a/b) study of housewives with young children provides an insight into the specific constraints that impinge upon women's leisure time in the early years of married life. The most obvious of these relates to domestic management and child-care. The women in Oakley's sample worked on average seventy-seven hours per week on household tasks including shopping and child-care. Moreover, this is only a notional figure since it is much harder to separate non-waged work from leisure than it is to separate waged work from leisure. Oakley suggests that the roles of good wife and mother exert an invasive influence over the spare-time activities of women. For husbands and fathers, leisure time is one of the main pay-offs of regular work. In contrast, for wives and mothers who are involved in household management and child-care, finding time to participate in leisure outside the home is a major preoccupation and popular fantasy.

In their study of leisure behaviour among young, working-class mothers Griffin *et al.* (1982: 111–12) found that the overwhelming majority were habituated, albeit reluctantly, to staying at home. Domiciled leisure, usually in the form of watching television, was almost universally accepted as part of the price to be paid for being a good homemaker. The women in their sample did not have a real notion of 'time off'. They had a self-image of being, at all times of the day, at the beck and call of their spouse and children. The time constraint that women experience in their leisure is fully reflected in the physical space which is allocated to them for leisure. There has not been much research into this matter. But what does exist suggests that if the home is now the major site for leisure experience, it is territory where private space for women is at a premium. As the authors of one study put it, 'characteristically, bathrooms are the only women-only spaces in our society. Male bars or clubs, football matches and the night out with the lads which cannot be interrupted – even the streets to hang around at night – have no female equivalents' (Griffin *et al.* 1982: 104).[4]

The conclusion that derives from these data is as follows. At every stage in the life cycle, the leisure time and space of females is obstructed by constraints that do not intrude so insistently upon the leisure preserves of men. Women's leisure experience is dominated by the consciousness that they are on display as potential life mates or as the 'better halves' of their husbands or boyfriends. This is reflected in the things that they spend their disposable income on, the way they dress, their manner in public, and their conversation. Their consciousness of the need to maintain and reproduce a feminine persona in public is also continuously accentuated by capitalist industry through its representatives in advertising, fashion, and women's magazines.

The case of women reveals the limitations inherent in the concept of free time as the basis for leisure theory and research. The leisure or 'free' time of women is conditioned by their position in a male-dominated society. The housewife can have time off only when her household duties have been satisfactorily fulfilled. Even then, she is subject to the ethos of sexism which supports some female activities and dismisses others. For example, it may be legitimate for women to devote their leisure time to playing bingo, but it is 'unfeminine' to drink excessively in public. Of course, there are always exceptions to the rule. We are referring here to the basic structural characteristics of leisure relations in capitalist society. It is in this general context that statements on the 'free' time of women should be compared, tested, and shredded.

The Organization of Leisure in Modern Capitalism

Throughout this book I shall exploit and develop two minimal methodological positions. First, it is fundamentally wrong to study leisure as an immediately given datum of human experience. Leisure shapes, and is shaped by, history and the interplay of social interests. Second, all views of leisure which devote themselves to uncovering universal laws which enshrine time-less qualities of leisure behaviour must be abandoned. Leisure practice must be thought of in terms of dynamic relations, i.e. relations that change over time.

The stress on process and change can easily lead to the con-clusion that leisure relations are all too dynamic: they can never be pinned down. Accordingly, the purpose of this section is to forestall such a construction by itemizing the deep-rooted histori-cal tendencies which give contemporary leisure relations their specific organizational form. I believe that four key tendencies should be differentiated: privatization, individuation, commer-cialization, and pacification. Let us consider them in turn.

PRIVATIZATION

The home is now the major site of leisure experience in capitalist society. The main catalyst behind this process has been the mass production of cheap home entertainments in the shape of tele-vision, radio, audio, and video equipment. If one looks closely at the design and marketing trends in these entertainment forms, two things rapidly become apparent. First, there has been a persistent tendency to miniaturize the unit size of equipment. Second, and at the same time, there has been a tendency to design units where entertainment functions are combined, e.g. music centres, radio cassette receivers, personal stereo equipment, etc. The microchip has revolutionized the scope available to pro-ducers and designers for accelerating these tendencies. Nowhere is progress more evident than in the case of television. Small, com-pact sets are now widely available. They combine a number of leisure functions. For example, they can be used to: (a) receive commercial and public service broadcasts, (b) process infor-mation via the various teletext systems, (c) play back video-recordings, (d) receive cable transmissions, and (e) act as monitors for computer packages. One corollary of privatization is the increased capital intensity of leisure activity. I shall return to this point when I consider commercialization and leisure.

INDIVIDUATION

Individuation refers to the historical and material processes which demarcate the individual as a specific person who is publicly recognized as separate and distinct from others. Forms of individuation include name, date of birth, nationality, marital status, home address, national insurance number, club membership, and academic qualifications. The groundwork of the individuated personality is laid in the socialization process which begins in the family and the school. The registration of birth, christening, school registers, and school reports are, *inter alia*, devices for differentiating individuals and 'distilling' their essence in standardized systems of retrievable information. Turner (1983: 163) has commented on the double-edged character of individuation. 'By making people different and separate,' he writes, 'it makes them more subject to control.' How is individuation expressed in modern leisure relations? Two related points need to be made. First, the specialization and differentiation of persons find a corresponding reference point in the specialization and differentiation of leisure pursuits. The institutionalization of leisure, in the shape of members' rules, newsletters, festivals, and competitions, has extended the power of discipline throughout leisure activities. The individual pays homage to the obligations of his chosen leisure enthusiasm almost as a condition of participation. This is obvious where the voluntary consent of the individual is given to the rules of a particular sport or leisure association. But some authors argue that even in privatized forms of leisure, such as TV watching, the choices that an individual may exercise are very few. For example, Adorno submits that,

> 'We are all familiar with the division of television content into various classes, such as light comedy, westerns, mysteries, so-called sophisticated plays and others. These types have been developed into formulas which, to a certain degree, pre-establish the attitudinal pattern of the spectator before he is confronted with any specific content and which largely determine the way in which any specific content is being perceived.'
> (Adorno 1954: 226)

For Adorno, the individuation of content, which is represented in the enumerated classes of programmes, exploits and develops the individuated attitudes and inclinations of the viewers. In 'the totally administered society', the production and scheduling of broadcasts is calculated to achieve a planned response. Perhaps Adorno exaggerates the passivity of viewers. Even so, his work does highlight an important point about individuation and leisure: the leisure industry can manipulate people's emotions even in contexts where they feel most free, e.g. the home.

This leads on to the second point. The leisure industry encourages and reinforces the narcissism of the individuated identity. Mass-produced leisure commodities are presented to the individual as unique and exciting accessories of personal lifestyle. For example, Chambers (1983) has investigated some of the marketing ploys of the luxury motor-bike industry. The motor bike, she argues, is advertised and sold as a personalized, symbolic expression of the 'transcendental woman'. Bikes are, for example, 'long legged and easy to live with' (Moto Guzzi); 'full of mounting excitement' (Kawasaki); and a pure 'thoroughbred/racebred' (Honda). From a Marxist standpoint, the individuation of commodities penetrates to the heart of alienation in capitalist society. Thus our consumption of commodities has the effect of separating and differentiating us further as individuals; this masks shared life conditions, and also marginalizes the whole question of how these conditions are materially produced and reproduced.

COMMERCIALIZATION

Leisure is increasingly run on business lines. Roberts (1978: 20) argues that the top five leisure pursuits in Britain today are television, alcohol, sex, tobacco, and gambling. These are not only pursuits that engage people's faculties and energies; they are also multimillion-pound industries which are organized to produce a continuous profit for the social interests who own and control them.

The leisure industry consists of the conglomerate of business units which aim to produce and reproduce consumer demand for leisure goods and services. Its branches include tourism, catering, sport, outdoor recreations, and the huge area of mass communications, including pop music, video, television, radio, magazines, and books. The leisure industry seeks to organize leisure activities on strict market principles, i.e. in pursuit of the accumulation of profit rather than the satisfaction of social need.

PACIFICATION

Modern capitalist society is based on the complex division of labour. This is associated with distinctive forms of power bonding and social integration. It would be wrong to say that we live in 'unexciting societies'. The revolutionary breakthroughs made in science, industry, and communications bring with them new opportunities for excitement and pleasure in work and leisure relations. However, they also presuppose degrees of administration and surveillance which make our experience of excitement and pleasure qualitatively different from the experience of people who lived in societies where the division of labour was less complex. Elias and Dunning describe the deep change which has occurred in the emotional drives and bonds of people in the advanced industrial societies as a decline in 'the spontaneous, elementary and unreflected type of excitement, in joy as in sorrow, in love as in hatred. The extremes of powerful and passionate outbursts have been dampened by built-in restraints maintained by social controls, which, in part, are built-in so deeply, that they cannot be shaken off' (1969: 60). In short, a comprehensive pacification of violent emotions has occurred.

Elias (1978a, 1982a) explores this idea more fully in his theory of 'the civilizing process'. This is considered in detail in Chapter 7 of this book (especially pp. 166–69). At this point, it is enough to state that the civilizing process refers to long-term changes in the social organization of deep emotions. Standards of restraint and thresholds of repugnance at the public display of naked physical aggression have risen. Similarly, in private life, most people feel embarrassed and self-conscious if their emotions get the better of them. The dominant inclination is not to express intense emotions but to keep them imprisoned in the garrison of the self.

Few theories in modern sociology have been so widely misunderstood as Elias's theory of the civilizing process. The theory does *not* argue that intense and violent emotions have disappeared from society. What it does submit is that, in adult life, the face of physical aggression has become more calculating and discreet. As regards leisure practice, Elias and his followers have used the theory to make two related propositions. First, they argue that in a long time-scale of over half a millennium a clear, demonstrable tendency can be discerned for leisure forms to become less violent. For example, Dunning and Sheard's (1979) study of the development of rugby football shows that the institutionalization and professionalization of the game correlate with a marked reduction in aggressive outbursts. Second, they suggest that in the relatively pacified societies of today, certain leisure forms may perpetuate mock violence and so, in a relatively peaceful and controlled way, arouse the intense emotions in human beings that are necessary for vitality. I shall return to both of these propositions and consider them in more detail in Chapter 7.

Historicizing Leisure

In this section I shall attempt to substantiate my thesis that privatization, individuation, commercialization, and pacification have attained levels of development which are historically specific to modern leisure practice. I propose to do this by examining the influence of industrialization on the transformation of time consciousness and leisure relations. I shall use this discussion to move on to an examination of the characteristic mass leisure form of the Middle Ages: carnival. However, before I turn to these substantive matters, I want to consider the general value of a historical perspective in leisure study.

THE HISTORICAL DIMENSION: THE PROBLEM OF PERIODIZATION

A historical perspective in leisure study is the best defence against imagining that leisure relations are either unique to a specific period or common to all times. It enables us to see more clearly that modern leisure relations are the emerging outer rim of long-term waves of development. These historical processes are neither homologous nor unilinear. They consist of numerous criss-cross movements in continuous and discontinuous directions. Even so, viewed over a time-scale of centuries, certain trend-maintaining tendencies in leisure practice are evident. The previous section discussed four key trends in leisure relations. They show that the leisure practice that we take as 'normal' or 'natural' is, in fact, historically produced and reproduced. This insight is indispensable, for it immediately directs attention to the social interests which shape long-term patterns of development.

All the same, the use of a historical perspective in the sociology of leisure poses an obvious problem. What time-scale should we use in our work? There is no Ark of the Covenant that can be mechanically unlocked to determine what the right time-scale for study is or ought to be. This is important for, methodologically speaking, any insight that we gain from adopting a historical perspective is only meaningful in relation to the historical register that we select against which to compare our behaviour. For example, popular assumptions that there was an olden time when everyone was more polite, when youth was less disaffected, and when leisure was more fun, are not necessarily borne out when put to the test. In fact, as Pearson (1983) demonstrates in his study of hooliganism and respectable fears, such assumptions are rarely corroborated by historical evidence. By the same token, the adoption of an abbreviated timescale can seriously distort comparative historical analysis. For example, if we compare the holiday time available for working people today with that available in 1950, we find that it has increased substantially. But if we refer to English medieval records we discover a working year of forty-four weeks with Sundays off.[5] This suggests that, viewed over a long time-scale, the pattern of holiday time does not present a picture of continuous growth.

Most excursions into the field have adopted the period of industrialization as the central time-unit for study (see Burns 1973; Malcolmson 1973; Cunningham 1980; Roberts 1981). There are indeed good reasons for regarding industrialization as crucially important. In the words of Marx and Engels, the rise of industrial capitalism produced:

'constant revolutionizing of production, uninterrupted disturbance of all social conditions, everlasting uncertainty and agitation. . . . All fixed, fast frozen relations with their train of ancient and venerable prejudices and opinions, are swept away, all new-formed ones become antiquated before they can ossify. All that is solid melts into air, all that is holy is profaned.'

(Marx and Engels 1968: 38)

Later, I shall argue that there are problems with a consistent application of this apocalyptic view of industrialization to the development of leisure. Before reaching that point, however, I want to discuss one of the most imaginative neo-Marxist attempts to assess the impact of industrialization on leisure practice: E. P. Thompson's (1967) consideration of time, work discipline, and the rise of industrial capitalism.

INDUSTRIALIZATION AND TIME CONSCIOUSNESS:
THOMPSON'S VIEW

For Thompson, time in pre-industrial society was 'task oriented',
i.e. it was gauged practically in relation to people's personal
experience of habitual work and domestic chores. Activities
would be reckoned out by measures such as how long it took to
boil a quantity of rice, or prepare breakfast, or mend a broken
wheel. Work and free time were not sharply differentiated. Time
was not experienced as an external constraint, which is somehow
'outside' the self, and which structures life in a fixed and inflexible way.

All of this changes with industrialization. The factory system
imposes a system of labour discipline which is based on the regi-
mentation of time. Time-sheets, time-keepers, clocking-in and
-out times, piece-work, overtime, bonus systems for beating the
clock – these are some of the institutional expressions of this
process. Workers begin to formulate a distinction between their
time and the employer's time. A universal principle is gradually
established: 'The master's right in the master's time and the
workman's right in his own time.'[6] This becomes an important
consideration in collective bargaining. For the entrepreneur,
time is money; it is a prime management resource to be manipulated and used. For the labourer, a working day lost is a day's pay
lost. Thus, time is gradually commodified. People think of time in
terms of opportunity cost. They consider what they will lose in
wasted opportunities by using their time in one way rather than
another. The standard of comparison in deciding between opportunities is money. In this way capitalism enters into the very
units that people use to measure out their lives.

Three important caveats need to be added to Thompson's
position. First, it would be an error to suppose that time discipline was created by industrialization. Most people in pre-
industrial society worked on the land. They were well aware of
the distinction between work and time off. But the pace of their
lives obeyed time-honoured and seasonal rhythms instead of the
rational time discipline of the working week. They worked hard
when the requirements of domestic life, community life, cultivation, and transhumance made it necessary. Otherwise their
attitude to work was flexible and relaxed. Theirs was emphatically not a 'golden age of labour' (see Clayre 1974: 152–57).
Second, the connection between time and money was well

understood in pre-industrial societies. As Ariès (1981: 173–96) shows, prayers for the dead and endowment masses after burial were tied to the cash nexus. The rich and powerful were not guaranteed a place in heaven, but their pious and charitable donations were signs of 'elective affinity' in this world which the poor could not match.[7] Third, it would be wrong to infer that industrialization effected a slash-and-burn clearance of all pre-industrial conventions and values. In their work on the history of leisure, Stedman Jones (1977) and Walton and Walvin (1983) emphasize the continuities in leisure practice that bridged the industrial divide. Nevertheless, it is certainly true that the idea of a normal working day which is bordered by ritualized clocking-in and -out times, and punctuated by agreed breaks and time off, becomes a universally established feature of occupational careers only with the rise of industrial capitalism. All 'continuity' in leisure activities is shaped by this fundamental fact.

Some writers have seized upon leisure as the child of industrialization. Thus, Dumazedier (1974: 14–16) insists that the idea of leisure did not exist in pre-industrial society. What did exist was a complex tangle of amorphous and ritualized non-work relations, which he describes as 'idle time'. There are problems with this designation, both in itself and as a basis for a general theory of leisure. In the first place, the work pattern of the medieval labourer may not have been framed by rigid work/leisure time-tables. But it did include a clear distinction between forced labour for the manorial lord, community labour, and holiday time. Similarly, leisure played an important part in the stratification and power system of medieval life. Luxuries of dress and the cultivation of leisurely habits of life were important to the rich, putting a distance between them and the poor who had to labour for a living. As Huizinga (1924: 38) puts it, in the Middle Ages, 'without leisure or wealth one does not succeed in giving life an epic or idyllic quality'. The concept of 'idle time' cannot easily encompass the effort, planning, and discipline which the 'leisured class' devoted to the ostentatious displays of finery, pomp, and unproductive knowledge which characterized their leisure. There is also the significance of carnival to be considered.

CARNIVAL IN THE MIDDLE AGES

Carnival was emphatically celebrated as non-work time by most people, and seemed highly valued precisely as a release from work. In today's community life there is no parallel to the spectacle and meaning of the medieval carnival. Bakhtin (1968) writes of carnival as a period of unrestrained merry-making in the lives of ordinary people. Work was suspended. The hierarchy of the 'official order' was overturned. The lowly mocked the high, and the high poked fun at the lowly. This was the people's 'second life' where, for days on end, jesting, drollery, and pleasure-seeking dominated social relations. The carnival brought people of all ranks and from all walks of life together to share in its 'universal spirit'.

The carnival tradition embodied a sense of immediacy, distracted sensuality, grotesque exaggeration, and colourful clowning that we might find infantile and naïve. Indeed, it is tempting to think of people who lived at this time as little versions of ourselves. Their pastimes seem childish, and what excites them seems simple and backward. Our greater sophistication, it might be said, is the most convincing explanation of why their behaviour seems so crude and infantile.

But that would be to misunderstand the place of leisure in the social and economic structure of medieval life. The lewdness and vulgarity of carnival were directly related to the low degree of control that people had over natural forces and their own emotions. People were openly interdependent upon each other for their bodily sustenance, well-being, recreation, safety, and pleasure. We can imagine how populations that could be plunged into crisis by seasonal droughts, floods, frosts, and other calamities of nature, might take an exaggerated pleasure in their mass leisure forms. The reciprocity and mutuality of social life were symbolized and reinforced by the image of the physical body depicted in carnival play forms. The image is of the grotesque body. As Bakhtin writes:

'The grotesque body is not separated from the rest of the world. It is not a closed, completed unit; it is unfinished, outgrows itself, transgresses its own limits. The stress is laid on those parts of the body that are open and outside the world, that is the parts through which the world enters the body or emerges from it, or through which the body itself goes out to meet the world. This means that the emphasis is on the apertures or the convexities, or on various ramifications and offshoots; the open mouth, the genital organs, the breasts, the phallus, the potbelly, the nose.'

(Bakhtin 1968: 26)

The grotesque body is, above all, a living body. It is, Bakhtin says, 'ever unfinished', 'ever creating'. The imagery directly represented the two principal features of the relationship between the social body and the natural world: interdependence and change. The mass consciousness of the precarious stability and interdependence of social life in the Middle Ages was oppressively insistent. Huizinga (1924: 30) writes of the 'sombre melancholy' that 'weighs upon people's souls'. Carnival played a part in lightening this burden by making the precarious aspects of society objects of comedy and play.

FROM CARNIVAL TO THE WALKMAN: A REVOLUTION IN LEISURE?

As Eagleton (1981) and Thompson (1983) point out, the pleasures of carnival derive from one source: the licensed transgression of the everyday rules of social life. Carnival was fun because it was a crowd affair, an all-inclusive affair. The delight of its pastimes, which mimicked and teased the established order, lay in the fact that everyone was an accomplice. Anxieties were less tormenting because they were shared anxieties. Play was less threatening because everyone joined in. The suspension of ordinary, official life was all encompassing.

In the complex industrial societies of today, leisure relations are very different. The crowd remains a characteristic feature of modern leisure forms. But when crowds gather to participate in a leisure event today, they are accompanied by the police, the squad car and the walkie-talkie. The crowd is now a collection of people with a specialized interest. The interest may be in sport, pop music, or a community festival. The details do not matter. The general point is that the rest of society does not share this specialist interest. Society therefore requires specialized units of surveillance and control to protect itself from the crowd, and to protect the participating crowd from hostile crowds. Privatization and individuation have divided us into distinct and separate individuals. Few people find this strange or worthy of comment. Yet, viewed historically, it is an amazing development. As Ariès explains, 'until the end of the seventeenth century nobody was left alone. The density of social life made isolation virtually impossible, and people who managed to shut themselves in a room for some time were regarded as exceptional characters' (1962: 398).

Today, our own room is often the first place we think of when we want some leisure. Nor is this confinement, this shutting away of the self, limited to domestic leisure activity. A sense of solitariness in crowds is familiar to everyone. Individuals barricade themselves behind the pages of a newspaper, or blank out others with the headphones of a Walkman. Our leisure is indeed more privatized, individuated, commercialized, and pacified than it has ever been before.

What would a carnival reveller make of it all? Doubtless, he or she would be incredulous at the sheer range of our leisure pursuits and the wonders of the capital equipment we use to relax and have fun with. At the same time, however, he or she would be struck by how privatized, differentiated, and self-contained our stock leisure activities are. The question of what caused this fundamental transformation is one which the carnival reveller would be entitled to ask. It is to this question that I now want to turn.

Leisure and Class: A unified problematic?

At the outset, I confess to an act of deception in broaching the question as if it could be answered in a few words. In one way or another the question recurs in all of the subsequent chapters of the book. Why is modern leisure like this? The answers vary with the assumptions and methods that mark out each given paradigm. I shall consider their validity as and when they arise. In recent years, however, the bid to ground the sociology of leisure in the unified problematic of class has attracted considerable attention.[8] In view of its influence and the controversy which surrounds it,[9] I shall devote the whole of this section to appraising its significance.

My treatment is designed to underline the increasing critical prominence given to class-centred approaches in the field. It also seeks to illustrate the defects involved in the attempt to reduce the complex tissue of leisure relations to a single problematic. As I shall show later in the book, the defect is not confined to neo-Marxist approaches. Indeed, within the sociology of leisure, neo-Marxist approaches have developed in reaction to the conventional wisdom which regards the development of leisure as a consequence of the general phenomenon of industrialization. For example, as Roberts puts it, 'leisure [is] an unintended and unwanted by-product of industrialization. An industrial society unavoidably generates leisure whether individuals welcome it or not' (1978: 90).

This view represents the formalist tradition in leisure theory. I shall examine it in more detail in Chapter 4 of this book. What needs to be noted here is that it has been regularly criticized by Marxist sociologists for its voluntaristic notions about social action, and its pluralist assumptions about power. Marxists have sought to expose the ideology of leisure in capitalist society. The important point, for them, is not the surface quality of leisure relations but their structural locations in the social, economic, and political context of modern capitalism. This has culminated in an attempt to interpret the enumerated characteristics of modern leisure practice, namely privatization, individuation, commercialization, and pacification, as facets of the class struggle.

No one would deny that class is anything other than a fundamental influence on the production and reproduction of leisure relations. Above all, the class approach has taught us that we cannot speak of the subjective experience of leisure in the singular because no one exists in the singular; still less can we attempt to label leisure relations in isolation because no social event occurs in isolation.

Even so, there are problems involved in trying to ground the sociology of leisure into the problematic of class. Writing from within the Marxist tradition, Stedman Jones (1977) has argued that the concept of class control often leads to a 'one-sided' view of the class struggle. Thus, the dominant class is seen as monolithically exploiting the subordinate classes in society. The effect of this is that class struggle under capitalism is made to seem less contradictory than it actually is. In particular, the capacity of the working class to launch counter-attacks against the capitalist class is seriously underestimated. Similarly, he refers to the 'real danger of over-politicizing leisure as an arena of class struggle' (1977: 170). Not every football riot or flare-up at a community carnival can be seen as an expression of class conflict. More generally, the tendency to aggrandize the concept of class in leisure study results in its losing all pretence of analytical precision. Stedman Jones does not argue that the concept of class is misplaced in the sociology of leisure. On the contrary, he argues for a more critical and rigorous application of the concept in the analysis of how leisure relations are historically and materially structured.

Foucault, writing from a diametrically opposed theoretical position, makes a similar point. 'Anything', he writes, 'can be deduced from the general phenomenon of the bourgeois class' (1980: 100). For him, the conceptual roominess of class analysis is the ally of exactly that form of circular reasoning which begins by positing a governing power relation in social affairs, and proceeds empirically by finding instalments of confirmation everywhere.

My own view is that class-based models are deficient because they underestimate the importance of levels of social integration in leisure practice and general social life, which supersede class relations. The three most important of these levels refer to nationalism, sexism, and civilization. Let us briefly examine them in turn.

Marx never took nationalism seriously. He dismissed it as a mere epiphenomenon of class society. As he and Engels explain in *The Communist Manifesto*, 'the bourgeoisie by the rapid improvement of all instruments of production, by the immensely facilitated means of communication draw all, even barbarian nations into civilization. . . . National one-sidedness and narrow-mindedness become more and more impossible' (1968: 39). Virtually the whole record of twentieth-century history and contemporary world affairs contradicts this judgement. Even in a comparatively narrow area like leisure relations, an analysis of the political economy of mass sport and tourism would be highly defective if it ignored the issue of national power bonding.

On the question of the sexual domination of men over women, class models appear to be on firmer ground. There is, at any rate, a well-established Marxist critique of the bourgeois family.[10] But even here, there are dangers in reading off relations of sexism from a class model of society. As Anderson has pointed out, 'sexual domination is much older historically, and more deeply rooted culturally, as a pattern of inequality, than class exploitation' (1983: 90). And who, except the most trusting Marxist, can believe that the socialization of housework, the enforcement of equal pay, and the elimination of class will automatically sound the death knell of sexism?

The difficulties that the question of civilization poses for a class model of social development have been fully rehearsed by no less a figure than Freud. He uses two major arguments against the class model. First of all, he submits that its analysis of the main-spring of social conflict is falsely reductive. In his own words, 'aggressiveness was not created by property. It reigned almost without limit in primitive times, when property was still very scanty, and it already shows itself in the nursery almost before property has given up its primal, anal form' (1979: 50). This is, to be sure, a sceptic's retort to the vision of communist society.[11] Freud submits that the socialization of the means of production will not bring about a marked reduction in human aggressiveness. Conflict and violence in society cannot therefore be reduced to the class struggle. Second, Freud's view of how social order is maintained and reproduced precludes him from believing that the history of human society is the history of class struggle. He believes that the sacrifices demanded by civilization make no distinction between bourgeois and proletarian. All must submit to the basic social requirement of instinctual renunciation. The argument is used as an additional proof of the fallibility of the communist case. For even if a classless society can be attained, unhappiness and discord in civilized society will remain. For all civilized life maintains social order and progress by exacting the payment of instinctual repression. In Freud's view, a reversal of these conditions is a reversal to barbarism.

Conclusion

Leisure pursuits are not attributes that men and women are born with, as they are born with sexual characteristics, skin colour, parents, and racial affinities. On the contrary, in everyday life we see leisure activities as the most telling indication of who a person really is; more so than other labels such as occupation. After all, work is something that most of us have to do in order to gain a living. We engage in leisure activities because we want to. A core argument of this chapter is that the freedom and choice popularly associated with modern leisure practice are deceptive. The conventions of leisure relations are historically structured. They are tied to systems of legitimation which regulate what is permissible in leisure conduct. The more closely one examines the conventions governing habitual leisure practice, the more sharply is their ambivalence revealed. For example, pornography has established itself as a major leisure industry on the principle that it is OK to consume the product so long as the transaction and experience are relatively secluded. At the same time, overt pornography on the streets or in the mass media is abhorred. Illicit practices are allowed provided that they are secreted from the public gaze. Yet since the public is also the consumer of the dark product a paradox is created: the public is protected from itself.

I shall return to this paradox in the final chapter. The point has now been reached in my argument where it is necessary to explore the battle lines of multi-paradigmatic rivalry in more detail. My discussion is planned to lead logically to a consideration of the contemporary situation of leisure theory. This occupies the greater portion of Part Two of this book. The remainder of Part One is devoted to a reconnoitre of the submerged tradition in leisure theory.

2 LEISURE AND SOCIAL INTERVENTION: Marx and Durkheim

Although in most other respects Marx and Durkheim were signally opposed social theorists, they shared a belief in the conscious regulation of society. Both writers argue that rational planned intervention into social life could improve collective conditions. Marx held fast to this position throughout his intellectual career. Durkheim, for his part, grew more sceptical in his later years. Even so, as regards leisure theory, it is useful to compare and contrast their views in terms of the question of intervention. Marx and Durkheim were both complex writers. In order to discuss their respective views of intervention and leisure meaningfully, it will be necessary to outline the background assumptions and logic of their general social theories.

Karl Marx

Marx's theory of capitalist society is a theory committed to revolutionary intervention and change. Its central aim is to create a society that will enable 'the free development, intellectual and social, of the individual'.[1] At the heart of this position is the assumption that individuals are not free in their life activities under capitalism. They live within a conditioning framework, a 'realm of necessity'. The question of what this realm constitutes is basic to Marx's view of work and leisure. It might, for example, be the case that Marx regards the realm of necessity to be equivalent to human nature. If so the implications for social intervention are far reaching. For plainly, if human nature means anything it means an everlasting, determining influence on social action and development. Similarly, if individual competitiveness and acquisitiveness under capitalism are expressions of human nature, the prospect of maintaining and reproducing a social order which is capable of achieving the free and full development of all individuals must be adjusted accordingly.

THE PROBLEM OF THE 'EPISTEMOLOGICAL BREAK'

The problem of defining the realm of necessity is complicated by the 'epistemological break' which some authors believe occurred in Marx's intellectual development between 1845 and 1857.[2] On this reckoning, the pre-1845 work displays a streak of utopianism which is intellectually indefensible. Thus, Marx can be found arguing for the 'complete abolition of the division of labour', the 'resolution of strife between the individual and the species', and 'the positive transcendence of private property'. These themes climax in the *Economic and Philosophic Manuscripts of 1844*. But even in a work of the break, like *The German Ideology* which Marx wrote with Engels between November 1845 and October 1846, Marx seems to entertain seriously the idea that communist society will be a sort of affluent, self-regulating, post-industrial utopia. Consider the following well-known passage:

> 'In communist society, where nobody has one exclusive sphere of activity but each can become accomplished in any branch he wishes, society regulates the general production and thus makes it possible for me to do one thing today and another tomorrow, to hunt in the morning, fish in the afternoon, rear cattle in the evening, criticize after dinner, just as I have mind, without ever becoming hunter, fisherman, shepherd or critic.'
> (Marx and Engels 1965: 45)

This glimpse of life activity under communism scintillates with intriguing possibilities regarding the Marxian position on the future of work and leisure. Indeed, it points to nothing less than the dissolution of the established division between work and leisure. Under communism, individuals will be allowed to follow their inclinations as they please. The necessity to work for a living is relegated to a mere convenant of pre-history.[3]

Against this, the writings of the mature Marx, especially the three volumes of *Capital*, are widely held to pursue a more circumspect line of reasoning. According to Althusser (1969, 1976; Althusser and Balibar 1970), Marx devotes himself in these works to a scientific, structuralist analysis of social and economic relations. The concepts of social formation, mode of production, superstructure and ideology are cited as evidence of a new scientific realism.

There is no question that a good prima-facie case can be made to support the epistemological break thesis. But it is important to counter the impression that the break was cut and dried. A strong body of Marxist thought argues that Marx's theories underwent something more like a process of gradual evolution (Mészáros 1970; Rattansi 1982; Geras 1983). Thus, the early themes of alienation and human nature continue to reverberate in the later works, albeit in a more developed form. Geras (1983), for example, argues that Marx never rejected the idea of human nature. Furthermore, to suggest the opposite, as Althusser and his followers do, is an odd 'fixation'.

THE REALM OF NECESSITY

At first sight it looks as if the realm of necessity merely consists of the requirements of physical maintenance and reproduction such as sleeping, eating, and personal hygiene. Evidence to support this proposition can be found in *The German Ideology* where Marx and Engels mention a number of fixed natural wants that must be satisfied in human existence. The need for food, water, shelter, company, and sex are itemized as being paramount. They constitute the inalienable starting-point for social analysis at all times and in all places. It is, however, doubtful whether these needs can be properly described as restrictions on human freedom. After all, if people do not eat or drink, they die. When all is said and done, the satisfaction of primary needs is not an encumbrance upon human society, but a prerequisite of it.

Of course, this does not mean that the physical necessities of life are frozen and unalterable. Natural wants can be *modified* by social action. Indeed, one of Marx's central economic ideas is that the satisfaction of primary needs acts as a multiplier in the realm of necessity. Consider the need to satisfy hunger. This is a mundane consideration of life. Even so, it has led to the creation of specialized knowledge and conventions in land cultivation and stock rearing. In order to be maintained and developed these forces of production require the selection, training, and allocation of labour. In this way, the social and economic maintenance of the agricultural sector becomes a necessary requirement for satisfying the physical wants of large and diversified populations. The same is true of trade. By importing foodstuffs that cannot be grown in a national territory, trade alters dietary habits and builds up specialized branches of commerce to distribute and merchandise imported products. The satisfaction of the physical necessities of life thus increases the forces of production which satisfy these necessities.

Upon closer inspection then, it appears that the realm of necessity is, above all else, a realm of production. Production is made up of two components. One is physical, and consists of the energy and strength that are naturally given to labourers. This is a relatively inelastic quantity since there are strong physical and mental limits upon the length of time that peak energy can be expended in the act of production. The second Marx describes as the 'traditional standard of life' which is the basis of demand in an economy and hence a major influence on production. Marx says that this 'historical and social element entering into the value of labour may be expanded, contracted or altogether extinguished, so that nothing remains but the *physical limit*' (1968: 222). It is, however, unlikely that this element can be entirely extinguished under capitalism, except through unforeseen catastrophe.[4] This is because, as we shall see in greater detail when we consider Marx's remarks on the production system as a whole, the traditional standard of life is actually nothing other than the primary influence on the market for commodities, i.e. the foundation of capitalist production.

Marx defines production as 'an appropriation on the part of the individual within and through a specific form of society' (1973: 87). Production requires labourers to use their faculties and skills to transform the material world about them. In transforming the world, they transform themselves and the conditions of life for their progeny. It is a watchword of Marx's theory that production under capitalism obeys the imperatives of capitalist accumulation rather than the social wants of individual consumers. Capitalist enterprise is arraigned and condemned as a distorting influence on the market for goods and services. Specifically, it (a) confines the great mass of wage labourers to narrow, destructive activities at work and stultifies them at home; and (b) weaves a fabric of purely illusory freedom in the consumption of commodities which masks the real, exploitative basis of the production process.

The key to Marx's theory of the subordination of labour under capitalism is his concept of the commodity. We can use this concept as a way into the wider question of class exploitation in the labour process and the sphere of consumption.

THE COMMODITY: USE VALUE AND EXCHANGE VALUE

The product of labour is a commodity. A commodity, declares Marx in the famous opening chapter of *Capital I*, is a unit of wealth. Its value can be looked at from two points of view: use and exchange. The use value of a commodity refers to its utility, i.e. the use it has for someone. Where does use value come from? Marx sees no special difficulty in answering the question:

> 'Labour is the creator of use value . . . it is a necessary condition, independent of all forms of society, for the existence of the human race; it is an eternal nature-imposed necessity, without which there can be no material exchanges between man and Nature, and therefore no life.'
>
> (Marx 1977(I): 50)

Useful labour and the creation of use value are therefore indispensable elements of the realm of necessity. For at all times, and under every conceivable mode of production, they will be required for the satisfaction of human needs.

But use value shows only one face of what commodities are. The other face is exchange value, i.e. the form in which commodity transactions are expressed and calculated. In capitalist society, where a unified market exists, the normal unit of exchange value is money. It is important to understand clearly that exchange value presupposes a consumer who is separate from the producer of the commodity or the service; and further, that exchange value varies over time. Thus, the exchange value of a given commodity may change in proportion to (a) its relative scarcity or abundance, and (b) the way in which it is marketed by the producer for the consumer. These attributes of exchange value are important because they disqualify it from the realm of necessity and hence from the sphere of natural wants.

Marx's core critical position concerning the production of commodities in capitalist society is that it perpetuates exchange value as the dominant, meaningful form in which the value of labour is computed. This has definite effects on interpersonal relations. As Marx puts it: 'Activity, regardless of its individual manifestation, and the product of activity regardless of its particular make-up, are always *exchange value*, and exchange value is a generality in which all individuality and peculiarity are negated and extinguished' (Marx 1973: 157).

In order to pursue the link between Marx's concept of the commodity and his analysis of the class struggle under capitalism it is important to recognize that the circuit of class exploitation is fully integrated. Workers do not merely produce commodities, they also consume them. In consuming them they pay for articles which they themselves have produced and provide the capitalist with the means to enslave them still further.

The working class, in fact, is held to be intrinsically and exhaustively exploited under capitalism. Engels in *The Condition of the Working Class in 1844* fulminates against the pestilential circumstances of proletarian work and leisure in Victorian England:

> 'The proletarian is helpless . . . what [he] needs he can only obtain from the bourgeoisie . . . the proletarian is . . . in law and fact, the slave of the bourgeoisie. . . . [The capitalist class] deprives thousands of the necessities of life, places them under conditions in which they *cannot* live . . . its deed is murder just as surely as the deed of the single individual . . . murder against which none can defend himself, and which does not seem what it is because no man sees the murderer, because the death of the victim seems a natural one.'
>
> (Engels 1952: 76, 95–6)

Fortunately, there is no need to rely on Engels's oratory to support the point.[5] Marx's theory of surplus value provides a forceful rationale of why exploitation is inherent in the production process as a whole under capitalism. The labour process is central because Marx regards the workplace as the site of exploitation in industrial capitalism. Before they can enter into leisure activities, labourers must first earn a living which is sufficient to maintain and reproduce themselves and their dependants. In addition, as I have already suggested, Marx believes that it is through labour that individuals construct an image of their personal worth and an estimate of their standing in the sight of others. What does Marx believe actually happens to labourers in the course of the normal working day?

THE LABOUR PROCESS UNDER CAPITALISM

To begin with, it is necessary to recognize that workers sell their labour power to the capitalist under sufferance. They do not *choose* to pledge their creativity, freedom, and energy for a mere cash transfer; they are *forced* to do so in order to gain the where-withal to satisfy the physical necessities of life. In Marx's view, the historical achievement of capitalism was to separate workers from their means of production. By systematically depriving them of wealth-creating capital, capitalism has forced the great mass of people to sell their skills and energy to the highest bidder. Marx traces this development back to the expropriation of the peasants from the soil. The process, he declares, is 'written in the annals of mankind in letters of blood and fire' (Marx 1977(I): 669).

Marx calls that part of the working day which the worker devotes to securing an income sufficient to ensure his own subsistence and that of his dependants, and *ipso facto*, the working class, *necessary labour time*. 'The entire remaining portion of the working day,' he writes, 'the entire excess quantity of labour performed above the value of the labour realized in his wage is *surplus labour, unpaid labour*' (emphasis mine) (1977(III): 834). The surplus value thus produced is appropriated by the capitalist class as profit. Marx concludes that the whole capitalist system of production is based upon the principle that workers must always be paid an income which is less than the value of what they produce in the labour process. The basic link between capital and labour is therefore economic. There is a famous passage in the *Manifesto of the Communist Party* where Marx and Engels rail against the capitalist class for having reduced social and political relationships to 'the callous cash payment' and 'egotistical calcu-lation' (1968: 38). But it is perhaps in a less well-known passage from the *Grundrisse* that Marx most eloquently vents his spleen against the dehumanizing effects of capitalist organization:

'The social character of labour, as well as the social form of that product, and the share of individuals in production here appear as something alien . . . confronting the individuals, not as their relation to one another, but as their subordination to relations which subsist independently of them and which arise out of collisions between mutually indifferent individuals.'

(Marx 1973: 157)

This is not an attribute of social relations in all forms of class society. In his discussion of feudalism, Marx is at pains to point out the 'reciprocal' and 'all sided' duties and responsibilities which bind classes together and overlay economic ties (Marx 1973: 155–58). Only under the dominion of capitalism have impersonality and indifference escalated into routine features of life activities.

According to Marx, labour under capitalism is normally treated like a commodity which is bought and sold according to market opportunity and constraint. But labour is also quite unlike any other commodity in that its use value is realized only in the act of production. Workers do not sell their labour. Labour is embodied only in the act of production. What they sell is their labour power, i.e. their creative potential and energy.

For Marx, the stock employment contract issued by the employer is a legal bond which permits and endorses the *formal subordination of labour*.[6] Under its terms, the labourer is deprived of personal identity and treated as mere living labour capacity. They are put to use or made idle as and when market conditions dictate. Formal subordination is not an end in itself. The desire of the capitalist for constant accumulation of surplus value drives him to seek new ways of extending his web of discipline over labourers. Under conditions of generalized commodity production, capitalists are responsible for the recruitment, training, welfare, and reward of workers. When the capitalist exerts a monopoly over these functions, as was the case with paternalist capitalism in Marx's own day, conditions approximate to the *real subordination of labour*.[7] Under these conditions the extraction of surplus value is not confined to the workplace. In modern 'welfare' capitalism, significant levels of redistribution occur through pricing policy and taxation. The manipulation of the Public Sector Borrowing Requirement is no less a basis for class exploitation than a wage cut or a freeze on jobs.[8] Modern Marxist economists argue that Marx's ideas are not necessarily *passé*. In modern welfare capitalism, the extraction of surplus value may be said to be operational before an individual is old enough to receive a national insurance number, e.g. through state policy on education, health care, and social security.

For Marx, then, any understanding of the labour process in capitalist society must begin from the proposition that contradiction is at the root of the relations between capital and labour. The theory of surplus value lays out the formal reasoning behind this claim. Capital consumes labour power, the life stuff of workers. In Marx's own words 'capital is dead labour, that, vampire-like only lives by sucking living labour, and lives the more, the more labour it sucks' (1977(I): 224).

'DISPOSABLE TIME' AND CONSUMER CAPITALISM

Marx's discussion of necessary and surplus labour in capitalist society suggests that workers' leisure time is sufficient to (a) replenish their energies, (b) ensure the reproduction of the working class, and (c) provide an integrated market for capitalist production. On each count the working class is treated as a mere force of production to be exploited and developed at the behest of the capitalist. Their time is not free for their own development. It is converted by the capitalist class into a means for pumping out surplus value. Marx is scathing about the mechanics of this process. He denounces it as the 'tyrannical usurpation' of capital. For, as he puts it:

> 'Time is the room of human development. A man who has no free time to dispose of, whose whole lifetime apart from the mere physical interruption of sleep, meals and so forth, is absorbed by his labour for the capitalist, is less than a beast of burden. He is a mere machine for producing Foreign Wealth.'
> (Marx 1968: 219)

In this passage 'disposable time' is associated with real wealth. For through it, creative labour power is liberated to satisfy real social wants. As we have seen, Marx believes that the employment contract under capitalism puts forward fast and binding obligations that labourers must obey to remain in employment. Their labour power is pledged to the capitalist. Labour power is therefore disposable time under capitalism in so far as it submits to the requirements of capitalist accumulation. In fact, it is not 'free' time at all. Rather, for Marx, it is subjectively experienced by the labourer as an alien force which he does not fully control.

If disposable time has any meaning for the working class it is formally confined to non-work relations. Marx's discussion of consumer capitalism does not suggest that the realm of consumption is a sphere of freedom. To clarify his argument, Marx (1977(I): 536) distinguishes between two sorts of working-class consumption under capitalism:

(1) Productive consumption refers to the worker's consumption of the means of production in the labour process. In expending labour power the worker uses up raw materials and other resources. Productive consumption assists capital accumulation in a twofold way: (a) it converts the resources consumed into products with a higher value, and (b) it creates a demand for the renewal of expended resources which is supplied by other branches of capitalist industry.
(2) Individual consumption refers to the labourer's own consumption of commodities with the money paid to him for his labour power. As we have already noted, Marx believes that this sum is normally sufficient to ensure the subsistence of the labourer and his dependants. It might therefore be argued that individual consumption is actually a disguised form of productive consumption. For it may involve the labourer in maintaining and reproducing his labour power simply in order to meet the requirements of work.

Marx draws these themes together in a powerful, declamatory passage which appears in *Capital I*:

'The fact that the labourer consumes his means of subsistence for his own purposes, and not to please the capitalist, has no bearing on the matter. The consumption of food by a beast of burden is none the less a necessary factor in the process of production because the beast enjoys what it eats. The maintenance and reproduction of the working class is, and ever must be, a necessary condition to the reproduction of capital. But the capitalist may safely leave its fulfilment to the labourer's instincts of self-preservation and propagation.'

(Marx 1977(I): 537)

On the face of it, this seems to display a most topsy-turvy form of logic. As already noted, Marx himself understood the prescriptive character of the capitalist employment contract. At the same time, everyone knows that the market does not force individuals to buy commodities. On the contrary, market organization allows individuals to follow their own inclinations with minimal let or hindrance.

Marx fully accepts that this is the commonsense view. It is consistent with the dominant academic view of the political scientists of his own day. They represented the market as a model of free choice and self-determination. They invoke an 'invisible hand' which silently, and without much fuss, ensures that the individual pursuit of self-interest satisfies the individual interests of all, i.e. the general interest. Marx introduces three arguments, one sociological, one empirical, and one philosophical, to falsify this position. Let us examine these arguments in turn.

In the first place, he submits that the statement that all individuals have private interests is unsatisfactory. It is a tautology. All that it says is that private interests are things which individuals have. This is a necessary condition of being an individual, and is hence not a significant insight in itself. In every case, the questions which the statement evokes are potentially more penetrating. What is a private interest? Where do private interests come from? How are they defended and reproduced in society? Marx's vital proposition is that 'private interest is itself already a socially determined interest, which can be achieved only within the conditions laid down by society and with the means provided by society' (Marx 1973: 156). This is manifestly not a tautology. Indeed it automatically suggests an agenda for research. It indicates that private interests have social origins and that they represent social interests.

The second argument which Marx puts forward refers to the empirical level. The consumer market, he argues, obeys the imperatives of capitalist accumulation above and beyond the social requirements of consumers. Indeed, under fully developed, generalized commodity production, the use value of some commodities almost vanishes as an element in economic transaction. Commodities are distinguished from each other only by their exchange value and brand name, and the artifice and contrivance of the individual merchant in presenting them to the consumer. Marx notes that the production of needed commodities is propagated by an important branch of capitalist industry. Through advertising and marketing, he writes, each capitalist 'searches for means to spur them [the consumers] on to consumption, to give his wares new charms, to inspire them with new needs by constant chatter etc.' (Marx 1973: 287). Hence the all-powerful drive of the capitalist to accumulate, even beyond the acquisition of the most discrete objects of desire, is legitimated. Accumulation becomes an end in itself.

Marx's third argument requires us to consider a couple of concepts from his social philosophical writings. The first is *commodity fetishism*. Under advanced capitalism the commodity form and the currency of exchange value have become the basic elements in the capitalist market. Commodities appear as impersonal, ready-made objects. They are, precisely, *dehumanized* objects. Any conscious awareness of them as expressions of human labour and definite social relations is either secondary or absent. In some cases, neither the immediate producer nor the consumer sees the commodity that knots them together. Small wonder that Marx compares commodity fetishism to 'the mist enveloped regions of the religious world' wherein 'the productions of the human brain appear as independent beings endowed with life, and entering into relations both with one another and the human race' (Marx 1977(I): 77). Thus the normal relations of production, distribution, and exchange under capitalism correspond to a popular consciousness which is dominated and shaped by 'thing-like' relations.

The second concept that we need to consider is *reification*. This refers to the process whereby definite social and historical relations are translated into ahistorical states of being. A crimped and reduced conception of individual rights, capacities, and general human potential passes for a 'realistic', 'no-nonsense' approach to life. Class exploitation is treated as a natural expression of justice. By laying down a general impression of what is and is not possible in human relations, reification imposes artificial barriers upon innovation and intervention.

It is, of course, right to stress that Marx observes a basic schematic distinction between the material life conditions of each class. Thus, the material conditions of the capitalist class are viewed as generally superior to those of the working class. This is, after all, no more than a necessary corollary of the theory of surplus value. It is also right to note that Marx argues that it suits the capitalist class to portray the strife-ridden conditions of work and property relations under capitalism as a primordial 'God-given' state of affairs. For this is a massive disincentive to collective organization and working-class action. Indeed, in those places in his work where Marx discusses the function of bourgeois ideology he constantly stresses its power to demoralize and suffocate working-class movements. It does this mainly by implying that the existing distribution of wealth and the division of labour are basically unalterable.[9]

Marx sees commodity fetishism and reification as corrosive influences in capitalist society, however. Their effects cannot be confined to a single class. In being duped by the snares and delusions of the commodity form, the capitalist class is as much prey as predator. True, in material terms, the capitalists are better off. But the enjoyment of their material wealth is tempered by the consciousness that 'time is money', and that undue slackness or a relaxation of guard will be paid for by a loss in competitiveness. The capitalist class cannot therefore be fully free in its leisure time. On the contrary, the capitalists are perpetually encumbered by the obsessive need to practise surveillance and to be one step ahead of the pack.

BEYOND 'THE REALM OF NECESSITY'

Marx's vital analytical insight for leisure theory was his recognition that under capitalism, relations of leisure are tied to property relations.[10] Leisure time is not a thing in itself. It has to be demarcated and financed from the proceeds of the working day. The working class can have leisure only if it fulfils the production requirements of capital. The capitalist class can only maintain its leisure relations if it ensures that in the long run more surplus value is extracted at source, i.e. by intensifying the exploitation of labour.

But capitalist exploitation is finite. Marx and Engels constantly emphasize the self-destructive aspects of capitalist accumulation. Thus, they compare the capitalist to 'a sorcerer who is no longer able to control the powers of the nether world whom he has called up by his spells' (Marx and Engels 1968: 40). The three volumes of *Capital* are sprinkled with complex technical arguments which prove, at any rate to Marx's satisfaction, that capitalism must fail. He mentions, *inter alia*, the crisis tendencies of capitalist production; the tendency for the absolute rate of profit to fall; the growth of bankruptcies in the capitalist class; the replacement of human labour with machines; the emizeration of the working class; and the creation of a 'reserve army' of unemployed. These are visible symptoms of capitalism's decay. What they show, thunder Marx and Engels, is that 'what the bourgeoisie, therefore, produces, above all, is its own grave diggers' (Marx and Engels 1968: 46).

In Marx's view the elimination of class society is equivalent to the real liberation of productive forces. This does not occur automatically. Marx's rebarbative attack upon Lasallean communism in the *Critique of the Gotha Programme* (1968) is the most systematic discussion of post-revolutionary conditions that he ever committed to print. In it he quite clearly distinguishes between a stage of socialist construction (the dictatorship of the proletariat), which is transitional, and real communist society. The dictatorship is needed to lay the foundations, economic, political, and social, of real communist society.[11] But Marx's discussion is notoriously vague. Its vision of the future form of society is confined to minimal propositions, so spare that their meaning dissolves to vanishing point, or floats away in billowing generalities. For example, a key submission that he makes refers to the mechanism for allocating reward during the period of socialist construction. According to him, the amount of labour which the individual expends in society will be returned to him in the form of a certificate which he can use to draw from the 'social stock' of the means of consumption. But how will this system be administered? What laws will be enforced to prevent abuse or double-dealing? Who determines the value of the labourer's contribution to society? To do him justice, Marx consistently maintains that all speculation on the precise structure of communist society will necessarily be utopian and ahistorical in character until the material and social preconditions for its existence have been established. However, we can glean more of his vision of communism by considering one passage from the last volume of his monumental work, *Capital.* In it Marx sets forth his view on the limits of social intervention and revolutionary transformation:

'The realm of freedom actually begins only where labour which is determined by necessity and mundane considerations ceases; thus in the very nature of things it lies beyond the sphere of actual material production. Just as the savage must wrestle with Nature to satisfy his wants, to maintain and reproduce life, so must civilized man, and he must do so in all social formations and under all possible modes of production. With his development this realm of physical necessity expands as a result of his wants; but at the same time, the forces of production which satisfy these wants also increase. Freedom in this field can only consist in socialized man, the associated producers, rationally regulating their interchange with Nature, bringing it under their common control, instead of being ruled by it as by the blind forces of Nature; and achieving this with the least expenditure of energy and under conditions most favourable to, and worthy of, their human nature. But it none-theless still remains a realm of necessity. Beyond it begins that development of human energy which is an end in itself, the true realm of freedom, which however, can blossom forth only with this realm of necessity as its basis.'

(Marx 1977(III): 820)

This does not support the impression that communist society will be a society of leisure. Marx states, unequivocally, that 'direct labour' which is 'determined by necessity and mundane con-siderations' is a feature of 'all social formations, under all poss-ible modes of production'. The realm of necessity will never 'wither away'. For it is a precondition of the satisfaction of the essential physical, economic, and social necessities of life 'laid down' by society and subject to the means provided by society. Its format under fully developed communism will, however, be qualitatively different from its format under capitalism. The individual labourer will be reconciled with his or her social being. Labour will therefore cease to be alienating since it will follow objectives which are socially determined and regulated.

Marx elaborates the concepts of 'labour' and 'disposable time' in the context of capitalism. Thus, neither concept can be simply transposed to post-revolutionary social formations. Marx indeed believed that the old division between work and leisure will have no salience under communism. Even so, he appears to deliver a real hostage to fortune with his somewhat Talmudic statement that the 'true realm of freedom', in which the 'development of human energy' exists as an end in itself, lies beyond the realm of necessity. All attempts to elucidate what Marx means by this seem destined to break down. The statement is indeed essentially tautological. What it says is that the realm of freedom will not be like the realm of necessity because it is the realm of freedom. Secondary interpretation seems to be confined to the prison house of circular reasoning.

Marx represents the whole movement of society as contradic-tion. Productive activity transforms human wants and, in trans-forming them, it is transformed itself. This is the essence of

Marx's method of dialectical reasoning. It is in the nature of the method that it can be retained even if all of the propositions and predictions that it advances are falsified.[12] Hence we have the spectacle, to be considered at length in Chapter 5, of present-day Marxists continuing to exploit and develop Marx's ideas, even though most of his original predictions regarding the future of class society have been compromised by events.

Emile Durkheim

Durkheim's remarks on social development make it plain that rational social intervention is sometimes necessary to correct malign tendencies in social life. Unlike Marx, he stopped well short of arguing that revolutionary class action is required. I shall submit that his position on intervention is essentially pragmatic. He believed that intervention in work and non-work relations developed in response to abnormalities in the division of labour. As we shall see, the scope for intervention is conditioned by the functional exigencies of what Durkheim called 'the normal division of labour'.

There is no simple way of summarizing Durkheim's view of human nature. The problem is that he shifted his position a number of times during his intellectual career. Hawkins (1977) usefully distinguishes three stages in Durkheim's thought on this matter. In the early writings, prior to 1895, he appears to reduce human history and action to exclusively *social* origins and imperatives. He formulates this view by way of a critical assault upon established theoretical positions. Thus, he criticizes Bentham, the Utilitarians, and the classical economists for taking the isolated individual as the starting-point of their considerations. Such approaches, argues Durkheim, reduce society to a 'mechanical aggregate' of contractual relationships. The law and the state cannot explain everything that happens in social life. He is no less critical of naïve socialists who promote the idea that class revolution will effect a great change in the structure of social relations. This underestimates the complex social forces and mechanisms which animate social life.

Between 1895 and 1911, Durkheim works through this position and seems to modify his standpoint. Throughout this period his thought on the question of human nature is larded with ambiguity and tension. In *Le Suicide* (1897) he postulates that some elements of the suicidal personality may be 'pre-social', or biological, in origin. Thus, he appears to depart from his original argument that society, and not biology, structures human action and development. Equally, however, Durkheim maintains that human wants are constantly remade and developed by the social means used to satisfy them. His lectures on socialism (1895–96) portray human wants as insatiable, i.e. free of all 'natural' limits (Durkheim 1959). In his own words, 'we will not succeed in pacifying roused appetites because they will acquire new force in the measure they are appeased. There are no limits possible to their requirements' (Durkheim 1959: 93). That Durkheim is referring to social and not biological limits to human wants here is corroborated by a passage later in the same work where he asks, 'how [are we to] fix the quantity of well being, comfort, luxury that a human being ought not to pass? Nothing is found either in the organic or psychological constitution of man which sets a limit to such needs' (Durkheim 1959: 244). At one and the same time then, Durkheim appears to be advancing the contradictory propositions that (a) human nature structures social behaviour, and (b) history and social action have broken free from nature's yoke. The factor which, above all others, caused Durkheim to change his position on the question of human nature was, by his own account, his research into religion. Lukes quotes a letter that Durkheim wrote to the director of the *Revue Néo-Scolastique* in 1907, in which he explains that:

> 'It was not until 1895 that I achieved a clear view of the essential role played by religion in social life. . . . This was a revelation to me. That course [his lectures on the sociology of religion] of 1895 marked a dividing line in the development of my thought, to such an extent that all my previous researches had to be taken up afresh in order to be made to harmonize with these new insights.'
>
> (Durkheim quoted by Lukes 1973: 237)

By 1912 the harmonization was more or less complete. As Hawkins puts it, 'from 1912 until his death in 1917, Durkheim unequivocally adopts a *homo duplex* model of human nature' (1977: 243). In this third stage of his thought, Durkheim sees human beings as riven between the need to satisfy 'egoistic' or 'personal' desires, and the 'moral' obligations that society requires in order to make collective life possible. 'The duality corresponds to the double existence that we lead concurrently: the one purely individual and rooted in our organisms, the other social and nothing but an extension of society' (Durkheim quoted by Bellah 1973: 70). The relationship is basically contradictory. Thus, egoistic desires undermine the requirements of social order, and social order is a real barrier against the satisfaction of egoistic desires.

LEISURE AND THE MORAL REMAKING OF SOCIAL LIFE

Durkheim's position on the function of leisure in industrial society remained consistent throughout his intellectual career. But his views on how social intervention might organize non-work relations underwent the same three-point movement that marks his theory of human nature. If Durkheim began his intellectual life believing that concerted planning could achieve integration between the individual and society, he ended it convinced that the dualism which he had unearthed in human nature ensures that the relationship between the two is one of perpetual contradiction.

Durkheim argues that the development of leisure is interdependent with the division of labour. As he puts it, 'it appears in the nature of things [that] sport and recreation develops side by side with the serious life which it serves to balance and relieve' (Durkheim 1933: 26). Leisure here is assigned a compensatory function. It restores the energies and faculties spent in the 'serious life' of labour. Elsewhere, he expands upon the point. Leisure forms, he notes, are associated with 'simple merry making' and 'pure fancy' (Durkheim 1965: 425). In contrast to work, leisure relations are regarded as 'foreign to all utilitarian ends; they make men forget the real world and transport them into another where their imagination is more at ease; they distract' (Durkheim 1965: 425). The fact that Durkheim situates leisure as the complement to the serious side of life is no pretext for assuming that the function which it performs is trivial. Durkheim uses two arguments against such an interpretation.

In the first place, he submits that the relationship between work and leisure is anything but haphazard. On the contrary, everything he writes indicates that necessity, not chance, has brought work and leisure together in their distinctive modern form. Each requires and conditions the other. Their relationship is one of *functional interdependence*. It follows that the part which work plays in reproducing and developing collective life could not be maintained without leisure. To repeat: theirs is 'a side by side' existence (Durkheim 1933: 26).

Durkheim's second argument requires lengthier discussion. It relates to his comments on the origins and development of leisure forms. These are expressed, albeit sporadically, throughout his writings (see Durkheim 1933, 1957). However, they are undoubtedly most fully developed in *The Elementary Forms of Religious Life*. In the closing chapters of that work, Durkheim makes an elaborate comparison between secular non-work relations and religious life. Consider the following passage:

> 'Every feast, even when it has purely lay origins, has certain characteristics of the religious ceremony, for in every case its effect is to bring men together, to put the masses into movement and thus to excite a state of effervescence, and sometimes even of delirium, which is not without a certain kinship with the religious state. A man is carried outside himself and diverted from his ordinary occupation and preoccupations. Thus the same manifestations are to be observed in each case: cries, songs, music, violent forms, movements, dances, the search for excitants which raise the vital level etc.'
>
> (Durkheim 1965: 427–28)

Durkheim does not soft-pedal the analogy. Indeed, he works through it to the notable conclusion that 'recreation is one of the principal forms of moral remaking' (1965: 427).

Of course, it is well known that Durkheim claims the same function for religious activity. In his view, the belief systems, ceremonies, and rituals of religious observance are collective expressions of the sacred element in social life. They involve surrendering the self to an entity which is represented as a superior, all-knowing moral force. This view is, in itself, worthy of comment in respect of Durkheim's intellectual development. In his early writings, Durkheim sees the law as the expression *par excellence* of moral remaking. This is because the law appeals to collective sentiments of right and wrong, normality and pathology. Therefore, observance and enforcement of the law necessarily reinforce moral life because they signify the action of collective solidarity. Durkheim is quite clear on the point:

> 'Law and morality are the totality of ties which bind each of us to society, which make a unitary, coherent aggregate of the mass of individuals. Everything which is a source of solidarity

is moral, everything which forces man to take account of other men is moral, everything which forces him to regulate his conduct through something other than the striving of his ego is moral.'

(Durkheim 1933: 398)

By the time of the *Elementary Forms*, Durkheim was arguing that religion went much deeper than the law in performing this function. For in that work he contends that the details of the sacred which are venerated in religious observance are no more than collective representations of the 'aggregate mass of individuals', i.e. society itself.

Durkheim recognized that leisure activities do not ultimately rely on a higher presence such as a God or spirit for their meaning. Nevertheless, the symbolism and ritual of many collective leisure forms are reminiscent of religious behaviour. They also have a similar effect. For example, leisure activity can draw the individual outside the self and dissolve him or her in the immediate collective life of the leisure form. The feeling of being liberated from the armour of everyday life irresistibly invites comparisons with religious experience. Durkheim explains the similarity in terms of the same cause. 'It is', he writes (1965: 425) 'a well known fact that games and the principal forms of art seem to have been born of religion.' Thus the emergence and descent of leisure forms are traced back to religious belief and practice.

Durkheim's argument is complex and connects up repeatedly with his general thesis regarding the progress of the division of labour. Essentially, however, he maintains that leisure emerges out of religion through a two-way process. First, historically, the sentiments of pleasure generated through religious activity are so 'intense and tumultuous' that they cannot be contained by religious forms. As he explains:

'A surplus generally remains available which seeks to employ itself in supplementary and superfluous works of luxury, that is to say, works of art. There are practices as well as beliefs of this sort. The state of effervescence in which the assembled worshippers find themselves must be translated outwardly by exuberant movements which are not easily subjected to too carefully defined ends. In part, they escape aimlessly, they spread themselves for the mere pleasure of so doing, and they take delight in all sorts of games.'

(Durkheim 1965: 426)

Durkheim's second argument is more subtle. Structurally, he insists, the canopy of religious symbolism cannot be tied down to fixed religious belief. The very exuberance that religion generates ensures that a distance will emerge between symbols and what they express. In Durkheim's own words, 'religion would not be itself if it did not give some place to the free combinations of thought and activity, to play, to art, to all that recreates the spirit that has been fatigued by the too great slavishness of daily work' (1965: 426). Durkheim's analysis suggests that leisure acts in conjunction with religion to accomplish this function in modern industrial society.

Durkheim makes these remarks on the function of leisure in the context of his general analysis of religion in primitive societies. In *The Division of Labour* he made an important distinction between two forms of social cohesion: mechanical and organic solidarity. Mechanical solidarity refers to the general condition of social bonding found in primitive societies. Such societies are characterized by the simple division of labour, uniform shared symbols and rituals, close identification between the individual and the group, and repressive law which functions to uphold collective sentiments. One of the major effects of industrialization is to expand structural and functional differentiation in society. A complex division of labour is elicited, values and beliefs become fragmented, individualism grows in power, and a new restitutive principle regulates the law. In brief, mechanical solidarity is replaced by organic solidarity. As regards leisure practice, the consequence of this deep change in social relations is that leisure activities become more structurally and functionally diversified. Leisure forms multiply. The rules and resources governing leisure grow likewise: 'To avoid all collisions [between leisure forms] it is necessary that each particular group have a determined portion of space assigned to it: in other terms, it is necessary that space in general be divided, differentiated, arranged, and that these divisions be known to everybody' (Durkheim 1965: 492). The division of leisure space was, of course, a feature of social relations under mechanical solidarity. Durkheim himself notes that 'every summons to a celebration, a hunt or a military expedition implies fixed and established dates, which everybody conceives in the same fashion' (1965: 492). But in modern 'organic' societies, the divisions are incomparably more complex. Social relations are based on the principle of *difference* in work and leisure. This principle permits a vastly increased range of leisure practices and values. It also serves to make a categorical distinction between leisure under organic solidarity and leisure under mechanical solidarity.

ABNORMAL FORMS OF THE DIVISION OF LABOUR AND LEISURE

Durkheim had a highly developed sense of the fragility and complexity of modern social order. He regarded society as a delicate, finely balanced organism. One facet of this general view is his belief that the goal of social harmony is not reached by the road of excess. For this reason he would have been vigorously opposed to the idea of the 'leisure society'. Too much leisure, he argues, is a 'sickly phenomenon' and a 'danger' to society. It increases the attraction of 'idleness' and tempts individuals to be chronically work-shy (Durkheim 1933: 240–41).

This is not to be interpreted as blind adherence to the work ethic. Durkheim would have been equally incensed by any social policy which sought to lengthen the working day arbitrarily. He genuinely believed that there is 'a normal intensity of all our social needs, intellectual, moral, as well as physical, which cannot be exaggerated. At each moment of history, our thirst for science, art and well being is defined as are our appetites, and all that goes beyond this standard leaves us indifferent or causes suffering' (Durkheim 1933: 240).

For Durkheim, the natural tendency of the division of labour in conditions of advanced industrialization is to ensure that 'society is constituted in such a way that social inequalities exactly express natural inequalities' (1933: 377). He refers to this as 'the normal division of labour'. Durkheim sees this as an immanent process in society. He recognizes that it has not been realized as an established fact in any industrial society.[13] What can be found empirically in modern societies are three 'abnormal' forms of the division of labour: anomic, forced, and dysfunctional co-ordination. Let us briefly examine each one with special reference to its relevance to leisure theory:

(1) *Anomic:* Durkheim describes anomie as a state of moral deregulation. Under it, the rules governing collective life are inadequate to maintain an equilibrium between relations. This is true of all social change. But where change is deep-seated and rapid, *anomie* may become pathological in its effects.

Durkheim believed that industrialization had destroyed traditional values and institutions but neglected to replace them with new ones. In the hiatus, social life is filled with sentiments of meaninglessness and purposelessness. Nihilism and dissatisfaction rush into all areas of social life, including leisure. Thus, leisure becomes self-destructive and anti-social. The profane style of the punk movement in British youth culture, which grew up in the context of high unemployment, contracting opportunities in education, and 'no future', may be cited as an example (see Hebdige 1979: 106–12).

(2) *Forced:* The 'forced' division of labour corresponds to a condition of inequality in which there is a mismatch between an individual's aptitudes and the social functions that he or she is required to perform. 'For the division of labour to produce solidarity', explains Durkheim (1933: 375), 'it is not sufficient . . . that each have his task; it is still necessary that the task is fitting.' This obviously does not happen in the case of class or caste societies, and Durkheim is explicitly critical of them (1933: 378–81). However, his argument has a wide range of application. It is intended to apply to all cases where social positions are not distributed in accordance with meritocratic principles. How does the forced division of labour apply to the question of leisure? Once it is remembered that leisure is an expression of the division of labour, everything falls into place. Thus, *forced leisure* is equivalent to a situation in which there is (a) a mismatch between the individual's inclinations and the leisure activity he or she performs, or (b) material deprivation in terms of the outlets available to an individual to exploit and develop his or her faculties and interests. As an example of the first instance, one may cite the highly structured and timetabled leisure activities that individuals are forced to participate in if they are inmates of a 'total institution' such as a school, prison, or army barracks.[14] The second case is most commonly encountered in the predicament of the long-term unemployed.

(3) *Dysfunctional co-ordination:* Durkheim gives scant consideration to this third form. It occurs where 'movements are badly adjusted to one another, operations are carried on without any unity; in short solidarity breaks down, incoherence and disorder make their appearance' (Durkheim 1933: 389). In places, Durkheim's discussion itself breaks

down and appears to be logically pre-empted by his prescriptive remarks on anomie. What he seems to have in mind is a
situation where the constituent parts of a given activity
develop discordantly, without centralized control. Dunning
and Sheard (1979) fasten upon a good example in their examination of the development of rugby football in Britain.[15]
According to them, the game developed from an unruly,
rough pastime as a result of being assimilated and reorgan-
ized by the public schools. Of particular interest here is their
analysis of the split between rugby union and rugby league.
The pattern of historical events here is reminiscent of the
maladjustment and disorder that Durkheim describes.[16]

It is widely accepted that Durkheim's discussion of the abnormal
forms of the division of labour is the weakest link in the chain of
his writings on modern society. The critical points have been well
rehearsed by other commentators, so I will be brief.[17] First,
Durkheim's construct of the normal division of labour is not
empirically based. This weakens the authority of his arguments
for it encourages the charge that they are idealist in character.
However, this weakness is further aggravated by the fact that the
overwhelming weight of empirical evidence falsifies his case.
The abnormal forms which he identifies as transitory are, in fact,
the general forms in modern industrial society. Second, the state
of normality that Durkheim invokes appears to give a limited
reading to the active, creative capacity of individual subjects.
Indeed the concept of individual or group interests seems to be
negated. Instead, Durkheim appears to suggest that individual
action simply exemplifies the functional requirements of the
normal form.

SOCIAL INTERVENTION: THE ROLE OF 'OCCUPATIONAL
GROUPS'

If Durkheim has shown that the normal division of labour
includes self-correcting devices which ensure cohesion and
regulation, what role remains for group participation in creative
planning and intervention? Durkheim's answer is as follows. 'It
is true that social functions simultaneously seek to adapt themselves to one another, provided they are regularly in relationship,
nevertheless the mode of adaptation becomes a rule of conduct

only if the group consecrates it with its authority' (1933: 4). In other words, it is not sufficient for the rules of social conduct to be accredited in society, they must also be firmly imprinted upon the mind and soul of the individual. Only an institution which is at once both moral and close to the individual can regulate, define, and sanction the rights and duties of individuals in collective life.

According to Durkheim, three institutions in modern society discharge this function: the family, the state, and occupational groups. The demands and opportunities of advanced industrial life combine to increase the prominence of occupational groups in this area. For example, the penetrating changes in the labour market associated with the creation of an industrial infrastructure have the effect of dismembering the family. Compared with traditional societies, individuals now need to be highly mobile in order to pursue their trade or profession. The relatively short-lived character of family life in modern society seriously weakens the capacity of the family to 'consecrate' the rules of social conduct. For its part, the state is too far away from most people to elicit close identification. Citizens rely on the state to administer social affairs, protect civil liberties, and formulate legislation. But its success in these matters depends on its ability to maintain solemnity, i.e. to be 'above' sectional interests. This necessarily limits its capacity to intervene, at every instant, in the minutiae of everyday social and economic relationships.

What the dynamic conditions of modern industrial life require, Durkheim concludes, is the establishment of strong intermediate collectivities situated between the family and the state. These middle layers of society must be permanent and morally relevant in the lives of the individuals who are attached to them. Only the occupational group, writes Durkheim, 'is a moral power capable of containing individual egos, of maintaining a spirited sentiment of common solidarity in the consciousness of all of the workers, of preventing the law of the strongest from being brutally applied to industrial and commercial relations' (1933: 10). His enthusiastic advocacy of nationwide professional and trade associations is the practical outcome of this theoretical position. Durkheim believes that these groups would be well placed to regulate social and industrial matters, such as wages, industrial relations, appointments, health, safety, and promotion. At the same time, the remit of their role is designed to extend well beyond the workplace. Occupational groups would perform educational, welfare, and leisure functions. They would organize courses, concerts, and dramatic presentations. In general, they would become an essential base for political and non-work life as well as a source of workplace regulation.

Durkheim's published thoughts on the varied functions of occupational groups were complete by 1912. We may infer from the *homo duplex* model of human nature that he embraced in the last stage of his thought that his belief in them as effective agents of conflict resolution diminished. He came to regard the pre-social appetites of egoism as fundamentally at odds with the moral requirements of collective life. The future of work and leisure in the 'higher' organic societies is regarded to be riddled with tension and stress in spite of the ministrations of occupational groups. Even so, there is little evidence to suggest that Durkheim *abandoned* his position that corporate associations are necessary in order to manage and contain conflict. Instead, it is probably nearer the truth to maintain that Durkheim moved towards a position which identified the function of occupational groups as vital in its purpose, but limited in its effects.

LEISURE: THE SECULAR FORM OF MORAL REMAKING?

Again and again in his writings, Durkheim emphasizes that modern industrial societies are going through a stage of profound transition. The power of the time-honoured values and ceremonies that upheld and reaffirmed collective sentiments in earlier times is waning. Instead of finding new ones, society is filled with anxiety and perturbation. 'In a word, the old gods are growing old or already dead, and others are not yet born', (Durkheim 1965: 475).

In particular, Durkheim is sceptical of the idea that individuals under organic solidarity will any longer be prepared to prostrate themselves *en masse* before the mysteries of religious belief. In *The Elementary Forms of Religious Life*, Durkheim looks forward to new, secularized feasts and rites which will anoint social life and unify moral solidarity in industrial society. Specific forms of leisure, such as games and group pastimes, are too narrow and discontinuous to maintain and affirm moral life in society as a whole. However, Durkheim does envisage collective leisure events in the future which will be able to discharge this function. His analysis of the origins of leisure suggests that leisure forms are capable of performing the same function at the secular level that religion performs in the realm of the sacred. According to Durkheim (1965: 475), there is no essential difference 'between an assembly of Christians celebrating the principal dates of the life of Christ, or of Jews remembering the exodus from Egypt, or the promulgation of the decalogue, and a reunion of citizens commemorating the promulgation of a new moral or legal system or some great event in national life'. In both cases the moral remaking of collective life is accomplished by the ceremony of reunion between individuals who are in close sympathy with each other.

The French Revolution gave a glimpse of the shape of things to come. It established a cycle of holidays which were designed as leisure ceremonies to celebrate the secular values of equality, fraternity, and liberty. The institution was not long lasting, 'because the revolutionary faith lasted but a moment' (1965: 476). Even so, Durkheim argues, it was the ancestor of the secular form of moral remaking that is destined to become the mass means of upholding and reaffirming collective sentiments in the fully developed industrial societies of the future: leisure-based rites and ceremonies organized around 'the cult of the individual'.

Durkheim regards the cult of the individual as the necessary corollary of the normal division of labour. It refers to the supreme value that society places on the dignity of the individual. It is reinforced by correlative beliefs in the importance of the principles of meritocracy, equality of opportunity, and social justice. Leisure events in the fully developed, organic societies of the future will be organized in such a way as to mete out reverence for this value. At the same time, it must be repeated that the prospect of individual happiness and satisfaction in leisure relations is subject to the contingencies of the *homo duplex* model of human nature. In the view of the mature Durkheim, leisure can be sociologically understood as a symptom of a morbidly divided society, as well as a sign of social health.

3 *LAISSEZ-FAIRE* LEISURE: Weber and Freud

The work of Weber and Freud pulsates with pessimism regarding the possibility of effective social intervention into collective life. Weber argued that bureaucratic organization and the development of rational knowledge compels individuals to surrender all utopian enthusiasms for the future of work and leisure. Freud was equally severe. 'The intention that man should be "happy" ', he declares (1979: 13), 'is not included in the plan of "Creation".' All that each writer hoped for was that individuals could be persuaded that real freedom lay in the recognition of invulnerable limits to social action. This highly reduced view of freedom and happiness was the most that intelligent people could expect from life. In each case this sombre conclusion is based on a densely argued analysis of modern social conditions. Let us try to unravel the main strands of each argument, and assess their bearing on leisure theory.

Max Weber

The substantive relevance of Weber's social thought to the sociology of leisure is threefold. It can be stated thus in summary form: (1) the analysis of work in capitalist society; (2) the rationalization thesis; (3) the concept of lifestyle. These points comprise the subheadings for my consideration of Weber's contribution to leisure theory.

It would, however, be a grave injustice to the depth and penetration of his thought if one proceeded by implying that these points can be divorced from the shaping themes in his sociology. Weber is, by a wide measure of consent, *the* sociologist of the infernal grove.[1] His grinding realism on questions of power, autonomy, and radical change still corner the sociological market in melancholy. For this reason it is necessary to preface my remarks on his contribution to leisure theory with a brief discussion of the keynotes of his thought. Purchase can best be gained on this complicated question by focusing on a central dichotomy in his writings: the dichotomy between fate and choice.

FATE AND CHOICE

Weber's discussion of fate and choice continues to ignite controversy. Simply put, the matter is as follows. It is often said that life is ruled by fate. If this is indeed the case, the questions of what we shall do, and how we shall live, are superfluous.[2] For fate decides life irrespective of the choices of individuals. Weber rejected the view that social life is governed by powerful metaphysical forces. To accept such a position would have forced him to support a non-social explanation of social behaviour. This, Weber was not prepared to do. Nevertheless, his thought is clearly marked by the belief that social life is fatefully determined. As his wife Marianne said of his work, Weber sought to teach the lesson that 'in its earthly course, an idea always and everywhere operates in opposition to its original meaning' (Marianne Weber 1975: 357). In other words, Weber argues that subjective choice between means and ends in social action *is* possible. But individual control over the *consequences* that arise from putting choices into effect is not. Fate, in Weber's work, is therefore an eminently sociological concept. It refers to the tangible social forces that the individual unleashes by making specific choices. The melancholy of his thought lies in the realization that these forces operate in the long run to violate the intentions that motivated choice in the first place.

What then, does it mean to make a choice in Weber's view of social conduct? No automatic or simple answer can be given to this question because Weber distinguishes no less than four types of subjectively meaningful action, i.e. action which is meaningful from the actor's standpoint.[3] Before we go deeper into the question of choice, it is necessary to set out what these types of meaningful action are.

Weber's typology is, of course, meant to be exhaustive in its terms of reference, i.e. it is intended to apply to all forms of social action. Since this book is concerned with leisure practice I have elected to illustrate each type with examples drawn from the field of sport. The four types are:

(1) *Traditional action:* This is determined by habit, custom, and convention, e.g. the practice of the winner(s) applauding the loser(s) off the field of play.

(2) *Affectual action:* This is associated with the discharge of intense emotions, e.g. violent foul play, or crying with joy at victory.

(3) Wertrational *action:* This arises from a commitment to an ultimate value or end, regardless of the cost involved in making this commitment, e.g. the refusal of some players to participate in games held under the jurisdiction of a political system of which they disapprove, such as apartheid or state socialism.

(4) Zweckrational *action:* This is calculative behaviour intended to align instrumental action to a desired end, e.g. the selection of tactics to deal with given climatic conditions.

In respect of the last two types only, Weber introduces a companion concept: 'objectively correct rationality' (*objektive Richtigkeitsrationalität*) (see Brubaker 1984: 53). *Wertrational* and *Zweckrational* action refer to forms of rational conduct which are defined solely from the actor's standpoint. Objectively correct rationality is based in scientific knowledge, i.e. a type of rationality which is neutral from the subjective standpoint of the actor. Weber's prime sociological interest is in the subjective meaning which individuals make of social phenomena. It follows that what exercises him most in his analysis of social action is the form and network of interdependencies associated with the subjectively rational types. In this respect he constantly stresses the limits of instrumental rationality. An example might help to get the point across. It may be valid to determine rationally what is technically the best move to make at a given stage in a game of chess. But it is invalid to expect rational thought to determine the outcome of the game, and consequently to predict all the moves that should be made in order to win. No body of technically correct knowledge can deprive the opponent of choice. The exercise of choice, in response to external opportunity or threat, can frustrate even the best laid plans made through instrumental rationality.

The example is trivial. The principle in Weber's thought that it illustrates is fundamental. There is no scientifically correct means of determining what the ultimate ends of life should be. As Weber puts it, 'the ultimately possible attitudes in life are irreconcilable, and hence the struggle can never be brought to a final conclusion' (1970: 151–52). Weber's sociology is therefore a 'forlorn' enterprise in at least three senses:

(1) It regards the individual as the ultimate social reality. The individual exists in the midst of others but is, none the less, profoundly alone in life.
(2) It defines social life as intrinsically confrontational. The individual is fated to live by a code of values which necessarily clashes with that of others who hold contrary values.
(3) It works on the principle that the original intentions behind a given course of action will always produce unforeseen and, often, undesired consequences.

The individual is not powerless. Weber fatalistically commits modern humankind to frustration on the ultimate questions in life in perpetuity. He nevertheless believes that there are ways in which this damnable position can be borne psychologically. For example, the scientist, who sees the world as it 'really' is, must embrace all of the contradictions that his/her knowledge brings. Weber rejects art and religion as viable sanctuaries for the embattled rational mind. Instead, the scientist must be stoical and honest, and 'bear the fate of the times like a man' (Weber 1970: 155).

Prima facie, Weber's account of the development of capitalist society might seem to suggest that the dilemma which he particularizes for the scientist is, increasingly, becoming generalized to the masses. A complex industrial society requires everyone to make basic choices. How to earn one's living, whether to save or to spend, how to protect one's interests – these are among the thousand and one decisions that people must make on a day-to-day basis. Weber does not, in fact, believe that these choices beat a path to the real questions of life. On the contrary, he regards them as the 'white noise' of 'average' existence, interfering with and blanking out the possibilities of making decisive choices about the self and society. Weber does not shrink from following through the severe implications of this position. He distinguishes between a 'heroic ethic' and an 'ethic of the mean' in social life. As he puts it:

> 'All systems of ethics, no matter what their substantive content, can be divided into two main groups. There is the "heroic" ethic, which imposes on men demands of principle to which they are generally *not* able to do justice, except at the high points of their lives, but which serve as signposts pointing the way for men's endless *striving*. Or there is the "ethic of the mean", which is content to accept man's everyday "nature" as setting a maximum for the demands which can be made.'
>
> (Weber 1978: 385–86, his emphasis)

Weber clearly believes that the scientist lives by the heroic ethic. In attempting to grapple with the contradictions of life, the scientist shakes a fist at the essential meaninglessness of human existence. For their part, the masses toil under the ethic of the mean. Their habitual work and leisure relations conform to the requirements of a merely mundane existence. As we shall see in Chapter 5, elements of this view can be found in the Frankfurt School's approach to leisure.

Brubaker (1984: 98) points out that this 'aristocratic moral philosophy' is founded upon a 'disturbing paradox'. Apart from its élitist and dismissive view of the masses, it consigns even the best of 'the ethical virtuosi', who strive to follow a heroic ethic in life, to ceaseless torment. As Brubaker explains:

> 'The truly human life is [defined as] one that is guided by reason. To live a life informed by reason, an individual must become a personality. To become a personality, he must commit himself to certain fundamental values. But this commitment . . . cannot itself be guided by reason, for in Weber's view there is no rational way of deciding among the plurality of conflicting possible value commitments. Every rational life, in short, is founded on non-rational choice.'
>
> (Brubaker 1984: 98)

All ideas of constructing a rational social order, where work and leisure are balanced to enhance the well-being of society as a whole, are dismissed as mere grace-notes to deluded fancy. For Weber, the fate of the individual in modern times is to find that all rational choice rests upon irrational presuppositions. In the shadow of this fundamental fact, irony is perhaps the only relief given to us, the only heroism that the best among us may display.

Weber's reduced view of happiness and power is the essential context for an understanding of his contributions to leisure theory. I now want to turn to a systematic examination of the details of this contribution. I shall organize my discussion around the three subheadings itemized at the beginning of this chapter.

WORK IN CAPITALIST SOCIETY

Weber's thesis that rational action is based upon irrational pre-suppositions is fully reflected in his analysis of work in industrial capitalism. Work, he argues, obeys 'the impulse to acquisition' (Weber 1976: 17). This impulse is expressed in a number of different forms. In the capitalist entrepreneur, it is so highly developed that it shapes the course of his entire existence. Yet, as Weber observes, the pursuit of profit is a 'peculiar ethic' to live one's life by (1976: 51); peculiar, because it is thoroughly irrational As Weber explains:

> 'the *summum bonum* of this ethic, the earning of more and more money, combined with the strict avoidance of all spontaneous enjoyment of life, is . . . thought of so purely as an end in itself, that from the point of view of the happiness of, or utility to, the single individual, it appears entirely transcendental and absolutely irrational.'
>
> (Weber 1976: 53)

To put it differently, the compulsion to pursue profit is irrational because it can never be assuaged. It is an all-consuming passion.

Weber submits that the pursuit of profit as an end in itself is: (a) specific to capitalism, and (b) related to 'a type of feeling that is closely connected with certain religious ideas' (1976: 71). What does he mean by this? Three points need to be made:

(1) The entrepreneur is devoted to the accumulation of profit. This involves the renunciation of immediate gratification, the temperance of pleasure, and a fixation upon opportunities for future financial gain.

(2) The entrepreneur's devotional attitude to accumulation promotes a rugged attitude in decision making and a regime of sobriety in the consumption of goods and services. The

same spirit of emotional reserve and rational calculation that governs his attitude to work and the market suffuses his leisure relations.

(3) The entrepreneur's business activity is conducted as a test of the individual's inner resources and personal worth. The accumulation of profit becomes a mark of the individual's worthiness.

The burden of Weber's discussion is that an 'affinity' exists between the capitalist spirit of accumulation and the Calvinist ethic of puritanism and predestination. The merits and defects of this controversial theory have been explored elsewhere (Smith 1981; Marshall 1982; Poggi 1983). Debate has turned on matters of historical accuracy and analytical rigour. The question of leisure has been almost wholly neglected. Yet Weber's thesis does have far-reaching implications for leisure theory. After all, Weber argues that the typical capitalist entrepreneur is quintessentially 'work centred'. Work is venerated as a means of making wealth grow and displaying one's piety and virtue to others. Weber finds the direct historical precedent for this in the attitude of the Puritan who truly valued 'not leisure and enjoyment, but only activity [which] serves to increase the glory of God' (1976: 157). At all events, the capitalist certainly regards industriousness and application as morally superior to pleasure seeking and relaxation. His attitude is that we are all on the earth for a short period, and it is our duty to make the best use of our time. Rest and recuperation have their place in the capitalist worldview. But when they lead to idleness and undisciplined merry making they are reviled. A passage from Foster's *Essay on the Evils of Popular Ignorance* (1821)[4] illustrates this value judgement very clearly. The passage concerns his observation of the leisure-time activities of manual workers. They have, he writes,

> 'several hours in the day to be spent nearly as they please. And in what manner . . . is this precious time expended by those of no mental cultivation? We shall often see them simply annihilating those portions of time. They will for an hour, or for hours together . . . sit on a bench, or lie down on a bank or hillock . . . yielded up to utter vacancy and torpor . . . or collect in groups by the roadside, in readiness to find in whatever passes the occasions for gross jocularity.'

Impulsive enjoyment, killing time, voluptuous pleasure seeking – these are the deadly sins of capitalist leisure time.

This is indeed a parsimonious view of leisure. It certainly fits in with Weber's thesis that the value system of capitalism is historically structured by the Protestant ethic. However, it is a serious misunderstanding of his position to suppose that he believed that the spirit of capitalism was solely, or even mainly, determined by religious influences. Poggi (1983: 29–37) has pointed out that Weber believes that the genesis of modern capitalism involves a complex causal matrix. Other important factors that Weber mentions are changes in scientific and technical knowledge; specialized units of law and order; a state bureaucracy run by trained officials; the growth of individuation; and improvements in systems of communication. A convenient way of bringing these themes together is to consider Weber's discussion of the rationalization process. I shall argue that his discussion of rationalization distances him absolutely from any meliorist position on the development of leisure. Weber did not believe that leisure is an inherently progressive force in society. Rather, it is subject to the contradictions and tension associated with rational action and organization enumerated earlier. I shall also argue that Weber connects the growth and spread of rational calculability in work and non-work relations with the requirements of capitalist industry for a disciplined labour force. He therefore fully anticipates a core argument made by contemporary neo-Marxist historians of leisure; namely, that the rational organization of leisure obeys the accumulation and productivity requirements of the capitalist class (see Thompson 1967; Malcolmson 1973; Bailey 1978; Cunningham 1980).

THE RATIONALIZATION THESIS AND LEISURE PRACTICE

Weber's rationalization thesis is extremely complex. Rationalization does not refer to a single process, but to a plurality of many-sided processes which represent different values and impulses. This plurality includes, *inter alia*, the spread of calculability in personal relations, secularization, legal formalism, the development of scientific and technical knowledge, and bureaucratic administration. In truth, each qualifies for a commentary in its own right. Here I am simply concerned to address the rationalization process as it directly applies to the question of leisure. On this basis, I shall focus on the following selective themes: (1) rational discipline and modern leisure practice; (2) charisma, disenchantment, and leisure.

Rational Discipline and Modern Leisure

For Weber, industrial capitalism depends on the rational conditioning and training of the labourer. The workplace is a model of rational discipline. Its complex system of incentives, rewards, and punishments is synchronized with the mechanization of plant, and the architecture of the work system. The capitalist aims at imposing a structure of control and discipline upon the labourer in order to enhance the regularity of production and to maximize profit. It was Weber who argued, long before Foucault, that the discipline of the factory leaves its mark on the body of the labourer. Under its regime, 'the individual is shorn of his natural rhythm as determined by his organism; in line with the demands of the work procedure, he is attuned to a new rhythm through the functional specialization of muscles and through an optimal economy of physical effort' (Weber 1968: 1,156). But rational discipline extends much further than the confines of the workplace. Indeed, one of Weber's central arguments is that social life under capitalism is dominated by it. He develops this idea most fully in his discussion of bureaucratic administration.

Weber's claims for the significance and influence of bureaucracy are very great. Its importance derives from its technical superiority as a form of administration. As Weber puts it:

'Experience tends universally to show that the bureaucratic type of organization . . . is, from a purely technical point of view, capable of attaining the highest degree of efficiency and is in this sense the most rational known means of exercising authority over human beings. It is superior to any other form in precision, in stability, in the stringency of its discipline, and its reliability.'

(Weber 1968: 223)

In its fully developed, ideal form, bureaucratic administration is based on a hierarchy of 'offices', each differentiated from the other on the basis of the technical expertise of the staff. The remit of official duties is laid down in the terms of the employment contract, and the house rules of work conduct. Work responsibilities are executed in a spirit of 'formalistic impersonality', i.e. with regard to standardized methods and calculable action.

Selection and recruitment of salaried officials proceeds strictly on the basis of technical qualifications. Weber does not use half-measures in his judgement of the effect of bureaucratic adminis-tration. 'The whole pattern of everyday life', he writes (1968: 223), 'is cut to fit this framework.'

It follows that leisure relations are included in this statement. Their 'fate' is also to be increasingly shaped by high levels of calculability, formalistic impersonality, standardization, and observance of routine. Guttman (1978) exploits and develops this Weberian insight in his thesis that there has been a consistent historical movement away from ritual towards rational standards in the organization of play. The privatization, individuation, commercialization, and pacification of leisure relations, which I examined in Chapter 1, may also be interpreted as concomitants of the rationalization process. The fact that leisure and work are increasingly shaped by the same social forces is no pretext for arguing that leisure and work are destined to converge. In Weber's view, the administration and subjective meaning of leisure are structured by the requirements of the individual's career and the sources of his or her income. Indeed, it might be said that the rational discipline of bureaucratic capitalism requires work experience to be demarcated from leisure as a functional necessity of social organization. For this enhances the allure of home life and spare-time activities, and hence increases the necessity to work.

Charisma, Disenchantment, and Leisure

Weber's discussion of pre-bureaucratic domination, notably patriarchalism and patrinomialism, stresses the highly personal-ized character of social relations. The individual's commitment to a cause is not bartered for an allegiance to rational standards of equality and justice. On the contrary, people follow traditional rights and duties and the principle of 'strictly personal loyalty'. The patrimonial official is not interested in the bureaucratic distinctions between public and private life, work and leisure. Rather the organization of his time derives from a purely per-sonal submission to the ruler. The subject is prepared to place everything at the disposal of the ruler, including his possessions and even his life.

All of this changes with the rise of rationally administered societies. Under modern bureaucratic systems of rule, the rights and duties of workers and employers, and governments and citizens, are carefully circumscribed by a complex juridical system. People no longer give themselves wholly to a leader. Similarly, few leaders in rationally administered organizations either seek or expect total commitment of this sort.

There are numerous differences that separate traditional types of authority, such as patriarchalism and patrinomialism, from modern bureaucratic systems. Even so, Weber stresses the importance of recognizing the basic common denominator between them. They are all systems of authority which govern *everyday* relations. For Weber, they are structures orientated to the satisfaction of routine, habitual needs by ordinary means. Contemporary leisure relations clearly exhibit the same emphasis on routine. As I argued earlier, the most popular leisure activities are organized rationally, in order to make a profit for the social interests who own and control the leisure industry. At the same time, leisure relations include more than their fair share of instances of extraordinary behaviour, i.e. behaviour where the individual is transported, taken outside himself, elated. Everyone has had the experience of being moved by the work of a particular writer, musical performer, or actor. Weber's discussion of authority types takes account of precisely this sort of experience. He identifies charisma as the bestowal of exceptional and perhaps even supernatural qualities by an assembly of people upon an individual or group of individuals. The charismatic individual is seen as being, superlatively, beyond the common ruck.

Weber's discussion of charisma fastens upon its role as 'the specifically creative revolutionary force of history' (1968: 1,117). More narrowly, the concept is a valuable addition to leisure theory. Charisma inheres in leisure practice under capitalism in the form of 'the fan club', 'the star system', and the various cults that surround famous people or groups. Empirically, it can be studied in such cases as the rise of successful sporting personalities, authors, actors, and pop stars. These individuals are seen as superhuman, and sometimes their followers endow them with magical powers. The late John Lennon complained that in the heyday of the Beatles, the group was often besieged after performances by cripples wanting to be touched. More generally, the phenomenon of wanting to see and touch a famous person is widely understood in modern society.

Weber's view of charisma is that it is an extremely unstable form of authority. Everything depends on the personal qualities of the charismatic individual. These qualities may easily be tarnished or weakened by events. For this reason, Weber believed that 'it is the fate of charisma to recede before the powers of . . . *rational discipline* [this] eradicates not only personal charisma but also stratification by status groups, or at least transforms them in a rationalizing direction' (Weber 1968: 1,148–149, his emphasis). In modern leisure activities the shift in a 'rationalizing direction' can be studied empirically with reference to the mass communication and rational management of charisma. The creation of an industry producing artefacts and mementoes of the famous person transforms the personal basis of charisma into the impersonal form of market transactions. Weber regards these tendencies as symptomatic of the rationally administered society. 'The fate of our times', he writes, 'is characterized by rationalization and intellectualization and, above all, by "the disenchantment of the world"' (Weber 1970: 155). Rational administration promotes impersonality and dehumanization. The bureaucratic official is reduced to playing the part of a small cog in a ceaselessly moving machine which he cannot control and is relatively powerless to influence. The highest expression of rational thought is science. Yet, as Weber repeatedly emphasizes, the rational, calculable interrogation of life has done nothing to advance human happiness. It may have increased human control over nature but, at the same time, it has deprived the world of the charms and mystery that our ancestors knew and worshipped. The progress of scientific knowledge shows, ever more insistently, that life is without meaning. Weber explicitly denounces the orthodox Marxist belief that changing the power structure of capitalist society will alleviate the disfiguring aspects of rational administration. As Weber genially explains, the effect of socialist revolution upon a rationally ordered officialdom is merely 'to change the top officials. It continues to operate because it is in the vital interest of everyone concerned' (1968: 989).

Sociologists often portray Weber's rationalization thesis as a thoroughfare for minatory thoughts about the future. However, what is really chilling about his thought is its austere appraisal of how far industrial society has already succumbed to disenchantment. All social policy, including leisure policy, is compromised by the fate of the times. The central motif of his argument is that this fate is not susceptible to rational corporate control. The disenchantment of play, the growth of urban rootlessness, and the imposition of routine in leisure are all parts of a widening gyre.

THE CONCEPT OF LIFESTYLE

One of Weber's most durable legacies to the sociology of leisure is the concept of lifestyle.[5] Initially, he raises the matter in the context of his discussion of status. Status, for Weber, refers to claims of negative or positive prestige and honour in social life. Specifically, these claims may be attached to relations of heredity, education, marriage, and commensality (the right to eat at the same table as others). The concept of lifestyle may be interpreted as an attempt to generalize these various properties sociologically for a given social position. In Weber's own words, 'in content, status honour is normally expressed by the fact that above all else a specific *style of life* is expected from those who wish to belong to the circle' (1968: 932, his emphasis).

The composition of lifestyle varies with the empirically given circumstances. One important dimension of it in all cases and at all times is the conspicuous consumption of commodities and leisure time. Weber himself alights on the case of games in the life of the feudal knight as an example. Weber assigns a dual function to the playing of games in this warrior status group. First, it acts as a means of training for military service. Games function to reinforce the dominant values of the knight's central life interest, i.e. aggression, enthusiasm, and discipline, which are required in warfare. Second, the playing of games and the consumption of luxury commodities categorically set the knight apart from all others who are obliged to labour for a living. Weber's argument recalls some of the basic tenets put forward by Veblen (1925) in his theory of the 'leisure class'. Thus, Weber submits that for the knight leisure 'constitutes a counterpole to all economically rational action'. Leisure, in this sense, is 'an important power instrument for the sake of maintaining one's own dominance through mass suggestion' (Weber 1968: 1,106). Weber's discussion of lifestyle is relevant to the modern debate on leisure in at least two major ways: (a) it equates leisure practice with a subjectively meaningful affiliation to a specific value position, and (b) it defines the lifestyle attached to a given leisure form as a symbolic expression of power.

In modern societies, the configuration of leisure lifestyles and the mediation of leisure values are far more complex than in preindustrial society. But the same principles of closure and exclusivity obtain. Each of the leisure status groups that he alludes to, namely clubs, house parties and voluntary associations, apply these principles. They distance themselves from others, notes Weber, by certain 'honorific preferences'. For example, he mentions the privilege of wearing certain costumes, eating special dishes which are taboo to others, and, above all else, manipulating 'totemic' objects such as estates and leisure commodities.

Sigmund Freud

Freud produced something unique for leisure theory: a theory of play whose main purpose is to affirm the existence of the unconscious. I shall consider his contribution in two stages. First, I shall examine his model of the main principles of mental functioning. The mere mention of this topic is apt to induce colossal weariness in some readers. The Freudian view of the mind has been so widely discussed and summarized in modern literature, cinema, and drama, as well as in social science, that it has become part of western popular culture. However, I do not believe that it is possible to skip the material. For one thing, it is the basis of all the exploits in social theory that Freud engaged in during the last years of his life. In addition, it includes his discussion of the pleasure principle as a primary process in mental life. One of the central arguments of this book is that Freud's work on the pleasure principle is indispensable for modern leisure theory. I shall take up this point in the last chapter, when I consider some new rules for the sociology of leisure. In the second stage I shall explore Freud's position on the regulation of pleasure in modern society. This will entail an examination of the Freudian view of the function of play and leisure in industrial civilization.

THE THREE PRINCIPLES OF METAPSYCHOLOGY

In his essay 'The Instincts and Their Vicissitudes' (1984), Freud maps out a framework through which to approach his thought on the structure and functions of the mental system. He invites the reader to consider the mental apparatus in terms of three principles of mental functioning: (1) subject/object, (2) pleasure/unpleasure, (3) active/passive. Let us examine these in turn.

Subject/Object

Freud's view of the mind adheres to a fundamental assumption of western social philosophy (at least since the time of Descartes), i.e. that a radical separation exists between subject and object. For Freud, 'the basic situation' in psychology and sociology is the individual (subject) confronting the external world (object). What is radically unorthodox about Freud's view is that he sees the subject as inherently *fragmented*. Freud calls the conscious part of the subject the 'ego'. It stands as the gatekeeper between 'inner' mental activity and the external world of physical and cultural stimuli. For Freud, the conscious ego is the mere surface of the mental apparatus. The greater mass consists of the 'unconscious'. The unconscious is, by definition, inaccessible from normal consciousness. It is the dark castle which dominates mental life and which is fortified against the gaze of consciousness by a series of barriers of repression and resistance. These barriers are occasionally breached in the subject's contact with the external world. In such instances the unconscious becomes visible through dream memories, slips of the tongue, disruptive mental lapses, and, in extreme cases, forms of mental pathology.[6] Freud schematizes the unconscious as consisting of three parts: the id, the super-ego and the ego.[7]

At this point an obvious difficulty arises. How can Freud maintain that the ego is simultaneously part of the conscious *and* the unconscious? The apparent inconsistency is resolved if we think of mental life in *developmental* terms. The individual organism comes into the world with the congenital drives and instincts of the id nakedly on display. If these elementary demands are left in the raw state they confer selectional *dis*advantage upon the organism. For without regulation they are discharged in a chaotic manner. Socialization provides this regulation. It is in the early stages of socialization that the conscious ego has its origin. It develops out of the id, through the two-way traffic between the id and the external world, e.g. through the acquisition of language and the internationalization of the rules of everyday life. The conscious ego has its roots in the unconscious. The ego may be divided, says Freud, into a conscious part which 'goes to sleep at night', and an unconscious part which 'behaves exactly like the repressed' (Freud 1984: 339–407). Freud refers to the super-ego as the fount of conscience in the human subject. It emerges through the child's perception of parental and societal judgemental standards. The super-ego functions to supervise the plans and actions of the ego and exercises censorship over them.

Pleasure/Unpleasure

Freud argues that the various component parts of mental life are animated by the pleasure principle, i.e. they are generically structured to produce pleasure and avoid unpleasure. This does not mean that the human subject in Freud's theory is merely a hedonist. The stricture to 'avoid unpleasure' is just as important as the aim of producing pleasure. Freud had hypostatized an aggressive and destructive instinct in mental functioning in his pre-war discussion of sadism (see Freud 1905, 1909). It was not until *Beyond the Pleasure Principle* (1984) that he firmly located the death instinct and identified it as a principle in the mental apparatus which sought to reduce 'the restlessness of life' to a stable, 'inorganic' state. In that work, Freud reiterated his belief that 'the mental apparatus endeavours to keep the quantity of excitation present in it as low as possible or at least keep it constant' (1984: 277). Freud calls this principle of mental functioning 'the principle of constancy' or 'the Nirvana principle'. In his work after 1920 he attributes increasing importance to it. We will consider this matter at greater length in the discussion of Freud's view of the requirements of civilization and the organization of play. At this juncture, it is necessary to emphasize that the Nirvana principle functions to obey the demands of the death instinct; similarly, the pleasure principle expresses the inclinations of the life instinct. This is important because it implies that social action is shaped by the original, concurrent, and mutually opposing dispositions of these two instincts. Freud thus attributes an instinctual basis for the historical gyrations of conflict and order.[8]

Active/Passive

The instincts, Freud argues, are not simply mutually opposing, they are also hydra-headed in themselves. For example, the instinctual aim of accumulating pleasure develops alongide the wish to be used as a source of pleasure for others. The active aim (to experience pleasure, to seek pleasure) is enmeshed with the passive aim (to please others, to be used for pleasure). The polarity between the active and the passive is a characteristic feature of Freud's psychoanalytic method, and he applies it to investigate a wide range of psychological problems, notably narcissism, masochism, sadism, and exhibitionism (Freud 1984: 124–32). He also uses it, less successfully, to lend legitimacy to the sexist prejudice that men are 'naturally' active and women 'naturally' passive creatures. Thus, for example, he asserts that 'the coupling of activity with masculinity and of passivity with femininity meets us, indeed, as a biological fact'.[9]

As far as play and leisure are concerned, the polarity has a number of intriguing implications which Freud himself partially followed through in his ambitious experiments in social theory after 1927.[10] Chief among them is the idea that the active aim of accumulating pleasure expresses itself through play, and also establishes the basis for aim reversal (being a spectator of play). The transformation of playing into watching corresponds to the operation of the dynamics between the active/passive principle in the mind.

PLAY, LEISURE AND INDUSTRIAL CIVILIZATION

Freud regards play as an expression of the pleasure principle. The play of infants articulates the initial drive of the id to accumulate pleasure through the body. This is why the central metaphor of childhood play is the body and its artefacts. The child's play world offers pleasure from three analytically distinct sources: (1) the individual's own body, (2) the external physical world, (3) the external social world. These are not only sites of pleasure, they are also controls on action. Children may tirelessly play repetitive games which give them pleasure. But adult society permits children to be in this state of unbridled 'sensuous gratification' for only a short period of time. Freud speaks of a moment in everyone's life when 'shame and anxiety awoke, expulsion followed, and sexual life and the tasks of cultural activity began' (1976: 343).

This moment in the life of the individual is, of course, the Oedipal crisis. The Oedipal stage, which begins with the collision between the child's ceaseless demands for instinctual gratification and the taboos of the adult world, ends in the child's identification with that world. After this stage, the child can no longer relate to the play world as the outer extent of his own body. Instead, play and pleasure become increasingly timetabled, individuated experiences which correspond to adult values and incentives. Freud believes that the Oedipal crisis is the key cultural reference point in the structure of civilization. Through it, the infant ceases to be 'polymorphously perverse', and internalizes the values of acceptable public behaviour which make civilized life possible.

The important thing about adult play is that it normally consists of *permissible* fun and pleasure. Children may cut the whiskers off a cat for 'fun', or lock up their brothers and sisters in play; but adults do not do that kind of thing. The pleasures of adult life are, in fact, closely codified and regulated. Freud calls the social mechanism responsible for this, the *reality principle*. It imposes certain obligations and responsibilities upon all adult individuals regardless of their social position. Freud mentions, *inter alia*, the need to work, to keep the peace, to defer gratification, and to restrain violent emotions. When Freud affirms that 'civilization is built upon the renunciation of instinct', it is to the work of this principle that he is referring (1979: 34).

For Freud, civilized life is skewered on the prongs of the dialectic between the pleasure and reality principles. The individual is instinctually constituted to accumulate pleasure. However, civilization depends on order and discipline for stability and growth. The structural basis for conflict and unhappiness in everyday life is therefore palpable. Even so, Freud recognizes that civilized life would not be possible without some institutionalized outlets for pleasure. Individuals cannot live by work and sobriety alone. This is why Freud argues that the reality principle does not function solely to block pleasure. Its action is more akin to the work of a drawbridge: permitting some forms of pleasure in certain contexts and excluding others. In Freud's own words, the reality principle

'does not abandon the intention of ultimately obtaining pleasure, but it nevertheless demands and carries into effect the postponement of satisfaction, the abandonment of a number of possibilities of gaining satisfaction and the temporary tolerance of unpleasure as a step on the long indirect road to pleasure.'
(Freud 1984: 278)

The social organization of leisure in advanced industrial society obeys the reality principle. It is based in a complex network of economic, political, juridical, and cultural power which permits the mediation of pleasure in approved social contexts. The main function of leisure is to provide an outlet for the inhibited aims and repressed desires of everyday life. Leisure allows the individual to 'become the hero, the king, the creator, or the favourite he desired to be, without following the long round-about path of making real alterations in the external world' (Freud 1984: 42).

Freud's thesis on pleasure and the reality principle eludes plain judgements. One cannot say that the reality principle exerts a positive or negative effect in social life; or that leisure is a reduced expression of the pleasure principle. It is true that the moderation of vital aggressive and sexual instincts which civilization demands, exacts a burden of unhappiness and suffering in the community. At the same time, the renunciation of instinct is the enabling device for community stability. Freud even argues that renunciation produces the means for the sublimation of thwarted energies into the arts and sciences (1979: 34). It therefore acts as the means of driving civilization on to new heights of achievement. Similarly, leisure activity in industrial society is controlled by the limits of permissible behaviour. To this extent it represents a shrunken form of the pleasure principle. At the same time, however, leisure 'offers substitutive satisfactions for the oldest and still most deeply felt cultural renunciations, and for that reason serves as nothing else does to reconcile a man to the sacrifices he has made on behalf of civilization' (Freud 1961: 14).

Freud's insistence on the importance of the reality principle in industrial civilization has led some observers to argue that work is the central category of meaningful experience in his theory of human relations. Thus Riesman (1954: 310–33) has argued that Freudian man is 'work centred'. On this basis he claims that Freud believed in the rigid segregation of work and leisure experience. Such arguments fundamentally misunderstand the generalized property of the struggle between the reality and pleasure principles. 'Civilized man', writes Freud, 'has exchanged a portion of his happiness for a portion of security' (1979: 52). The point applies to all social relations. The reality principle does not stop working when the factory gates or the office doors close. This is important, for Riesman's argument can easily lead to the false conclusion that work is the cause of unhappiness and dissatisfaction in modern society and that the reorganization of work will increase general life satisfaction. It is true that Freud argued that most people have an aversion to work, and only engage in it by dint of necessity. But if the opposite argument is used, and it is assumed that society is dominated by a leisure ethic, there is absolutely nothing in Freud's theory to suggest that people would, *ipso facto*, be happier and more fulfilled. The scope for radical intervention in social policy is therefore limited.

If Freud argues that instinctual renunciation is a necessary feature of industrial civilization, he nevertheless recognizes that renunciation is stratified. Some groups and classes in industrial society have more freedom in their work and leisure relations than others. Freud's arguments in this context provide an additional proof of his scepticism on the question of intervention. Freud writes:

> 'It is just as impossible to do without control of the mass by a minority as it is to dispense with coercion in the work of civilization. For the masses are lazy and unintelligent; they have no love of instinctual renunciation, and they are not convinced by arguments of its inevitability. . . . It is only through the influence of individuals who can set an example and whom masses recognize as their leaders that they can be induced to perform work and undergo the renunciation on which the existence of civilization depends.'
>
> (Freud 1961: 7–8)[11]

Freud's theory therefore includes the intriguing idea that the work and leisure preoccupations of the masses should be manipulated by élite groups so as to ensure the well-being of society as a whole. Freud himself never followed through the radical implications of this position. As we shall see in Chapter 5, it was left to the central figures in the Frankfurt School to do so, with their ambitious marriage between Freud and Marx in their approach to leisure.

LEISURE AND THE STRUGGLE BETWEEN 'LIFE AND DEATH'

After the publication of *Beyond the Pleasure Principle* Freud argued consistently that the reality and pleasure principles were themselves localized expressions of the general struggle between the life and death instincts. 'This struggle', he writes, 'is what all life ultimately consists of, and the evolution of civilization may therefore be described as the struggle for life of all human species' (1979: 59).

What did Freud mean by this momentous struggle? The question can best be approached by a closer look at his view of the content and function of the two instincts. Freud's evidence for the life instinct (Eros) is based on the belief that the individual organism in all species will ordinarily struggle to maintain life. The idea can be readily confirmed by observation of an individual organism which is subject to illness or external threat. Upon this basis, however, Freud makes the more contentious claim that the purpose of the life instinct is 'to combine single human individuals, and after that families, then races, peoples and nations, into one great unity, the unity of mankind' (1979: 59). All that attracts, all that encourages co-operation and development is part of the life instinct. The rationale behind this claim is rather weak. 'Why this has to happen,' admits Freud, 'we do not know' (1979: 59). Even so, it is possible to regard the inclination to engage in group leisure pursuits and to develop skills in games and recreations as expressions of this instinct.

The clinical evidence for the death instinct (Thanatos) rests largely on the phenomenon that Freud termed 'repetition compulsion', i.e. the practice of repeating unpleasant or destructive behaviour.[12] To place oneself in danger or to punish oneself is in such striking opposition to the aim of the pleasure principle that it cannot easily be thought of as a derivative of the life instinct. Instead, Freud argued that the death instinct is an 'original', 'universal', and 'self-subsisting' disposition in all animate forms: the desire to return to a quiescent, inanimate state. It is not easy to think of examples of this instinct in the field of leisure. Perhaps the failure to learn from one's mistakes or the stubborn refusal to make the most of one's opportunities come close to it.

CONCLUSION

This last shift in Freud's thought serves to underline his view of the nugatory prospect of any improvement in work and leisure in industrial society. The subjective goal of personal life satisfaction is incompatible with the objective requirements of civilization. The most that can be hoped for is that the individual can be partially reconciled to the emotional frustration engendered by the repression of desire and the deferment of gratification. Leisure activity is one of the major ways in which this process of reconciliation occurs. However, the burden of Freud's argument is that the individual can never be fully recompensed for the possibilities of instinctual discharge and pleasure accumulation which civilized life compels him or her to forgo. The Freudian view of leisure in modern society is therefore founded on the assumption of the historic *austerity* of experience. The pleasure principle is mediated through a complicated system of filtration which civilization applies to regulate and stabilize collective life. This is not to imply that findings of life satisfaction and personal happiness in modern leisure experience testify only to the false consciousness of the respondents. There is nothing in Freud's argument to suggest that when people testify to experiences of pleasure and contentment they are referring to anything other than genuine emotions. The point is that these emotions are meaningless unless they are analysed in terms of the prevailing standards of the day. Viewed historically, these standards can clearly be shown to have involved a moderation in the range of permissible pleasurable and unpleasurable behaviour. According to Freud, both the incidence and intensity of instinctual discharge can be shown to have receded.[13] The compensatory function that leisure performs in modern society must be understood in the context of this long-term process. Freud's theory leads us to infer that in civilized society, leisure experience is normally controlled by a network of regulatory mechanisms which compel relations to obey a comparatively low level of intensity. In the industrial-urban societies of today, the experience of raw pleasure is confined only to infants and individuals bidden by certain forms of madness.

PART TWO
LEISURE THEORY AND
MULTI-PARADIGMATIC
RIVALRY

4 SOCIAL FORMALISM AND LEISURE

The use of the term 'social formalism' to describe the work of a range of writers as diverse as Dumazedier, Burch, Kaplan, Kelly, Neulinger, Roberts, and Parker, requires some justification. For one thing, there is no evidence that they see themselves as members of a unified school of thought in leisure theory. Certainly, no agreed programme or manifesto has emerged from their ranks. Even so, their work represents the dominant research tradition in the field. In the words of one commentator, it constitutes the 'conventional wisdom' in leisure theory against which all rival paradigms must be measured and judged (Parry 1983: 74–9).

I shall consider social formalism under two general subheadings: (1) the methodology of formalism, and (2) domain assumptions about the nature of leisure.

The Methodology of Formalism

Social formalism is committed to the *scientific* study of social life. The methodological and practical superiority of science over all other forms of knowledge is assumed. This is expressed procedurally in an emphasis on the importance of quantifiable concepts and propositions in theory and research. Survey methods dominate the field. They are recommended as the best means for systematically assembling hard data on leisure. Hard data is the life stuff of 'good' formalist theory.

The formalist approach begins with the question of defining leisure. Dumazedier has done more than most to insist on the absolute importance of a rigorous, scientific definition for the entire 'scientific' status of formalist research. A scientific definition of leisure, he argues (Dumazedier 1974: 67), must exhibit four basic properties:

(1) *Logical consistency:* it must permit the specialist to ascertain the dividing line between the object of research (leisure) and other relations in society. In Dumazedier's own words, the definition 'should enable its object to be located in the genus to which it belongs, while being distinguished from other objects within it by the least ambiguous specific difference' (1974: 67).[1]
(2) *Validity:* it must relate to the major social processes which animate social life in the present day.
(3) *Operational proficiency:* it must have the capacity to be put to practical use in empirical research.
(4) *Precision:* 'it must take account of the division of labour within sociology between various specialized branches (industrial, political, etc.) and define its object as clearly as possible to demarcate it from that of other specialisms' (Dumazedier (1974: 67).

I shall go into the question of how formalists have examined leisure in the next section. At this stage in my discussion, my main concern is to attempt an exact elaboration of the central methodological preoccupations which characterize the approach. In this respect, Dumazedier's account is exceptionally helpful. His stipulations regarding an objectively adequate sociological definition of leisure go far beyond a simple devotion to the ideals of clarity and precision. They underwrite nothing less than a commitment to construct a pure science of leisure which aims to treat its object of inquiry as 'a total social fact, linked with all others' (Dumazedier 1974: 73). This semi-autonomous discipline will seek to explain and predict relations in the world of leisure by searching for regularities and causal relationships in its constituent parts. This does not preclude inquiry into other sectors of social life. However, it does demand that leisure activity should be taken as the basis from which society as a whole may be explored.

The quintessential achievement of this approach to leisure theory is twofold. It has (a) illuminated how our personal consumption and leisure change through the life cycle, and (b) quantified the relationship between the distribution of leisure and associated variables such as, *inter alia*, income, property, occupation, sex, education, religion, and race (Kaplan 1975: 89–105).

I want to look more closely at the distinctive research procedure employed here. After considering some case studies, I shall return to examine its validity critically and at length. I shall argue that social formalism's main defect in this respect is its tendency to separate its object of inquiry from the rest of society. Social formalism neglects to convey the dynamic interdependence between leisure relations and society as a whole. Indeed the only ambassadors of society which gain admittance into formalism are the 'associated variables' of leisure, i.e. relations which are defined in terms of leisure itself.

PATTERNS OF LEISURE: PARKER'S VIEW

I noted in my introduction that academic sociology has tended to neglect the question of leisure. In Britain the standard bearers have been few and far between. Perhaps the most prominent figure in their midst, certainly in terms of output, is Stanley Parker.[2] In this section I shall treat Parker's work as being at the forefront of the formalist tradition. I shall develop this proposition by examining his typology of leisure patterns in contemporary society.

Parker's core research interest is the relationship between work and leisure. In exploring this field, he invites us to make a basic conceptual distinction between the individual and society. As he explains, 'the functions which leisure serves for society are rather different from those which apply to individuals: the former are to do with maintaining the social system and achieving collective aims, the latter provide relaxation, entertainment and personal development' (Parker 1983: 41).

The distinction logically implies that relationships at the societal level have relative autonomy from those at the individual level. Thus, it is possible for sociologists to locate a 'fusion' or 'polarization' between work and leisure relations in the organization of society, without a corresponding development at the individual level.[3] Parker does not state that the conceptual distinction represents the division between diachronic and synchronic analysis, but in trying to understand the typology I have found it helpful to think in these terms. Thus, at the societal level, changes in the work–leisure relationship refer to historical changes and can best be studied developmentally. In contrast, relationships at the individual level refer to present-day conditions and can best be studied in terms of the structural distribution between work–leisure relations. What then are the main types of relationship between work and leisure at the individual level?

Parker employs a threefold typology. The *extension pattern* refers to a situation where work and leisure activities in the individual's life are similar in content, and no sharp dividing line can be drawn between work and leisure. The *opposition pattern* describes a situation where work and leisure relationships are polarized, and the demarcation between work and leisure is unambiguous. Finally, under the *neutrality pattern* work and leisure are held to be distinct, but not polarized. There may be areas of partial convergence between the two. But the neutrality pattern is definitively set apart from the other two by the neutral feeling which individuals express concerning work and leisure, i.e. a feeling which exhibits no strong attachment to either sector of life.

It is important to recognize that Parker's typology is based upon empirical research into selected occupational groups.[4] His fieldwork included an examination of work and non-work variables and their causal relationship with attitudes to leisure. Among the work variables that Parker identifies are autonomy in the work situation, use of personal faculties, and involvement with work colleagues. As regards non-work variables, education, duration of leisure, and social contacts are singled out. On this basis he puts forward a number of propositions regarding the functional connections between patterns of work and leisure relations. For example, individuals who experience high autonomy in their work are likely to exhibit an extension pattern, and those with low autonomy a neutral pattern. A close friendship network at work is positively related with an extension pattern and negatively related to a neutrality pattern. Individuals who manifest an extension pattern were found to have the highest levels of education, and those with the opposition pattern were found to have the lowest. Finally, Parker submits that personality development is a main function of the extension pattern. In the neutrality pattern the function of leisure is identified with 'relaxation'; and in the opposition pattern with 'recuperation'.

SOCIAL FORMALISM: THE FRAGMENTS AND BEYOND

Parker's work has exerted a great influence in the field of social formalism. But it is by no means alone. In fact, the work–leisure relationship is a central preoccupation of formalist excursions in the sociology of leisure. In an influential initial statement of the relationship, Wilensky (1960) distinguished between 'spillover' and 'compensatory' leisure hypotheses. 'Spillover' models emphasize the determinant effect of work experience on leisure behaviour. Basically they suggest that the deprivations of work are reproduced in leisure. For example, workers who are physically exhausted and alienated by their work are likely to have a passive, sedentary leisure pattern, e.g. watching television. 'Compensatory models' argue that leisure can act as a compensation for the deprivations of work.

Wilensky intends his work to be used as a heuristic device in exploring problems in the sociology of work and leisure. He therefore does not anticipate that empirical research will reproduce his typological model in every particular. However, a number of studies exist within the formalist tradition which appear to support his basic ideas. For example, Friedmann's (1961) famous study of the leisure activities of French miners includes propositions about compensatory work and leisure relationships which fit Wilensky's schema. Similarly, Meissner's (1971) study of the effect of working in a job where there is low opportunity for social participation with others, found a 'spillover effect' in 'unsociable leisure' patterns.

The spillover and compensatory typology has had an obvious influence on Parker's thought. His threefold typology of work–leisure relationships may be seen as an attempt to refine Wilensky's basic model. Further afield, the typology continues to exert an influence in current research (see Kelly 1976; Staines 1980; Roberts 1981, esp. 56–66). Since there is a strong element of repetition in this work I do not propose to attempt a comprehensive survey of research findings here. I shall, however, examine a representative study which illustrates the typical research approach and the kind of findings produced. Champoux's (1978) study is based on a sample of 178 employees of an American pharmaceutical firm. His working hypothesis is that individuals may be meaningfully compared and contrasted according to their perceptions of the value of work and non-work experience and their own 'self-concepts'. Respondents were asked to frame their replies according to a survey set of twenty-five 'semantic differential scales'. The research aim was to investigate the correspondence or divergence between an individual's self-concept and his or her perception of work and leisure.

Abstracting from the data, Champoux concludes that it is useful to distinguish four personality types in work–leisure relationships. Individuals whose self-concept conforms more closely to work experience than non-work experience are classified as *spillover work oriented*. Those whose self-concept conforms more closely to non-work experience are classified as *spillover non-work oriented*. Individuals who are strongly attached to their work but who find their leisure unexciting are described as *compensatory work-oriented* individuals. Finally, individuals who find excitement and stimulation chiefly in their non-work activity, and experience their work as a means to an end, are termed *compensatory non-work-oriented* individuals.

I shall take up some of the defects of Champoux's work in the course of the next section which consists of a critical examination of formalist methodology. At this point in my argument, I want to correct the impression that I may have given that formalist approaches to leisure are only concerned with the work–leisure relationship. There is, for example, a strong formalist research tradition in the sociology of leisure and the life cycle. The Rapaports (1975) assembled a great deal of information from different age-groups relating to leisure behaviour which leads them to conclude that each stage of the life cycle is associated with a distinctive leisure concern. Adolescents demand leisure which is varied, exciting, and based in peer groups. Much of their leisure-related spending goes on items of conspicuous consumption such as clothing and beauty products. The leisure activities of the young are thought to help them to adjust to new work and family roles. During the period of marriage and procreation leisure activities are organized around the family and the responsibilities of home ownership. In later years, when children have left the family, the leisure pattern of parents changes yet again.

The Rapaports emphasize the central importance of the family in the organization of leisure. This is a well-established theme in formalist research literature. The family is seen as the primary agent of leisure socialization (Cheek, Field, and Burdge 1976; Kelly 1978). It is also regarded as the major unit of consumption for leisure goods and services (Collins and Strelitz 1982). On the question of family life and leisure satisfaction, research by

Presvelou (1971) and Orthner (1976) suggests that joint conjugal participation in leisure activity correlates positively with higher marital satisfaction scores.

Of related interest in the formalist tradition is the work done on leisure and social stratification. Research findings here are not easy to assimilate. They are voluminous, but somewhat inconclusive. For example, Young and Willmott (1973: 217) submit that there is no significant connection between socio-economic criteria and leisure activity, whereas Cheek and Burch (1976: 51) argue that income is a direct, determining influence on the sort of leisure activity that an individual will indulge in. In an important critical review, Wilson (1980: 26–9) submits that social stratification is a key influence on leisure conduct. He argues that there is a marked inconsistency between formalist studies regarding the criteria used to isolate and differentiate strata. For example, status rankings are treated as being equivalent to census-based occupational categories; and no account is taken of the effect of social mobility on leisure behaviour. These strictures point to deficiencies in the basic methodology of social formalism. It is to a more systematic appraisal of these deficiencies that I now want to turn.

A CRITIQUE OF THE FORMALIST APPROACH

Parker's study of leisure and work stands in the closest possible relationship with orthodox functionalism. In this, his work is no different from the bulk of survey research that occupies the commanding heights of social formalism.[5] The sociological objections to functionalism are well known (Benton 1977; Elias 1978b), and I do not propose to cover old ground here. Nevertheless, in the course of this critique it will be necessary to make some theoretical connections explicit, because social formalists have neglected to situate their own work in a coherent tradition of social theory. I have already argued that the formalist approach as a whole has tended to trivialize the true extent of multi-paradigmatic rivalry in the sociology of leisure. Had they addressed some of the critical debates on values and research, they might have been less vulnerable to the first criticism that I want to make.

In Chapter 1 I suggested that statistical correlations between leisure activity and socio-economic variables can provide useful information on the distribution of leisure in society. The formalist approach as a whole tends to confirm this point. However, the survey method *per se* runs the risk of assigning quantitative data a priority in analysis and policy formation which they neither warrant nor sustain. The conventional line of defence of quantitative methods is that they reveal hard facts about social reality, and do not seek refuge in the rarefied sensibilities of the discourse on values *contra* values. But this point of view is undermined by the assumption that pronounced statistical regularities in social behaviour provide a satisfactory yardstick with which to ascertain the nature of social reality. This assumption takes for granted precisely that which is most problematic, i.e. the social genesis and mediation of leisure practice and the 'scientific' knowledge which relates to it. By restricting its brief to an interrogation of leisure relationships as they are found in contemporary capitalist societies, the survey method, and the formalist theory which surrounds it, confine the scope of critical discourse to questions of methodological procedure. The vital question of how the interplay of social interests combine, historically and materially, to produce and reproduce leisure relations is falsely construed as a 'second-order' problem. Thus, the vaunted 'precision' of social formalism becomes transfixed in the measurement of the immediate surface rules of leisure relations. And thus social formalism participates in the reproduction of the basic generative structures of power in society (including sexism and class). In this context, it is worth noting that Parker's typology has been roundly attacked for (a) marginalizing the significance of women's leisure, and (b) restricting the meaning of work to waged labour (see Griffin *et al.* 1982: 91–4; Coalter and Parry 1982: 11).

Further purchase on this point can be gained by another look at Champoux's discussion of work and leisure relationships. He argues that there are two sorts of compensatory relationship. First, leisure can compensate for an unexciting work life. Second, work can compensate for an unrewarding leisure life. There is certainly a pleasing symmetry about this formulation. Compensatory work-oriented individuals are described as having work experiences which are 'considerably more varied, creative, challenging, orderly, pleasant . . . cheerful, companionable and friendly than their non-work experience' (Champoux 1978: 415). By contrast, compensatory non-work-oriented individuals are seen as having work experiences which are 'less varied, creative, challenging, pleasant, cheerful, companionable, and friendly, and slightly more orderly than their non-work experiences' (Champoux 1978: 415).

But what is being compensated for here? Consciousness of the world as it is and might be, or the lack of it? Champoux neglects to situate the self-concepts of his respondents into a recognizable historical and material social context. No consideration is given to how self-concepts are constructed, maintained, and reproduced. As a result, individuals appear as free agents, who possess a coherent worldview but lack a biography. I want to give a simple example which illustrates my objection to Champoux's research and the train of formalist methodology that it represents. The example is meant to be absurd and should in no way be taken as a comment on Champoux's survey sample. Imagine that battery hens could speak. Would they describe their work as compensating for an 'inadequate' leisure life? Would they be classified as hens with 'compensatory work-oriented self-concepts' on the grounds that they spend all day working and do not seem to gripe about it? Of course not: for only in the grotesque sense of the words can they be said to have a meaningful history of non-work life.

Battery hens cannot speak, but humans can. Yet the principle still holds. If, as some Marxists claim, it is true that the life experience and room for personal development of most people in capitalist society are confined and retarded by reason of their want of property and other material resources, what can they speak of except their own confinement and deprivation? And if they speak positively about their experience of confinement and deprivation in work and leisure, in what sense is it meaningful? The question is not whether individuals identify positively or negatively with their leisure or work but, on the contrary, whether they have had access to a sufficient range of comparative experience in their life history to make their statements stick.

I now want to turn to the question of the relationship between the formalist approach and functionalism. Functionalist ideas break through the crust of social formalism in a number of places. Already in this discussion I have had occasion to refer to two instances. The first pertains to Dumazedier's yearning for a 'pure science' of leisure. The problem recalls the 'leisure without society' issued alluded to in the introduction of this book. It lies in the false idea that leisure can be studied semi-autonomously, i.e. as a well-defined sector of social reality, divorced from its total societal context.

The second instance refers back to Parker's conceptual dichotomy between the individual and society. This is, of course, a very familiar opposition in the history of social thought. But it suffers from a number of weaknesses which make it eminently expendable as a useful heuristic device for modern social theory. I shall list the two main theoretical defects in summary form, and then apply them to Parker's analysis. The two main defects are:

(1) The dichotomy tends to reify society, i.e. it gives society a 'thing-like' status. Society no longer consists entirely of individuals acting with and against each other; on the contrary, it appears to exist 'outside' or 'above' individuals.

(2) The dichotomy fails to incorporate an adequate concept of power into its frame of reference. Power is presented either as (a) a one-way relationship, emanating from society and moulding the conduct of individuals, or (b) a wholly constraining and limiting influence upon human choice and action. The concept of the individual as a knowledgeable, capable actor who understands the routine features of social life and bases his actions around them is conspicuously absent.

The sociological critique of functionalism centres on the charge that the concept of 'need' is invalid when applied to the level of the social system. Empirically, individuals can be shown to have a variety of needs. More or less automatically, one thinks of the need for food, water, shelter, warmth, and social relations with others. This is a complicated issue, but basically functionalism confuses the concept of 'social need' with the concept of 'group interest'. The point can be clarified by means of an example. Marx argued that the ruling class has an interest in presenting its ideas as the ruling ideas in society. This enables the ruling class to establish its ideological dominance over all other classes. But this is quite different from suggesting that the ruling ideas in society are functionally required by the social system. To prove that thesis one would have to show that the social system has independent needs which express themselves regardless of the wishes and policies of the dominant power groups in society.

How do these criticisms of functionalism relate to Parker's analysis? To begin with it should be noted that, to his credit, Parker is uncomfortable with the idea of a division between the individual and society. He proposes a connecting link which, he believes, conceptually restores the relationship between them to one of dynamic contact. The connecting link is philosophy. According to Parker:

> 'Each of us has a philosophy of life, whether or not we consciously think about it. In considering the ways in which work and leisure pose problems for us in our lives we tend to adopt one outlook rather than another. The sort of solutions we prescribe for ourselves or for other people stem from the particular philosophy we hold. Whether these prescribed solutions "work", whether they can be put into practice, depends on how closely they fit the conditions and trends in our society or community.'
>
> (Parker 1983: 86)

On this basis, Parker (1983: 97–8) identifies two sorts of philosophy, each of which implies a distinctive pattern of work–leisure relations. *Holism* is a philosophy which regards social relations as interdependent. The holist is likely to manifest an extension pattern of work and leisure, and to live in a society or 'social circle' where work and leisure are 'fused'. *Segmentalism* is exactly the opposite. It is a philosophy of social life which sees relations as relatively autonomous. The segmentalist is likely to have an opposition work–leisure pattern, and to live in a society (or 'social circle') of polarized work–leisure relationships, or a neutrality pattern and live in a social formation in which work and leisure are 'self-contained'.

There are at least two aspects of the use of philosophy as the connecting link between the individual and society that require comment. In the first place, Parker does not explain where the philosophies of holism and segmentalism come from. It is as if the two philosophies represent spontaneous developments in advanced industrial organization. The whole matter is treated ahistorically. Second, there is a degree of tension between the voluntarism which he assigns to the action of the individual, and the determinant role which he seems to attach to society. Thus, he argues that individuals are free to choose the 'leisure futures' which they desire (1983: 137). At the same time, he submits that only those philosophies which 'fit the conditions and trends' that dominate society will prevail. There is a contradiction between these views which Parker neither fully recognizes nor explains.

THE FALSE CONCEPTUAL DICHOTOMY IN SOCIAL
FORMALISM

In my view the central weakness of formalism is the false conceptual dichotomy between the individual and society which is
situated at the heart of its methodology and theory. In assigning a
'thing-like' status to society, formalism commits what Alfred
North Whitehead[6] called 'the fallacy of misplaced concreteness',
i.e. it assumes that concepts which have been formulated for
heuristic purposes (the social system and its needs) must have a
real, tangible corresponding reference point in social life. The
result is that society is thought of as being 'above' individuals,
and individuals are presented as 'alone' or 'separate' from
society. What needs to be stated clearly is that no individual
exists alone, and society consists entirely of individuals.

I want to explore more systematically some of the defects
associated with this false conceptual dichotomy. In particular, I
want to examine how it affects the formalist view of power and
the function of leisure. Once again, I will refer to Parker's work
for source material. However, the criticisms I shall make apply to
formalism as a whole.

The question of power can be illustrated by referring back to
Parker's discussion of philosophies and leisure. According to
Parker, holism and segmentalism are corollaries of social systems
where work and leisure are either fused or polarized. The condition of fusion or polarization is represented as being a result of
the collective need of the social system in which it occurs. Apart
from the tautology involved in this line of reasoning (what it says
is that social systems are fused and polarized because they need
to be fused or polarized, in order to fulfil the aim of fusion and
polarization), this seems, precisely, to confuse the concept of
'collective need' with 'group interest'. Once again the point can
best be clarified by means of an example. A government of
'holists' might decide that workers who are happy in their leisure
are also more productive in their work. In that event, public
funds might be made available to bodies like the Sports Council,
the Manpower Training and Service Units, schools, and colleges
to encourage a fusion between work and leisure in people's
attitudes. But in that case it is patently *not* society which chooses
fusion. On the contrary, what has happened is that a powerful
group in society, acting from a received value position, has set out
to imprint its values upon less powerful groups. By basing his

analysis on the dichotomy between the individual and society, Parker marginalizes the role of group power struggles in the production and reproduction of leisure relations.

The question of power is also germane to the point I want to make about the formalist view of the function of leisure. The conventions and values of leisure practice are instilled in the individual through the socialization process. Parker defines socialization as 'the process by which people learn to play their part in society' (1983: 33). From the outset then, the emphasis is on people learning to discharge their roles in collective life, rather than on interpreting and remaking them through social interaction. Parker regards successful socialization in leisure as performing three functions: (1) it teaches people how to behave in leisure activity; (2) it helps to achieve collective societal goals; (3) it maintains and reproduces integration in the social system.[7] These three achievements of successful socialization also represent the three main functions of leisure in society as a whole. I want to raise three objections to this view of leisure. First, it omits conflict from its frame of reference. It is therefore objectively inadequate because it ignores a major fact about leisure relations in contemporary society.[8] Second, it evokes a social system which is permanently in a condition of stasis or, at any rate, equilibrium. Thus, if individuals spend all their time in achieving collective goals, and maintaining and reproducing the social order, it is hard to see what basis remains for social change. Third, it gives a limited reading to human agency. The individual is presented as the living embodiment of the conventions and requirements of the social system. The point is illustrated in Parker's threefold typology. This seems to indicate that the wishes and desires of people for their leisure fit with the actual work–leisure patterns that they achieve like a dovetail joint. But as Clayre points out, 'people do not necessarily find either the work or leisure they want; so their needs and wishes cannot be necessarily assessed from their actions. There may be more people seeking "extension" or "compensation" in leisure than actually finding it' (1974: 198). This is indeed the case. However, to raise the question would involve facing the issue of power in social relationships head on. This would require social formalists to surrender a methodological prejudice to which they are deeply attached, i.e. the prejudice that sociology is chiefly about the study of the relationship between the individual and society.

Domain Assumptions About The Nature of Leisure

So far, I have argued that social formalism is methodologically disposed to endow leisure relations with the attribute of voluntarism. This disposition, however, exists in considerable tension with the deterministic explanation of how people learn about leisure, and how leisure conventions and values are produced and reproduced in society. In fact, the social system is regarded as the main determining influence on leisure practice. This leads to a host of untenable propositions regarding human agency and power.

In this section I want to consolidate these points by systematically examining the formalist domain assumptions about the nature of leisure. 'Domain assumptions' is a technical term coined by the late Alvin Gouldner (1971: 31). It refers to the background assumptions of a given theory about the structure and form of social life under investigation.

Within the formalist tradition there have been a number of attempts to determine the nature of leisure experience. Dumazedier (1967: 14) associates it with relaxation, entertainment, and personal development. Burch (1971: 161) has associated it with tension release and opportunities to assess one's life and one's society. Kaplan (1975: 26) identifies it with self-determination, free time, and feelings of pleasure. Neulinger (1981: 21) has written that it represents the condition of 'perceived freedom'. And Kelly (1983: 198) sees leisure as social experience in which institutional constraints and obligations are minimized. However, perhaps the most comprehensive formulation made in social formalism to date is given in Parker's (1981) paper. He equates leisure experience with four concepts: choice, flexibility, spontaneity, and self-determination. This seems to distil the conventional wisdom of the field into a quartet of manageable proportions. For this reason I shall base my discussion of formalist domain assumptions upon it.[9] In the next section I shall examine how the question of leisure was treated in the ill-fated 'post-industrial society' theory of the 1950s and 1960s. This discussion is intended to serve as a case study of the limitations of formalist domain assumptions regarding leisure experience. Finally, I shall attempt to compare the theories of social formalism and Marxism on the questions of social intervention and leisure. This is in preparation for my detailed commentary on neo-Marxist approaches to leisure which takes up the whole of the next chapter.

CHOICE, FLEXIBILITY, SPONTANEITY, AND
SELF-DETERMINATION

Parker presents these four concepts as separate core features of leisure experience. My presentation will stress the interdependence that exists between them. My discussion will therefore involve considerable cross-referencing between the four concepts.

Choice

The proposition that leisure approximates to a condition of freely chosen activity is a stock in trade of social formalism. Thus Roberts argues that in leisure 'amid all . . . limitations on free will, individuals can feel that they possess scope for choice and this is one of the definitive features' (1978: 6). The problem here, as Bacon (1972: 87) has pointed out, is that concepts like freedom and choice are multi-dimensional. Their meaning is dependent on the cultural and subcultural context in which they are used. Thus, freedom and choice may be regarded as formal properties of collective life in the democracies of the west. Substantively, however, they are structured by a variety of socio-economic influences. For example, I have already argued that women's experience of leisure is structured by their subordinate power position in capitalist society. Similarly, only in a notional, and quite misleading, sense is it correct to say that the employed and unemployed live in identical contexts of freedom and choice. All leisure activity of the unemployed is dictated by the restriction of a subsistence-level income.

Flexibility

Flexibility is closely related to the concept of choice. It is therefore subject to the same reservations. Parker (1981: 325) uses it to refer to the 'mental attitude' which the individual brings to leisure. The capacity to switch roles at the same time as switching activities, he argues, is highly valued in the culture of modern capitalism. Changes in the occupational career structure and the work system are combining to increase its significance in social life. Parker fails to locate this mooted attribute of flexibility in the historical and material power structure of capitalist attitudes. Each individual's capacity and confidence to be flexible are shaped by his or her life experience in the family, school, and the community, and at work. This experience is not uniform throughout society. For example, Marxist critics of the capitalist education system have condemned it precisely for the inflexible, low horizon which it imposes on working-class children (see Bowles and Gintis 1976).

Spontaneity

Leisure activity, unlike work, is held to include opportunities for 'spontaneous' action. The essential objection to this standpoint was made in Chapter 1 of this book. My discussion of the social processes of privatization, individuation, commercialization, and pacification was intended to underline the fact that leisure practice is historically and materially structured. Leisure is not an isolated realm of society with laws and conventions of its own. On the contrary, it is fully integrated into the power structure of capitalist society. The inclusion of spontaneity as a key feature of contemporary leisure ignores this all-important fact. It directs attention away from the power context in which leisure occurs and instead heaps power on the individual. The result is a slide into idealism, in which the surface appearance of leisure claims the whole of social analysis, leaving the underlying generative structures of leisure wreathed in mist.

Self-Determination

The assumption that leisure practice is self-determined pervades the entire ethos of formalist leisure theory. As Dumazedier puts it, 'leisure is characterized by a search for a state of satisfaction, taken as an end in itself' (1974: 75). Similarly, Neulinger writes of 'pure leisure' as 'a state of mind brought about by an activity freely engaged in and done for its own sake' (1981: 31). Since the concept of self-determination starts from the basis of the free individual who can exercise free choice and flexibility, it is vulnerable to all of the criticisms made above. In particular, it is important to stress that self-determination is a multi-dimensional concept which cannot be used unproblematically. It also ignores the cultural and subcultural context of leisure practice, and therefore marginalizes the importance of the localized meanings of leisure under capitalism. The field of cultural studies and youth subculture research has shown something of the range and fecundity of leisure meanings and styles that exist under capitalism (Williams 1961, 1981; Willis 1978; Wutnhow *et al.* 1984; Hebdige 1979). Their work calls into question the whole area of a general meaning of leisure.

THE 'LOGIC' OF THE 'LEISURE SOCIETY'

A central article of faith in the various contributions to 'post-industrial society theory' in the 1950s and 1960s was that the advanced industrial societies were already approximating to the ideal of the 'leisure society' (Dower 1965; Dumazedier 1967; Kerr *et al.* 1973). This can be loosely defined as a society where choice, flexibility, spontaneity, and self-determination in mass leisure are maximized.

The faith in the coming of the 'leisure society' was sustained by a broad swathe of popular beliefs. For example, it was widely believed that the creation of the welfare state and full employment had solved the problem of real poverty. The *embourgeoisement* thesis predicted that the growth in affluence and the improved provision of state education was causing the old class antagonisms to wither away peacefully. At the same time, the automation of manual labour processes and the movement towards a shorter working week were combining to alter vitally the balance between work and leisure. For the first time since the dawn of the industrial revolution, the development of leisure as the central life interest of the masses was held to be a genuine possibility. Indeed, in the view of Clark Kerr and his associates (1973), it was more than a vague possibility; it was an immediate historical inevitability. Industrial society, they argue, is rapidly moving to a condition where 'leisure will be the happy hunting ground for the independent spirit' (1973: 276); the leisure society is an ineluctable consequence of what they call the 'logic of industrialization'. This is a multi-faceted concept. However, at its core lies the proposition that the automation of production has the dual effect of releasing individuals from routine work and increasing real income. Post-industrial society is not work-free. The 'logic of industrialization' thesis presupposes that individuals will be required to work in order to run the new technology, and perform essential administrative functions in society. There will also be requirements for labour in the vastly expanded knowledge and communications sectors, e.g. in the areas of

education, health care, social welfare, and science. It is important
to note that the 'logic of industrialization' is depicted as a
phenomenon which cannot be arrested, i.e. it expresses itself in
all industrial societies regardless of their current political and
ideological composition.

Post-industrial society theory presents an alluring set of ideas.
It strives to unveil a world where freedom of choice and flexibility are the distinctive values in human relations. Kerr *et al.*
refer to 'the new bohemianism' in leisure practice that will
flourish in the leisure society. The talents and energies of individuals will be unleashed and allowed to develop freely and fully.
Within the constraints of the law, individuals will have the time,
education, and disposable income to do their own thing in a
general social atmosphere of tolerance and support.

The theory was incapable of sustaining its initial momentum.
In the early 1970s structural changes in the world economy were
reintroducing short-time working and the phenomenon of mass
unemployment in the advanced societies. At the same time, the
spectres of runaway inflation and diminishing marginal utility in
the public sector were causing governments to immobilize the
Keynesian machinery which had traditionally been applied to
remedy shortfalls in the allocation of manpower. Even at the
dizzy height of its influence, it was evident that the 'logic of
industrialization' thesis had great difficulty in explaining the
persistent low incomes and reduced leisure time of specific
groups in society, e.g. the unskilled, women workers, and ethnic
minorities. Similarly, it was increasingly subject to basic criticisms regarding its ethnocentric bias (see Goldthorpe 1964;
Bendix 1966–67; Rojek 1980). It was all very well for Kerr *et al.* to
wax lyrical about the new bohemianism and the splendours of
the leisure society; but they did so at a time when the problem of
Third World poverty was becoming more acute, and the development gap between the rich and poor nations was increasing. The
International Labour Office (1976) reported that in the early
1970s, 460 million people suffered from severe protein malnu-
trition; 300 million were unemployed or chronically under-
employed; 700 million lived in conditions of acute poverty; and
between 1960 and 1970, at the very moment when the post-
industrial society theorists lectured on the inevitability of mass
literacy and leisure for all, the number of illiterates in the world
grew from 700 to 760 million people. There are few examples in
the formalist tradition which reveal more starkly the limitations

of an analysis which proceeds by severing leisure relations from the global context.

The central error of post-industrial theory was to situate the concept of 'industrialization' in the cockpit of analysis. This implied that the cure of social ills was the inevitable logical consequence of industrial development. What this neglected was the role of political, economic, and social power in influencing the distribution of social resources and opportunities. In capitalist society, the price mechanism plays a pivotal role in the allocation of labour, leisure, output, and incomes. From a Marxist standpoint the price mechanism does not work impartially. Rather, it operates to enhance the interests and power of the established dominant class in society and to reproduce the subordination of the dominated classes in society. I shall try to outline the main features of contemporary neo-Marxist thought on leisure and the reproduction of subordination in capitalist society in the next chapter. However, it may be helpful to contrast the Marxist and formalist approaches by a brief comparison of their positions on social intervention and leisure. This will throw into relief some of the most important divisions that exist between the rival paradigms in the field of leisure theory.

SOCIAL INTERVENTION: FORMALISM AND MARXISM

It is somewhat disarming to note that, on a prima-facie reading at least, there are a number of similarities between social formalism and Marxism. For a start, both assign the highest theoretical importance to leisure activity. Formalists regard it as a time for exercises in 'life satisfaction'; and Marxists see it as 'room for individual development', i.e. the space in life for developing creative faculties and interests. Even on the more contentious question of policy, there is a surprising measure of agreement on what should be done. Thus, Marxists and formalists both emphasize the need to maximize disposable time for individuals. Both submit that state education should play an important role in stimulating and developing leisure activity. Finally, both argue that the development of leisure requires a basic redistribution of wealth and a reorganization of social priorities. Marxists believe that this will ultimately be accomplished by 'historical necessity'. Formalists, for their part, argue that society needs to devise a fiscal policy which will ensure guaranteed minimum income entitlement to be disbursed as a 'social dividend' (see Neulinger 1981: 206–08; Martin and Mason 1984: 16).

There is, however, a fundamental difference between the two approaches which renders all these similarities superficial. Marxists are committed to achieving the emancipation of leisure relations and social activities as a whole, by means of the complete transformation of the existing capitalist power order. One important consequence of this is that they investigate leisure relations as a power resource to be exploited in order to raise class consciousness.

In contrast, formalists aim to improve leisure provision, and enrich the quality of leisure experience within the existing framework of capitalist society. In policy terms they approach leisure as: (a) a resource for commercial exploitation; (b) a social problem which requires specialized education programmes, e.g. on how to cope with more leisure time; and (c) a lever of social control, e.g. to suppress socially unacceptable forms of leisure such as stealing and vandalism (see Dower *et al.* 1981: 141–47; Martin and Mason 1982: 40–63). Social formalism continually stresses the need to place leisure policy in the context of the deep changes in leisure values and practice which are occurring automatically in society as a consequence of technological and economic changes (see Best 1980; Harriman 1982; Martin and Mason 1982). Hence the emphasis in leisure policy on educating people to take advantage of the new leisure opportunities and adjusting them to altered conditions. Debate turns almost entirely upon how the new technology should be applied. The question of who owns and controls it is conspicuously neglected.

The main Marxist objection to the formalist position is well known. In the words of Horkheimer, the social formalist is 'incorporated into the apparatus of society, his achievements are a factor in the conservation and continuous renewal of the existing state of affairs, no matter what fine names he gives to what he does' (1972: 196). The comment is reminiscent of Marx's mordant view of the political economists of his own day whom he summarily dismissed as the 'ideological representatives of the ruling class' (1977(I): 537).

The similarity in the basic terms used in Marxists' rejection of social formalism is misleading. It would be an error to suppose that Marxist thought has ossified since Marx's death. Much has changed in the structure of capitalist society. The increasing economic importance of leisure in the capitalist economy and the expansion of leisure time in the working class are two examples of basic changes in the organization of economic and social relations. Marxists have responded by making a number of critical departures from Marx's original theory. As regards leisure theory, some of these have been so fundamental that it is preferable to speak of 'neo-Marxist' approaches to the subject, i.e. approaches which are in the Marxist tradition, but which openly reject some of Marx's basic ideas. Neo-Marxists have not been content merely to criticize formalist theories of leisure. On the contrary, they have produced a series of ambitious theoretical alternatives which attempt to explain the structure and function of contemporary leisure relations in the context of the modern capitalist power structure. It is to this whole area that I now want to turn.

5 NEO-MARXIST
APPROACHES TO LEISURE

The 'Crisis' and Leisure

The 'crisis' of western Marxism has been the subject of considerable discussion (see Anderson 1976; Alvater and Kallscheuer
1979; Callinicois 1982). The issue is rather involved and I do not
propose to attempt a detailed survey of the terrain here. Even so, it
is important to try and establish the rudiments of what is at stake.
For the neo-Marxist approaches that I shall investigate in this
chapter have gestated and matured in the context of the crisis in
Marxist thought. The essential points can be stated in a few words.
   Marx, as everyone knows, predicted that the demise of capitalism would begin in the *heartland* of the system, i.e. in the economically advanced societies. In fact, the only real headway that
Marxism has made politically is in the *hinterland* of the capitalist
world system, i.e. in those countries which were relatively
underdeveloped at the time of Communist Party takeover. Mean-
while, class contradictions in the advanced societies have failed
to escalate into revolutionary class action. The developed capitalist societies have demonstrated a remarkable capacity to adapt
and grow stronger economically. For their part, workers in the
existing Marxist societies have not been 'freed from their chains'.
The socialist societies have not abolished wage labour; they are
still subject to strikes and industrial conflict; they have not
eliminated relations of gender domination; in short, they have
failed to advance very far down the road to the 'free and full
development of all individuals. Indeed, many post-revolutionary
states appear to have congealed into authoritarian power orders

where freedom of speech and association are at a premium.[1] The most important predictions of Marx's theory do not therefore appear to have been fulfilled.

Throughout the entire post-war period western Marxists have busied themselves with the task of working out a convincing theoretical response to allegations of failure. The response consists of many strands of detailed analysis concerning the changed economic, political and ideological conditions of capitalist society. But what Anderson (1983: 20) calls 'the grand Western Marxist tradition' has nucleated around a preoccupation with the new mechanisms of capitalist cultural integration.[2] Three major themes have emerged from this process of revaluation: (a) the importance of the welfare state in damping revolutionary class consciousness; (b) the fragmentation of the working class along lines of differential market capacity, skill level, strength of unionization, status interests, and leisure activities; (c) the significance of leisure as a mechanism of class control.

These themes are, of course, interlinked. But I want to concentrate here on the third one. At least three points need to be made. First, as I have already noted, the leisure industry has emerged in the post-war years as a huge and expanding sector of the capitalist economy (see pp. 2, 14–21). Marxists now see leisure as one of the central dynamics of the modern capitalist economy (see Harrington 1974; Hargreaves 1975).* On purely economic grounds therefore, leisure is a key factor in explaining the persistence of capitalist society. Second, Marxists have continually stressed the role that leisure plays in adjusting the working class to a subordinate position in capitalist society. Leisure relations are held to create the illusion of freedom and self-determination which is the necessary counterbalance to the real subordination of workers in the labour process. Contemporary Marxists have stressed in particular the capacity of modern leisure to mystify the working class, e.g. to present its subordinate position in the capitalist power structure as a form of freedom. In the words of Hargreaves, modern leisure is 'unique in its capacity to provide surrogate satisfaction for an alienated mass audience, while at the same time perpetuating its alienation and functioning as a means of political socialization into the hegemonic culture' (1975: 60). Third, the development of new forms of technology and economic organization in capitalism has reopened the important

* For reference to developments in this author's position see Hargreaves, J. (forthcoming) *Theatre of the Great: Sport and Hegemony in Britain.* Oxford: Polity Press.

question in Marxist thought of the dividing line between the realms of necessity and freedom. As we shall see in the last section of this chapter, at the heart of this debate is the question of the degree of freedom in leisure relations which is compatible with a modern, technical rational power order.

These themes recur throughout the chapter. But I want to structure my discussion of neo-Marxism and leisure into a tighter plan of exposition. In this way I hope to convey the contrasts within neo-Marxism on the question of leisure. I shall base my discussion on four general headings: (1) the universal market; (2) the culture industry; (3) hegemony and consciousness; (4) forced leisure and post-industrial socialism. These headings will draw on the work of the following distinctive neo-Marxist writers: (1) Braverman and Wallerstein; (2) Adorno, Horkheimer, Marcuse, and Habermas; (3) Althusser and Gramsci; (4) Gorz. For those readers who are familiar with the important contrasts between their positions, this listing may give a clear preview of the ground that I shall cover. For readers who lack such familiarity, I shall try and underline the different points of divergence between these approaches as and when it is relevant in the course of my commentary. Let us examine the four headings in more detail.

The Universal Market

Marx argued that capitalist production is based in the world market. Three aspects of this concept need to be differentiated. First, it is a *universal* market. It surpasses all national barriers and limits. Second, it is regulated by the *price mechanism*. Production is not the servant of social needs. Instead, it obeys market forces. Third, it is a *mass* market. Production is standardized and automated to cater for mass consumption.

I argued in Chapter 2 that Marx regarded reification and commodity fetishism as the two most important consequences of generalized commodity production in the world market. Both concepts figure prominently in neo-Marxist post-war leisure theory. The historical role of capital is theorized as aiming to run leisure activities on strict commercial lines by commodifying leisure pursuits wherever possible. As Braverman puts it:

> 'Corporate institutions . . . have transformed every means of entertainment and "sport" into a production process for the

enlargement of capital. . . . So enterprising is capital that even where the effort is made by one or another section of the population to find a way to nature, sport or art through personal activity and amateur or "underground" innovation, these activities are rapidly incorporated into the market as far as it is possible.'

(Braverman 1974: 279)

Like Gorz (1965) before him, Braverman appears to accept Marx's premiss that advanced capitalism has normalized the separation of the individual from the means of production. It has turned a historically specific set of relations into a 'natural', everlasting state, i.e. it has produced reification. One important consequence of this is that the overwhelming majority of individuals in modern capitalism are attached to their work on a strictly instrumental basis, i.e. they see it as a means to an end (the salary or weekly wage). Work is experienced as a burden or a drag on the self rather than as a means of personal creative development. This gives leisure an extraordinary significance in popular western culture. For it is in leisure rather than work that individuals see themselves as free to act and develop as they please. However, from a Marxist standpoint, this freedom is a snare and a delusion. Marxists believe that 'leisure is not really free time at all, but an organization of non-work time that is determined by the relations of capitalist production' (Frith 1983: 251). The fundamental arguments that modern Marxists use to substantiate this position do not depart very much from Marx's original analysis. Thus, every modern Marxist who is interested in leisure stresses that leisure opportunities and resources are bound up with property ties. In this sense, leisure acts to reproduce class society. Writing in this vein, Adorno and Horkheimer submit that:

'Amusement under late capitalism is the prolongation of work. It is sought after as an escape from the mechanized work process, and to recruit strength in order to be able to cope with it again. But at the same time mechanization has such power over a man's leisure and happiness, and so profoundly determines the manufacture of amusement goods, that his experiences are inevitably after-images of the work process itself.'

(Adorno and Horkheimer 1979: 137)

Similarly, Gorz (1965) and Braverman (1974) reiterate familiar Marxian propositions in their thesis that consumer capitalism perpetuates 'passive' leisure pursuits so as to distract workers from the assorted formal economic and political mechanisms of class subordination.

All this might suggest that modern Marxism has been content merely to reproduce the stock ideas from the canon of Marxian thought on leisure and power. In fact, Marxism has made notable progress in delineating the architecture of the universal capitalist market. The key work here has been Wallerstein's study of the capitalist world system. He argues that the capitalist world system remains a fully integrated totality. In other words, the socialist societies remain part of the capitalist world system. As Wallerstein puts it, 'none of the so-called socialist states are socialist. Nor could they be, for they are not autonomous systems, but remain part of the capitalist world economy, subject to its law of value and bound by the constraints of the inter-state system' (1982: 51). The main evidence for this startling claim is the persistence of wage labour, the phenomenon of wage drift and the extraction of surplus value from the workers by the state apparatus in socialist countries. For Wallerstein, the effect of socialist construction has been to boost economic output and turnover in the world system, as a result of the growth and modernization of markets via the spread of industrialization and urbanization.

Wallerstein divides societies in the world system into three types. This is done on the basis of their rank and function in production, distribution, and exchange. *Core powers* refer to the most economically and militarily advanced societies. These nations accumulate surplus by extracting wealth from the under-developed nations and reproducing their dependency on the core. The *periphery* consists of underdeveloped societies which constitute inelastic markets and cheap sources of raw materials and food for the core. The *semi-periphery* refers to societies which are structurally located between the core and the periphery. Their economic function consists of the production of luxury goods and invisible exports. However, their primary function in the world system is not economic but political. These countries present a complication to opposition movements and alliances in the periphery and hence promote the dominance of the core.

The question of leisure does not figure directly in Wallerstein's discussion. However, a position can be extrapolated from the general details of the world system approach. Thus, one can en-visage that the distribution of leisure resources and opportunities might be held to correspond to the division of power between the core, periphery, and semi-periphery. Certainly, the model seems to be a useful framework for exploring the interdependence of leisure relations in the universal market. We can have time off only if others sell their labour power to buyers. The core can increase its consumption of leisure commodities and expand its regime of disposable time only if more surplus value is extracted from the world economy, i.e. if the exploitation of labour is intensified and revolutionized. The empirical facts of a simultaneous growth in working-class leisure consumption in the core during the post-war period, and the intensification of exploitation in the periphery are quite consistent with these general propositions.[3]

Wallerstein's work has been subjected to numerous critical attacks.[4] In particular, three criticisms are penetrating. First, he is held to exaggerate seriously the importance of the class struggle as the motor of history. Second, and by extension, he is held to neglect the importance of nation states and warfare in international affairs. For example, at a time when nuclear capabilities in the superpowers have been expanded and modernized alarmingly, Wallerstein argues that the capitalist world system has risen to new heights of economic integration and output. Third, the location of particular nations into the major zones of the world economy is often quite arbitrary and misleading. Within the periphery there are metropolitan centres which maintain conditions that parallel lifestyles in the core. Likewise, within the core, pockets of poverty exist which mirror conditions in the less-developed zones of the world economy. By highlighting contradictions between economic zones in the world economy, Wallerstein is alleged to minimize the anomalies that exist within specific representative nations. Even so, there is little doubting the impressive sweep and thematic power of Wallerstein's argument. It alerts us to the incredible resilience and pervasiveness of capitalism. It also emphasizes the value of studying leisure relations within nations in an international context.

The Culture Industry

The concept of the universal market presupposes generalized capitalist commodity production. Among neo-Marxist approaches to the mass manipulation of leisure, the work of the Frankfurt

School on the culture industry is of front-rank importance. The basis of my discussion will consist of an examination of the writings of Adorno, Horkheimer and Marcuse. However, it is important to stress that a number of other writers were either loosely or directly involved in the development and refinement of these three writers' ideas.[5] They are excluded from discussion here partly for reasons of space, but also because the work of Adorno, Horkheimer, and Marcuse has exerted the greatest influence in the field. It should also be noted that although these three are often seen by others as a collective 'school' of thought, important differences exist between them. I do not propose to compare and contrast their respective positions here. But partly in recognition of the divergences between them, notably on the question of leisure and emancipation, I shall consider their output under separate headings. Finally, I shall include a note on the work of Jurgen Habermas in this section. Habermas's relation to Frankfurt Marxism is ambivalent. His ambitious attempt to 'reconstruct' historical materialism is widely thought to distance him in important respects from the Frankfurt tradition (Held 1980; Keat 1981; Anderson 1983). Even so, I have included his work in this section on the grounds that his formative work was clearly based in an engagement with the writings of Adorno, Horkheimer, and Marcuse.

ADORNO AND HORKHEIMER: 'LEISURE AS MASS
DECEPTION'

The term 'the culture industry' was coined by Adorno and Hork-heimer (1979) to refer to popular cinema, music, commercial theatre, sport, television, comics, magazines, storybooks, and related forms of mass entertainment. Its importance in consumer capitalism resides in its power to structure leisure relations in accordance with the requirements of the social interests which own and control it. Adorno and Horkheimer hold fast to the orthodox Marxian idea that capitalist society is dominated by the capitalist class. Their debt to Marx and his view of the totality of capitalism is evident in their methodological premiss that the culture industry is 'a system which is uniform as a whole and in every part' (1979: 20). To this premiss they add insights from Weber and Freud to create an alloy of neo-Marxist theory which is incomparably more pessimistic than the analysis of their progenitor.

From Weber they take the idea that the development of capitalism consists of the advance of instrumental rationality and the disenchantment of the world. Similarly, they argue that the greatly increased rationalization of social life since Marx's day has achieved the normalization of rational administration and mass enslavement to the bureaucratic order. Like Weber, they submit that these conditions cannot be alleviated simply by the installation of representatives of the Communist Party in the place of the capitalist class at the head of society. From Freud, they take the theory of the unconscious and of instinctual repression, and apply it to the class-based requirements of the universal market. Repression, guilt, and self-punishment in individuals are connected to the subliminal tendencies towards 'psychological regression' and the 'levelling down' of ambiguity and initiative in social relations perpetuated by the culture industry.[6]

Using these materials they construct a picture of the culture industry as a universal influence in the social life of advanced capitalism. The individual becomes its obedient subject from birth. For the culture industry today sets the context in which socialization takes place: 'None may escape. . . . Everybody must behave (as if spontaneously) in accordance with his previously determined and indexed level, and choose the category of mass product turned out for his type (in short) . . . the man with leisure has to accept what the culture manufacturers offer him' (Adorno and Horkheimer 1979: 123–24).

Several of the distinctive features that Adorno and Horkheimer attribute to the culture industry are contained in this passage. Adorno embellished them in a series of later essays on culture (see especially Adorno 1954, 1975, 1978). I shall try to convey their essence by listing them here in a fairly formal way. Adorno's elaborations will be incorporated as and when appropriate.

(1) The culture industry is universal. It enmeshes the individual, by default, on both the conscious and the unconscious level.
(2) The culture industry exploits the individual's leisure time. Its control is most complete when leisure experience has to be bought and sold. For this reason the culture industry aims at the commodification of leisure activities: 'The entire practice of the culture industry transfers the profit motive naked onto cultural forms' (Adorno 1975: 13).

(3) The culture industry also functions to induce uncritical mass obedience to the existing power order in society. Adorno expresses the point forthrightly:

'The concepts of order which it hammers into human beings are always those of the status quo. They remain unquestioned, unanalyzed and undialectically presupposed . . . the categorical imperative of the culture industry no longer has anything in common with freedom. It proclaims: you shall conform, without instruction as to what; conform to that which exists anyway, and to that which everyone thinks anyway as a reflex of its power and omnipresence. The power of the culture industry's ideology is such that conformity has replaced consciousness.'

(Adorno 1975: 17)

(4) The culture industry supports only the veneer of free choice. The customer's 'choice' amounts to little more than the received options which the culture industry lays before him. These options in themselves tantalize with images of pleasure and emancipation from the cares of everyday life. But the images are never allowed to become anything more substantial than mirages. The unbreakable principle upon which the culture industry works is stated by Adorno and Horkheimer thus: '[It] perpetually cheats its customers of what it perpetually promises' (1979: 139).

(5) The extravagant concern with the individuation of products, expressed in merchandising and design factors, is a mask to disguise their mass-produced origins. 'It is as if each thing's claim to be something special were mocking at a situation in which everyone and everything is incessantly subject to a perennial sameness' (Adorno 1941: 392).

The greatest criticism of the culture industry relates to its claim to keep the customer amused. Its allotment of administered pleasures and calculated distractions is condemned by Adorno and Horkheimer for its minimalist aspirations. The paralysis of critical thought, they argue, is the price exacted for the mere amusement of the individual. Leisure is mass deception. Free choice is not free; spontaneity is cynically manufactured to obey the cash demands of the manipulators of leisure; self-determination is a gimmick of the culture industry.

The use of the term 'culture' in this context is meant as a heavy irony. Originally the term was used to refer to 'that which goes beyond the system of self-preservation of the species' (Adorno 1978: 100). As such, it referred to activity which was inherently creative. For in exceeding the mundane reality of self-preservation (i.e. the normal, habitual order of reality), it exposed the cracks in everyday life. The administration of culture in modern industrial capitalism achieves precisely the opposite effect. It papers over the cracks in everyday life by making them objects of melodrama or hollow mirth. According to Adorno and Horkheimer the contemporary situation is one in which freedom is conventionally confused with slavery. As a result, it is sociologically necessary to consider not merely the quality of personal feeling today, but the more fundamental question of whether it is any longer meaningful to speak of 'the individual'. Thus, for example, Adorno and Horkheimer declare that 'in the culture industry the individual is an illusion not merely because of the standardization of the means of production. He is tolerated only so long as his complete identification with the generality is unquestioned. Pseudo individuality is rife' (1979: 154).

A number of writers have commented on the palpable élitism and elegiac form of Adorno and Horkheimer's argument (Jay 1973; Kellner 1975; Turner 1981). It is true that their thesis does indeed suggest that only the intellectual now has the critical consciousness to see through modern life. The masses are held to be thoroughly conditioned in their work relations to circumstances of relentless exploitation; and in their leisure relations they perpetually celebrate the vulgar, mediocre, and crass artefacts of the culture industry. These criticisms underestimate the importance of the social context in which the thesis was originally formulated. After all, Adorno and Horkheimer prepared the manuscript as German Jews exiled in the United States, and as the appalled heirs of Auschwitz, Bergen-Belsen, Dachau, and the Nazi 'culture industry'. There is also direct textual evidence against the charge of élitism. Adorno, towards the end of his life, wrote of the 'deep unconscious', and 'real' capacities of the masses to resist 'total control'.[7] I have a number of criticisms that I want to make about the culture industry thesis. However, because they also apply to Marcuse's analysis of modern leisure relations, I shall postpone them until I have elaborated his position.

MARCUSE: LEISURE IN ONE-DIMENSIONAL SOCIETY

Marcuse's view of leisure cannot be assimilated simply. The

main reason for this is that he developed a number of contrasting positions on the subject in the course of his intellectual career. Moreover, there is no obvious linear progression in the development of his theory of leisure. Indeed a strong case can be made that his thoughts on leisure exhibit a circular motion. Thus, his youthful view of leisure as a relatively autonomous sphere of human interaction which supports genuine creativity and personal fulfilment is recapitulated in his last book, *The Aesthetic Dimension* (1978). However, Marcuse is a complex thinker who has been ill served by snap judgements on his alleged intellectual opportunism (see MacIntyre 1970: 87–92; Turner 1981: 89–92).

His basic arguments relate closely to the culture industry thesis. Like Adorno and Horkheimer, he argues that leisure activity is structured by the requirements of capitalist production. Similarly, he identifies the culture industry as a key mechanism in modern capitalism for subduing critical class consciousness. Marcuse pulls these ideas together in a passage from *Eros and Civilization*:

'The basic control of leisure is achieved by the length of the working day itself, by the tiresome and mechanical routine of alienated labour; these require that leisure be a passive relaxation and recreation of energy for work. Not until the late stage of industrial civilization . . . has the technique of mass manipulation developed an entertainment industry which directly controls leisure time, or has the state directly taken over the enforcement of such controls.'

(Marcuse 1955: 49)

These themes are pursued to their negative conclusion in *One Dimensional Man* (1964a). Here Marcuse shows us a picture of leisure and work which is utterly permeated by instrumental rationality and bureaucratic administration. Consumer capitalism maintains and reproduces leisure forms which must never be allowed to deviate from

'a pattern of *one-dimensional thought and behaviour* in which ideas, aspirations and objectives that, by their content, transcend the established universe of discourse and action are either repelled or reduced to terms of this universe. They are redefined by the rationality of the given system and its quantitative extension.'

(Marcuse 1964a: 24 his emphasis)

Adorno could have written these lines. But unlike Adorno who, in his later years, dismissed radical change as nothing more than a marginal possibility, Marcuse insists that captalism inevitably creates the conditions for radical intervention by oppressed groups. He bases this view on two interconnected arguments: (a) the economic contradictions of capitalism intensify the exploitation of specific groups such as women, ethnic minorities, unskilled labourers, and the unemployed; (b) the cultural contradictions of capitalism involve the perpetuation of a dominant conformist ideology which itself ultimately has the effect of provoking critical consciousness, e.g. through subcultural reaction and art. Earlier, I argued that western Marxism has been thrown into turmoil by the apparent fragmentation of the working class. By a neat piece of formal reasoning Marcuse appears to snatch the promise of victory from the jaws of defeat. He retains the orthodox Marxist idea that only the working class can produce the negation of class society. But he introduces the new position that minority groups in the system, who are either temporarily or permanently beyond the control of the state apparatus and the culture industry, can act as the catalysts for revolutionary change. These arguments greatly enhance the importance of leisure relations in contemporary Marxist theory. For they suggest that the seeds of revolutionary transformation can be sown in struggles which are located in the *non-work* sphere. Thus, for example, the movements for racial equality and sexual liberation assume greater significance in the everyday relations of capitalist society. These 'free-time' struggles have the potential to start a chain reaction which ultimately exposes the economic and cultural contradictions of the system as a whole. Marcuse's rationale for these contentious propositions is based on a radical re-reading of both Freud and Marx.

Marcuse agrees with Freud that civilization is built on the reality principle, i.e. on the renunciation of aggressive and sexual instincts. These instincts are sublimated by various social institutions, notably the family and school, which are responsible for channelling libido into socially acceptable forms. Marcuse notes that Freud ultimately traces the origins of repression to the problem of scarcity in society. Civilized life requires repression so as to maintain order and production. What Freud ignores, maintains Marcuse, is what every Marxist knows, namely that in class society, repression is organized around the principle of class domination. In capitalist society the problem of scarcity is not one

of production (not enough wealth to go round), but one of distribution (the unequal share of wealth between strata). On this
basis, Marcuse submits that forms of repression exist which are
geared to the perpetuation of established systems of domination.
He calls these forms *surplus repression*. The term refers to the
controls on interpersonal conduct which are above and beyond
the basic repression necessary for the perpetuation of civilized
life. Marcuse mentions the relations of class, sexual domination,
and racial prejudice as examples. The existence of surplus
repression in capitalist society presupposes a change in how the
reality principle is conceived. It implies that repression no longer
merely obeys the laws of necessity, but is also regulated by the
social interests of powerful groups. In fact, Marcuse argues that
the dominant form which the reality principle assumes in
modern capitalism consecrates individual competition, self-
interest, and accumulation as intrinsically valid ends in social
life. He calls this the *performance principle*. Again the parallels
with Adorno and Horkheimer's culture industry thesis need to be
emphasized. For example, the performance principle demands
automatic obedience and the repression of critical thought. It
habituates the individual to society as it is, and dismisses alternative, transcendent views as unrealistic or naïve. It foments what
Marcuse calls the 'happy consciousness', which is inherently
conformist and fully integrated with the economic requirements
of consumer society (1964a: 78). Finally, it perceives leisure and
disposable income as the 'reward' for work. On the last point, the
sense of affront which seizes Adorno and Horkheimer on the
alleged 'freedom' of leisure in capitalist society ripples through
Marcuse's social analysis:

'In the "normal" development, the individual lives his repression "freely" as his own life; he desires what he is sup-
posed to desire; his gratifications are profitable to him and to
others; he is reasonably and often exuberantly happy. This
happiness which takes place part-time during the few hours of
leisure between the working days and working nights, but
sometimes also during work, enables him to continue his performance, which in turn perpetuates his labour and that of
others.'

(Marcuse 1955: 48)

It might be thought that Marcuse succumbs to the lofty pessimism
which characterized the writings of Adorno and Horkheimer in

their later years. Certainly, *One Dimensional Man* is sprinkled with rebarbative comments on the development of the 'totally administered society' which is 'without opposition'. Even here, however, as Geoghegan (1981: 94–6) notes, Marcuse's discussion of the ramifications of 'one-dimensionality' into all areas of social life is an exercise in 'worst possible case' analysis. It is merely one hypothesis about the future, albeit a real and important one. Simultaneously, Marcuse held the directly opposing view that the technical progress of advanced capitalism might create fresh opportunities of liberation from care and want. In particular, the growth of automation and the corresponding decline in the need for routine labour might force the contradictions inherent in the performance principle to climax in concerted social action. With it, Marcuse suggests, the tower of surplus repression would come tumbling down. Marcuse interpreted the sexual liberation and the increased social value placed on work in the 1960s as circumstantial evidence that the process was under way. Despite the 'events' of May 1968, which led him to conclude that social revolution was not imminent, his belief that it was an *immanent* feature of the development of capitalism never wavered. For example, in his last book, which consisted of a self-avowedly 'utopian' monograph on art, he argued that in advanced capitalism a new reality principle was emerging, precisely from the accomplishments and creative capacities of capitalism. The transformation of work meant that all people, even those in government, might support the creation of a society in which

'existence would no longer be determined by the need for life-long alienated labour and leisure, human beings would no longer be subjected to the instruments of their labour, no longer dominated by the performances imposed upon them. The entire system of material and ideological repression and renunciation would be senseless.'

(Marcuse 1978: 29)

These words recall the social vision of the young Marx. The influence of Marx's *1844 Manuscripts* on the development of Marcuse's social thought is indeed well known. It is worth spelling out just how heterodox his thoughts are in terms of the critical tradition in leisure theory. Marcuse argues that rationality and happiness are compatible in the leisure relations of modern civilization. He thus departs from Weber who believed that rational knowledge wraps social relations in fateful contradictions which marginalize the possibility of happiness. He also departs from Freud, who argued that the repression demanded by civilization might be a cause for stoicism and courage in the individual, but that it could never lead to happiness. In fact, it is only with the more orthodox theory of social formalism that the marriage between rationality and happiness in leisure activity is so heartily endorsed as a real option in the future of industrial societies.

THE FRANKFURT SCHOOL CRITICIZED

This completes my discussion of the contributions of Adorno, Horkheimer, and Marcuse to leisure theory. I shall now turn to a brief critical assessment of their work. Since most of these points have been well rehearsed in the extensive critical literature on the Frankfurt School (see Jay 1973; Connerton 1976; Slater 1977; Buck-Morss 1977; Held 1980), I shall outline them here in summary form. Once again, it is very important to emphasize that there are significant differences between these writers. I have deliberately side-stepped the whole question in my discussion because to explore it adequately would entail a major digression from the central concern with leisure theory. There are, as I have noted, a number of clear and concise secondary texts on this topic which are widely available.[8] With the *selective* basis of my commentary understood, it is necessary to make at least four critical points.

(1) The concepts of 'the culture industry' and 'one-dimensionality' forcefully affirm the important sociological fact that relations of leisure are also relations of power. The experiences of freedom, spontaneity, and self-determination which are often associated with leisure activity are only fully understood if they are situated in the total power context of capitalist society. The importance of the Frankfurt School in underlining this key fact is not in dispute. What is in dispute are the conclusions which they draw from it. The writings of Adorno and Horkheimer, and Marcuse's most pessimistic book, *One Dimensional Man*, threaten to install a new conventional wisdom which, in its fully developed form, is every bit as restrictive as the old one which it is trying to replace. What it says is that leisure practice continually functions to remake the power structure of capitalist society. It therefore neglects

to convey the two-sided action of leisure which operates both to undermine and to reproduce the conditions of class society.[9]

(2) The second point that I want to make relates closely to the first. The superficial comparison I made above, between Marcuse's vision of leisure and labour in the society of the future, and the position of social formalism on rationality and happiness, was no accident. There are several places in the arguments of Adorno, Horkheimer, and Marcuse regarding the relationship between work and leisure where assumptions and propositions of a functionalist type are deployed. For example, leisure time is said to re-energize the worker for more labour; and leisure commodities are shown to functionally integrate capitalism to new heights of consensus and class domination. In all of this the functional passivity of the consumer is assumed. The alleged mystifying and dehumanizing effects of leisure are deduced from a highly abstract examination of its theoretical role in the age of 'high capitalism'. The charge has led some commentators to make damaging comparisons between the Frankfurt School's model of advanced capitalism and Talcott Parsons's view of 'the social system'.[10] In both cases leisure relations are oversimplified and made to conform to an assigned theoretical function and shape.

It should be noted in passing that the work of Braverman, Gorz, and Wallerstein on 'the universal market', alluded to in the previous section, also displays the brand-mark of functionalist reasoning. Consider Gorz's statement that: 'capitalism civilizes consumption and leisure to avoid having to civilize social relationships. Alienating men in their work, it is better equipped to alienate them as consumers; and conversely it alienates them as consumers the better to alienate them in work' (1965: 349).

This is a rather magisterial summing up of the complex relationship between work and leisure under capitalism. The question is whether this theoretical functional relationship is actually reproduced empirically in leisure practice. There is, for example, a large and growing body of research in the field of deviance which indicates that capitalism is only partially successful in 'civilizing' leisure relations (see Cohen 1972; Hall et al. 1978; Mungham and Pearson 1976).

(3) In speaking of the 'totally administered society', 'one-dimensional' leisure, and society 'without opposition', the

writers of the Frankfurt School deliver a real hostage to fortune to their critics. If these statements are being used rhetorically they are misleading, since they do not correspond to empirical reality. Equally, if they are being used as factual statements about how the world is, they place the entire claim of the Frankfurt School to be engaged in 'critical' theory in jeopardy. For in the 'totally administered society' which is 'without opposition' all criticism must be specious, i.e. ultimately concerned with renewing the power of the existing dominant social interests in society.

(4) Adorno, Horkheimer, and Marcuse criticize both the 'heroic materialism' of leisure relations under capitalism and the 'authoritarianism' of work and leisure in socialist Soviet-type societies (Marcuse 1964b; Horkheimer 1973). At the same time they refrain from seriously engaging in the task of producing constructive alternatives to capitalism and state socialism. Instead, their work moved away from the orthodox Marxist concern with class struggle and the transcendence of class society, to a more general preoccupation with the struggle between society and nature. The solution for alienation was transferred from revolutionary class action to a general 'reconciliation with nature'. As Kellner points out, this shift in focus carried with it 'very quietistic and even mystical implications. It is highly unclear what they meant by reconciliation with nature in view of their dislike for irrationalism, naive Rousseauean or barbaric fascist nature worship' (1975: 148).

A NOTE ON HABERMAS

In recent years, the most ambitious programme of research and theory making that has emerged from the spoils of the Frankfurt tradition is the work of Jurgen Habermas. There are major interpretive problems involved in attempting to distil the relevance of his work to leisure theory. Habermas sometimes writes as if the whole weight of the crisis of western Marxism is on his shoulders. He has plunged deep into the Marxist tradition, contemporary western philosophy, social science, and political theory in an effort to lessen the burden. Similarly, he has made important contributions to structural linguistics, the theory of the state, the sociology of knowledge, the method of historical materialism, and the sociology of culture. In this note I shall restrict myself to a brief examination of his work on communication and 'speech acts'. I shall argue that this area of his voluminous publications is most relevant to leisure theory.

Habermas (1971) criticizes Marx for exaggerating the importance of material production in his theory of capitalist development. What is equally important for an understanding of social life, argues Habermas, is communication. In his early writings, Habermas appears to assign a very wide latitude of meaning to this term. Thus, Anderson (1983: 60–1) has argued that the meaning is so vague that it embraces all political and cultural forms (including leisure). The reason for this apparently self-defeating capaciousness derives from Habermas's strong desire to separate communicative action and culture from the production process. Communicative action cannot be reduced to labour. It is precisely this error which Habermas sees as the central flaw in Marx's theory.

In his more recent writings, Habermas (1979) gives a sharper focus to the meaning of communicative action. At its core is language. For Habermas, 'the significance of the medium of language is evident; in it individual and social consciousness are combined' (1979: 168). Language here is not merely envisaged as words on paper or sentences of speech. This is because all language presupposes a social context, and therefore tells us something about social order. This fact makes it an area of outstanding importance for sociological inquiry. As Habermas explains:

> 'We can examine every utterance to see whether it is true or untrue, justified or unjustified, truthful or untruthful, because in speech, no matter what the emphasis, grammatical sentences are embedded in relations to reality in such a way that in an acceptable speech action segments of external nature, society, and internal nature always come into appearance together.'
>
> (Habermas 1979: 67–8)

Language is the primary medium of human communication. For Habermas, this alone would make it of indispensable importance to sociological research and theory. But, additionally, he argues that language obeys rules and norms which are universal. The study of how linguistic communication occurs can therefore act as the main route for understanding universal features of social interaction.

What has all of this got to do with leisure? Before we can answer that question we need to look more closely at the concept of the speech act. At its simplest level, a speech act is a single sentence or intelligible utterance. But Habermas gives the term a more complex meaning, i.e. he makes it refer to any type of sustained social interaction. Examples might include watching television, conversing with someone, reading a book, or being the spectator of a game or event. The point is that all speech acts consist of communicative action which may include, but cannot be reduced to, speech *per se*. The relevance of Habermas's work to leisure theory is now easier to decipher: leisure forms may be studied as specialized types of speech act. They can be sociologically understood in terms of the *objective* rules and resources applied and developed in communicative action. The emphasis in social formalism, Weberian sociology, and Freudian theory, on subjectivity is therefore reversed.

The immediate objection to studying leisure 'objectively' as a speech act arises precisely from its claim to transcend subjectivity. Everyone knows that communicative action is never simple or transparent. Meanings can be ambivalent. Speech acts may obey certain 'universal' rules in logic. But the application of those rules can distort communication and misinform social action. Orthodox Marxists certainly recognize this. They argue that communication is systematically distorted by the fact of class in capitalist society. Communication is held to be suffused with power relations which are organized to perpetuate the domination of the ruling class. Habermas fully recognizes the force of this criticism. But he maintains that orthodox Marxist views are too naïve. Communication and leisure action are not structured merely by the class dialectic. An objectively adequate understanding of communication must recognize additional structuring influences on speech acts. Habermas distinguishes four sources of structuring in a given communication setting (1979: 66–7):

(1) *External nature:* the physical world of animate things. True and false statements are often measured against the observable 'facts' which the physical world 'reveals'.
(2) *Society:* the world of interpersonal relations, traditions, institutions, and culture. Proper and improper conduct, right and wrong action are assessed in relation to their norms and values.

(3) *Internal nature:* the world of the communicating self. This refers to the realm of physical desire, feelings, and wishes. It is the 'I' who interacts with others.

(4) *Language:* the grammatical, syntactical, and semantic rules of communication. Habermas argues that language is a reality *sui generis.* The technical system of language is a self-subsisting structure.

This typology leads Habermas to speculate on the nature of the 'ideal speech situation'. Abstractly, he suggests that it consists of a situation in which each participant engages in communicative action on the basis of: (a) rational agreement rather than force; (b) complete mutual understanding by participants; and (c) an acceptance of the right of all participants to communicate openly as equals.

The sphere in modern life which reproduces these features most faithfully is psychoanalysis. According to Habermas, in psychoanalysis, analyst and analysand are brought together in conditions of rational agreement; both are primarily concerned with mutual understanding; and both are encouraged to communicate openly and freely.

Habermas regards himself as a Marxist. However, within the congregation of contemporary Marxists this claim is challenged. Anderson (1983) submits that in identifying communication as the foundation of social life, Habermas has effectively put a match to any Marxist credentials he might have claimed for his work. Exploring communication leads to the impasse of idealist thought. The plight is illustrated in Habermas's concept of the 'ideal speech situation'. The concept is so rarefied that its application in social life is extremely limited. This point links up with another criticism that Anderson (1983: 66) makes. He argues that Habermas has an 'essentially pedagogic view' of human relations, i.e. a view which stands above the day-to-day struggles in communication and social life in general, and hence fails to engage meaningfully with them. Similarly, Gadamer (1975) submits that the main weakness of Habermas's work on communication is that it marginalizes the historical dimension of social relationships. It therefore underestimates the role of tradition and class in structuring all instances of current communicative action.

Fundamental criticisms of Habermas's work have also been made by Giddens (1977). He argues that the distinction between interaction (communicative rationality) and labour (instrumental rationality) that Habermas characteristically employs in his writings is not cut and dried. In fact, it is difficult to think of any area in social life where the two do not interpenetrate. For example, watching a film in the cinema may seem to approximate to the condition of communicative action and pure leisure activity. But producing the film, maintaining the cinema auditorium, and buying the ticket, all relate to questions of labour and labour interests. Similarly, Giddens casts doubt on the practicality of Habermas's theory. It is difficult to imagine the social conditions that might permit the ideal speech situation to be generalized in society.

These criticisms are well founded. Even so, it would be wrong to conclude that Habermas's work is of no value to leisure theory. Three points need to be made. First, it has accomplished a penetrating critique of subjectivism. After Habermas, it becomes harder to approach the study of leisure relations in terms of concepts such as perceptions of freedom, self-determination, life satisfaction, and spontaneity. Second, Habermas avoids the reductionism which many commentators locate in Frankfurt Marxism. Thus, following Adorno, Horkheimer, and Marcuse, Habermas submits that meaningful communicative action is only intelligible in the total societal context of class and rational administration. Unlike his progenitors, however, Habermas insists that this context is not a self-sufficient basis for explaining communicative action, i.e. there are influences on speech acts which relate to nature, personal history, and the technical system of language as well as the world of interpersonal relations. Third, Habermas's work on communication provides a useful counterpoint to the important work on signification to be considered in the next chapter.

Hegemony and Consciousness

Earlier, I argued that the crisis in western Marxism originated in part from the failure of basic predictions in Marx's theory to come true. It is no surprise therefore to find that the most heated controversies within neo-Marxism have centred on the question of determination and consciousness. In Marxian theory, determination refers to the causal relationship between levels of structure and forms of practice. The received wisdom in orthodox

Marxism has always accommodated the principle that there is a fundamental relationship between the economy and consciousness. We have already encountered this view in the neo-Marxist approaches to leisure enumerated above, notably in the proposition that forms of leisure practice and consciousness are determined by the material level of class relations. The rationale for this was supplied by Marx in his famous discussion of base and superstructure. The passage is crucial and deserves to be quoted in full:

'In the social production of existence, men enter into definite, necessary relations, which are independent of their will, namely relations of production corresponding to a determinate stage of development in their material forces of production. The totality of these relations of production constitutes the economic structure of society, the real foundation on which there arises a legal and political superstructure and to which correspond definite forms of social consciousness. The mode of production of material life conditions the social, political and intellectual life process in general. It is not the consciousness of men that determines their social being, but on the contrary it is their social being that determines their consciousness.'

(Marx 1976: 3)

This passage is widely held to have had a major influence on the development of Marxist thought. What it says is that the economic base determines social relations. The economy is therefore depicted as the mainspring behind social development. The difficulty is that it seems to set up a false conceptual dichotomy. There are innumerable 'superstructural' relations which cannot be reduced to the economic base. Leisure is one of them. I do not mean to imply by this that leisure relations have no economic basis. On the contrary, as I argued earlier, leisure can properly be regarded as one of the main dynamics of capitalist production. At the same time, however, leisure activity seems to include social relations which have little to do with the economic base. For example, it is difficult to see how the annual village cricket match or the urban community carnival can be seriously defined as a result of the economic requirements of capitalism. Applying the economy to everything that happens in society seems to deprive the concept of all determinacy and precision. At all events, Marxist sociologists now accept that the relationship between the base and superstructure is far more complex than Marx's initial formulation implied.[11]

The major routes out of this apparent blind alley have con-
verged in a resurgence of interest in the concept of ideology. The
leading theoretical innovations here are usually accepted to be
the concepts of 'relative autonomy' (Althusser) and 'hegemony'
(Gramsci). Both of these concepts have attracted considerable
critical attention in the secondary literature.[12] For this reason I
shall confine myself here to a brief account of their core
features.

The writings of Althusser and Gramsci have been a shaping
influence on the stimulating and important work of the Centre
for Contemporary Cultural Studies (CCCS) at Birmingham
University. Their work has looked at aspects of culture and
subculture including leisure relations. I shall consider their
contribution to leisure theory at the end of this section.

Before I begin to discuss the work of Althusser and Gramsci,
however, it is very important to cancel any notions that a unilinear
progression exists in neo-Marxist approaches to ideology. In fact,
many writers who regard themselves as Marxists unabashedly
denounce the 'structuralist' writings of Althusser and his followers. For example, E. P. Thompson (1978: 103–22) identifies a
major rift between forms of Marxist theory in which human
consciousness and action are 'read off' from their position in the
capitalist mode of production and his own 'Marxism' in which
consciousness and culture are centre stage, i.e. irreducible in the
last instance to the relations of the economic base. Thompson's
pugnacious and highly influential critique calls on Marxists to
recognize the 'protean' character of social action, and to study
history in terms of 'structural actuation' (1978: 110). This means
rejecting the idea of historical necessity and, instead, studying
history as an emergent process which occurs within a framework
of 'pressures and limits'. Action transforms existing conditions.
But in transforming them, it also transforms the conditions of its
own existence. It is important to note two things. First, the
emphasis that Thompson places upon the centrality in Marxist
thought of people's capacity to make sense of their own lives and
histories ('lived experience') is not unique to him. On the contrary,
its currency is so wide that it has been assigned a descriptive label
of its own: 'culturalism' (see Samuel *et al.* 1981: 375–408). Second,
point for point, and for that matter almost line for line, the
culturalist approach has been opposed by 'structuralist' Marxism
(see Johnson 1981: 386–96). For example, culturalism has been
criticized for its alleged 'empiricism', 'simple populism', and,

above all, its serious neglect of the role of economic categories in the determination of action and development.

All of this is mentioned to indicate the real differences that exist in neo-Marxism. It is against this backdrop that my discussion of Althusser and Gramsci should be located.

ALTHUSSER AND RELATIVE AUTONOMY

According to Althusser, Marxist sociologists of culture and ideology need to accommodate the tension generated by two opposing ideas: 'on the one hand *determination in the last instance by the (economic) mode of production*; on the other, *the relative autonomy of the superstructure*' (1969: 111). There are obvious difficulties with this statement. Chief among them is the fact that it presents a manifest contradiction. No object can have 'relative autonomy' if it is determined 'in the last instance' by the economic mode of production. Indeed if the autonomy of the superstructure is larded with the constraints of the economic base it is hard to see how the term 'relative' can be anything other than a misnomer. Similarly, if one approaches the matter from the economic base, the meaning of the term 'in the last instance' is rather ambivalent. Althusser himself compounds interpretive difficulties by observing that 'the lonely hour of the "last instance" never comes' (1969: 113). In my view, these conceptual difficulties severely militate against the value and utility of the base/superstructure distinction in leisure theory.

It is important, however, to note that many observers have suggested that Althusser's work represents a seminal advance in the base/superstructure problem, and furthermore, that the interpretive difficulties associated with it are more apparent than real. Thus, Wolff (1981: 82–3) submits that what Althusser means by the relative autonomy of superstructural levels (politics, ideology, leisure, religion, etc.) is not only the capacity of the superstructure to act reciprocally on the economic base, but also the relative autonomy of these levels *from each other*. For example, leisure relations have their own effective sphere of influence which is distinct from the sphere of the other superstructural levels. By the same token, leisure relations, and social relations at all levels of the superstructure, have the capacity to react on the base and actively change its structure. Thus, the historical development of a game like football, from amateur to professional

status, was patently situated in an economic context of constraint. But as the game became more professional, it began to
acquire its own relative social and economic power (via the
development of regular fixtures, leagues, established fan clubs,
and the introduction of spectator charges) which in turn fed back
into the base and caused modifications in the overall structure of
economic constraint. As regards the question of what the phrase
'the last instance' means, Wolff argues that this must be understood in the context of the different superstructural *levels* that
Althusser's theory denotes: 'The fact that the ''last instance''
never comes, only means that historically the economic is never
the sole determinant' (Wolff 1981: 82). But this hardly resolves
the problem of reductionism in Althusser's theory. For Wolff also
notes that the mutual determination between all superstructural
levels is 'ultimately' determined by the economic base.

The mark of reductionism in Althusser's work is most transparent when he applies his theory to the analysis of concrete
social processes. His inquiry into ideology and the reproduction
of subordination bristles with functionalist assumptions and
propositions. Thus, for example, he writes that 'the reproduction
of labour power requires not only a reproduction of its skills, but
also, at the same time, a reproduction of its submission to the
rules of the established order' (1971: 127). Althusser submits that
workers are inured to their subordinate position by dint of the
superstructure which continuously reproduces the relations of
economic domination. In exploiting and developing this idea he
introduces the celebrated distinction between the 'repressive
state apparatus' (RSA) and the 'ideological state apparatus' (ISA).
The former refers to the coercive mechanisms of state power, e.g.
the police, the army, the courts, the prisons, and the civil service.
The ISA includes, *inter alia*, the education system, the Church,
the family, the media, and the culture industry. According to
Althusser (1971: 143) the apparent diversity of the ISA structures
masks their common function in society which is to train and
allocate labour to positions in the labour market and to legitimate
the entire system. The effect of ideology is thus universalized. It
is a web which enmeshes everyone regardless of their rank in
society. The individual, whether bourgeois or proletarian, is
held, *in the last instance*, to exemplify the requirements of the
mode of production in his or her thoughts, feelings, and actions.

Althusser's work has been the subject of intense scrutiny in the
social sciences. I do not propose to survey the field in its entirety

here. In any case, for leisure theory the essential critical points are quite localized. Three points need to be made. First, whatever Althusser and his disciples say, the gist of his theory is to reduce the individual to 'a socially obedient cipher' (Hirst and Woolley 1982: 136). Second, it falsely represents the function of leisure as pathetically reproducing the status quo. Third, it is by no means clear that the theoretical distinction between the RSA (which functions by 'violence') and the ISA (which functions by 'ideological persuasion') can be corroborated empirically. Thus he warns his readers that a search for a 'purely ideological state apparatus' will prove to be futile. This calls into question not only the value of the original distinction but also its utility in social analysis.

GRAMSCI AND HEGEMONY

Mouffe (1979) argues that Gramsci's work anticipated Althusser in several respects. Thus, Gramsci's concept of hegemony is committed to a study of ideology as a real material force in the production and reproduction of social formations. Similarly, Gramsci emphasizes that ideology is not 'false consciousness', i.e. it is not a systematically distorted view of social reality. On the contrary, it is most effective when it is 'lived through' as a 'natural' expression of social reality. In Gramsci's own words:

> 'Hegemony works through ideology but it does not consist of false ideas, perceptions, definitions. It works *primarily* by inserting the subordinate class into the key institutions and structures which support the power and social authority of the dominant order. It is, above all, in these structures and relations that a subordinate class *lives its subordination.*'
>
> (Gramsci 1971: 164)

Hegemony is therefore to be understood as a type of domination which is based on the 'active consent' of the subordinate groups. This consent is typically engineered through the exercise of intellectual, moral, and political leadership. But it rests finally on the monopoly control of the repressive machinery of the state (e.g. the police, the army, and the legal system). In contrast to Althusser's position on ideology, which stresses the general framework of social domination, Gramsci's discussion is resolutely non-monolithic. It emphasizes the contingent and changeable nature of social rule. Above all else, hegemony is conceived of as a *histori-cally specific* phenomenon. A class or 'historical bloc' (alliance of classes or dominant groups) may lose hegemony when the power balance between itself and subordinate groups shifts. Gramsci's concept is therefore more flexible than Althusser's model of ideol-ogy and repression. He argues that hegemonic rule is mediated through a number of ideological apparatuses spread through the social formation, e.g. the schools, the Church, political parties, and the culture industry. These institutions are the locations for the transmission and elaboration of hegemonic rule. They are also the key sites of power struggle in the superstructure.

SUBCULTURE AND CONSCIOUSNESS: THE WORK OF THE
CCCS GROUP

The concept of hegemony is at the forefront of the approach to culture, leisure, and ideology associated with the influential CCCS group.[13] The group has acknowledged an indebtedness to the work of Althusser and Gramsci (see Clarke *et al.* 1976; Hall 1981). The Centre's research interest in leisure derives from its central theoretical concern to explore the mechanisms of cultural integration in modern capitalism. According to Hall *et al.* the work is based on the following idea: 'the conditions for (capital-ist) production – or what has come to be called *social reproduction* – are often sustained in the apparently "unproductive" spheres of civil society and the state' (1978: 202, their emphasis).

To date, the focus of research has been directed at leisure relations in working-class culture, racial minorities, and football supporters. In all of these areas, the work of the Centre has emphasized the function of subcultural styles as ritualized responses to the commodities of the culture industry. However, whereas Frankfurt Marxism was principally concerned with the production and manipulation of popular culture in high capital-ism and the resulting implications for Marxist theory, the work of the Centre is chiefly addressed to the question of the dynamics and variations in consciousness among working-class consumers. The change in focus produces a different way of looking at leisure. The weighty conclusion that Adorno, Horkheimer, and Marcuse draw from their analysis is that mass leisure activity involves the real capitulation of the working class. It is in their leisure, at the very moment when working-class consumers imagine themselves to be most free, that they are actually the most faithful servants of capital. Against this, the work of the Centre stresses the concept of the consumer as a skilled, knowledgeable actor who engages in relations of negotiation and resistance with and against the output of the culture industry. Working-class leisure is portrayed as a form of class struggle, and a continuous mode of transaction with the hegemonic culture. As Hall *et al.* put it, 'leisure and recreation seem to have provided a more nego-tiable space than the tightly disciplined and controlled work situation. The working class has imprinted itself indelibly on many areas of mass leisure and recreation' (Hall and Jefferson 1976: 50).

The Centre is highly critical of the conventional wisdom which associates leisure with 'free time and free choice'. The approach which it has developed emphasizes that all leisure experience occurs within a framework of economic constraint. Even so, the Centre defines leisure relations *à la* Althusser, as 'an area of *relative* freedom' (Clarke 1976: 175, his emphasis). As with Althusser, this formulation carries with it a number of diffi-culties. For example, Clarke submits that working-class leisure should be understood as a simultaneous release from, and repro-duction of, work discipline. Thus he declares that: 'the rigours of work are not forgotten when the indulgences of leisure begin. But the "relative freedom" of leisure has allowed the *displacement* of central class concerns and values, developed in work, to the symbolic activities of the leisure sphere' (Clarke 1976: 176). Prima facie, this appears to underline the freedom involved in leisure relations. However, the analytical weight of the passage is plainly stacked on the side of work as the determinant influence in shaping patterns of working-class leisure. When all is said and done, leisure activity is seen as structured by the demands of work, and hence is subject to the logic of class exploitation. In this context, the vaunted 'heroism' and 'energy' of subcultural groups in resisting hegemonic rule are noteworthy not so much for what they achieve, but for their underdog status in relation to the massed repressive and ideological forces of capital. Incidentally, it is worth noting in passing that Young (1983: 134–38) has attacked the whole CCCS output for falsely 'idealizing' the moral charac-ter of oppressed groups, an approach which tends to produce a naïve view of an 'unflawed historical subject' pitted against the Goliath of modern capitalism. The moral sensibilities of the CCCS group are not at issue here. Rather, I simply wish to submit that the vital interplay between work and leisure, which they espouse at the level of theory, appears to be remorselessly denied when the theory is applied to concrete empirical processes. Thus the 'resistance' of exploited groups in capitalist society appears to be played out in a societal context where working-class incorporation is already accepted as a *fait accompli*. The revolt is a revolt into style, expresses itself in cultural fashions and rituals, and in desultory episodes of violence such as random rioting, mugging, and street crimes. In letters which spell out the bleakest proofs of the prophecies of Frankfurt Marxism, the work of the Centre reveals in the 'subtext' of its research a view of the working class as effectively integrated into the system.

This is a real weakness; however, it should not be allowed to diminish the significance of the Centre's achievement. Two points in particular need to be emphasized. First, the work of the Centre has included some of the most imaginative attempts within the Marxist tradition to portray the real diversity of leisure values and lifestyles within capitalism. Second, it has made a genuine attempt to demonstrate the dialectical character of relations of race, class, gender, and leisure. I have argued that the CCCS approach is not entirely successful. However, I hope that I have also indicated through my general discussion of hegemony and consciousness, the prime importance of the attempt.

Forced Leisure and Post-Industrial Socialism

It is currently fashionable to use the euphemisms 'forced leisure' or 'involuntary unemployment' to describe the conditions of the long-term unemployed. From a Marxist standpoint, there are a number of insuperable difficulties in this terminology. In the first place, these individuals are unemployed not because they are unemployable, but rather because they are surplus to the requirements of capitalist production. Second, their condition is not one of 'forced leisure' but redundancy. If they were in a condition of forced leisure they would merely be deprived of labour. But they are not *merely* deprived of labour, they are also deprived of a wage or an income from the state that would enable them *both* to satisfy the necessities of life and to enjoy the free and full maintenance and development of leisure interests. Viewed from a Marxist perspective, the unemployed are objectively attached to the universal market, but are subjectively deprived of the individual purchasing power that would enable them to participate meaningfully in the consumption of the commodities and services that they are continually encouraged to covet by the organs of the culture industry.

At the same time, the view that leisure activity involves compulsion and force is implicit in all of the neo-Marxist approaches to leisure that I have considered above. However, this view of leisure activity refers to a social condition which is analytically distinct from the condition of long-term unemployment outlined above. As regards relations under capitalism, the concept of forced leisure hinges on Marx's discussion of individual and productive consumption. For Marx, the individual with leisure is continuously exposed to forms of popular amusement which pacify and retard creative faculties and interests. To turn away from these social forms of amusement is to isolate oneself from the quick of social life. This applies to all classes under capitalism. For example, the disposable time of the labourer is conditioned, above all else, by the absolute necessity to gain waged labour. Working-class leisure is fitted around the fact of waged labour, and reflects the assorted deprivations of work. However, the capitalist also experiences his leisure time as hedged in with business worries and the need to maintain a decorous social distance between himself and the representatives of other classes. In Marx's writings an identikit picture of the capitalist entrepreneur emerges. It shows us a 'private person', wary of others, calculating and oppressively conscious that a pleasure gained today must be paid for tomorrow. The neo-Marxist approaches enumerated above have taken up these ideas and greatly embellished them to fit the altered conditions of social life under capitalism today.[14] But their ultimate conclusion reaffirms one of the central arguments in Marx's theory: leisure under capitalism is intrinsically and exhaustively 'forced' in so far as its distribution, duration, and quality obey the iron laws of capitalist accumulation.

These remarks on forced leisure apply to social conditions under capitalism. But Marx looked beyond capitalism to labour and leisure under communism. As we have seen, Marxists today still wrestle with the meaning of his cryptic discussion of the 'realm of freedom' and the 'realm of necessity'. In recent years, largely under the impetus of the 'new' technology, Marxists have devoted more attention to the validity of Marx's analysis in the age of the microchip and mass communications. One of the most penetrating and stimulating contributions has come from André Gorz (1982). I want to look at his work in terms of (a) its 'in house' critique of Marxist thought on work and leisure, and (b) his discussion of the organization of work and leisure in 'post-industrial socialism'.

THE WEAKNESSES IN NEO-MARXIST APPROACHES TO LEISURE

Gorz argues that the importance which orthodox Marxism has traditionally attributed to workers gaining control of the entire labour process as the basis for real emancipation is no longer relevant to modern society. As he explains, 'for workers, it is no longer a question of freeing themselves *within* work, putting themselves in control of work, or seizing power within the framework of work. The point now is to free oneself *from* work by rejecting its nature, content, necessity and modalities' (1982: 67).

Gorz bases this statement on his analysis of the four principal features of work today. These can be listed in summary form thus:

(1) Capitalist industry has reduced its requirement for physical labour on a world scale. Production is now more mechanized and standardized than ever before. The invention of minia-turized, digitally controlled production systems has been a major factor in revolutionizing the production process.

(2) Capitalist industry attempts to organize its labour force on the principle of 'interchangeable labour'. Work tasks have been designed to reduce the workers' skill level and sphere of discretion in the work process. The 'deskilling process' has also been extensively discussed by Braverman (1974). Both writers submit that the historical role of capitalism is: (a) to reduce the dependence of capital upon labour, and (b) to standardize the skill level among workers, so that labour can be switched from one task and trained to fulfil another with the minimum of disruption to the overall production process.

(3) The enormous scale of modern capitalist production means that the labour process is no longer a sphere of social relations which the great mass of people look to for self-fulfilment and self-development. Individual producers may never consume what they produce. No urban centre is capable of meeting the

basic needs of its population through its own resources. People can no longer be persuaded to fight for the revolutionary transformation of society in order to become the 'associated producers' at the end of the day.

(4) The extension of the principle of economic interdependence and the concentration of power in the welfare state has induced a generalized mentality of 'dependency' in consumer society. For Gorz,

> 'the spontaneous reflex of the working class is to demand that this dependence upon the state be matched by duties of the state vis-à-vis the working people. Since the working class can do nothing for itself, it follows that the state should do everything for the working class. . . . The seizure of state power by the working class is replaced by state protection for the working class.'
>
> (Gorz 1982: 41–2)

Gorz's arguments are not meant to be exclusive in their terms of reference. He recognizes that in all societies, at all times, a small minority of highly trained and skilled workers will be found who identify themselves with their work and seek to realize themselves through it. But his central proposition is that the four principles of work in modern capitalism enumerated above are combining to reduce the size of this group drastically. For most wage labourers today, "real life" begins outside of work, and work itself has become a means towards the extension of the sphere of non-work' (Gorz 1982: 81).

As we shall see in the next section, the argument bristles with contingencies. The point to emphasize at this stage in my discussion is Gorz's contention that leisure is now the central sphere for adult self-realization in capitalist society. If this thesis is correct, it means that the propositions and policies of orthodox Marxism which assume that work occupies this privileged position are no longer valid. It also means that leisure relations are now the key site of neo-Marxist inquiry.

LEISURE IN 'POST-INDUSTRIAL SOCIALISM'

Gorz makes a number of practical proposals on the organization of work and leisure in post-industrial socialist society. These converge in his 'policy of time'. He argues that governments in all advanced industrial societies should implement policies designed to reduce working time. This is economically practicable because of the labour-saving innovations of the new technology; and it is also politically attractive, since most people resent their work and regard it as a burden. Under post-industrial socialism, time and life space should be organized on a principle of dualism. Individuals would live in 'two spheres': (1) the *heteronomous sphere*, which consists of relations that satisfy the necessities of life, in accordance with a voluntary and socially binding plan of production; (2) the *autonomous sphere*, which refers to the self-determined activities of individuals, e.g. relations of creative activity and self-determined 'convivial' enterprise.[15]

By present-day standards, the heteronomous sphere (the realm of necessity) would require a very low time input. Gorz (1982: 150) mentions the figure of twenty hours per week. This would leave the rest of the individual's time for personal development (the realm of freedom).

Gorz is, of course, assuming a fundamental change not only in the relationship between work and leisure, but also in the distribution of wealth, the system of allocating income, and the concept of 'occupational career'. The two biggest assumptions he makes are also the most sociologically questionable.

(1) He assumes that the future, libertarian, post-industrial society will be based on a 'time bank' system. Under it, time will be quantified into exchangeable units, and people will borrow or lend units of autonomous and heteronomous denominations just as they please.

(2) He assumes that post-industrial socialism will be run on the lines of the full collectivization of the means of production. The wealth liberated by the ending of the class system will be devoted to improving the system of social services and benefits, and also extending the principle of a guaranteed income for life to everyone.

I want to turn now to a critical estimate of Gorz's study. At the outset it should be said that his work is one of the few attempts within western Marxism to come to terms with the practical significance of the new technology for Marxist theory and the organization of work and leisure. His is indeed original and stimulating work. Even so, I shall argue that his work stands out, not so much for the questions in leisure theory which it answers, as for the critical contingencies which it passes over in silence.

In particular, I want to focus on three problems in his analysis relating to the question of the transition to socialism, the domination of the state, and the privileged status of leisure.

Gorz portrays the transition to post-industrial socialism as an automatic process. The question of the inevitable class confrontation that would ensue from any serious attempt to introduce and maintain the fiscal and redistributive measures capable of financing the 'time bank' policy is not adequately confronted. This raises doubts about the realism of his approach.

With regard to the issue of state domination, Gorz's study manifests ambivalence. He goes out of his way to declare that 'the "organization of leisure", where the state dragoons the young and the old, men and women workers, mothers, schoolchildren, etc. into carefully separated activities, is worth no more than the leisure organized by the merchants of escapism' (1982: 139). Yet one must point out that there is not a single important area in the organization of leisure under post-industrial socialism where the state's role is envisaged as anything less than central. For example, the state is charged with the essential task of regulating the 'time bank'. *Contra* Weber, Gorz invites us to believe that the state can discharge its duties without dominating the lives of individuals.

Finally, there is the question of the privileged status of leisure in most people's lives today. There are two aspects to this point. First, there is strong evidence that most wage labourers are instrumentally attached to their work.[16] The evidence that they are indifferent to what they do, or that the labour process under capitalism has wholly eliminated pleasure and satisfaction from the work experience of wage labourers, is less well founded. Second, Gorz's proposals regarding the restructuring of work and leisure under post-industrial socialism do not include the abolition of work. As long as individuals remain conscious of the critical conjunction between work and leisure, necessity and freedom, they will be prey to the stresses and tensions involved in switching from one sphere to the other. There is no reason to suppose that merely providing a guaranteed income and vastly increased non-work time will produce satisfying leisure experience.

6 LEISURE, SIGNIFICATION, AND POWER: Barthes and Foucault

Orthodox Marxism looks forward to the real liberation of man and womankind from lifelong alienated labour and leisure. As Marx repeated continually, the aim of socialist revolution is to create a society in which labour becomes not only 'a means to life' but 'life's prime want'.

In recent years, this whole line of reasoning has come under fire. 'Structuralist' and 'post-structuralist' writers no longer look forward to the reconstruction of society and the realization of the 'all round development of the individual'. Instead, these approaches express the view that 'the goal of the human sciences is not to constitute man but to dissolve him' (Lévi-Strauss 1962: 326). The writers that I shall examine in this chapter, Roland Barthes and Michel Foucault, are often referred to as representatives of this position. Certainly, their work draws attention to the problematic nature of the categories of 'subjectivity', 'meaning', and 'social order'. The human subject is indeed studied as a 'decentred' being, which has 'meaning' only in reference to 'the laws of desire, the forms of its language, the rules of its actions, or the play of its mythical and imaginative discourse'.[1] The individual 'exists' in the slipstream or the 'play' of these structures. Barthes's work on 'mythology' and Foucault's discussion of the successive historical 'atmospheres of discourse' (*episteme*), that supported some forms of knowledge and suffocated others, clearly have structuralist and post-structuralist overtones.[2] Even so, neither academic label embraces the full capaciousness and sheer incongruity of these writers' lifelong intellectual exploits.

Foucault (1977: xiv) openly abhorred being pigeon-holed. And every word that Barthes wrote proclaimed his self-image as the maverick of style.

A few explanatory words are owed to the reader who wonders why I have alighted upon the work of Barthes and Foucault as material which is of outstanding importance for contemporary leisure theory. The truth is that neither approach has generated a strong research tradition in leisure study. Also, the question of leisure is not addressed at length in the published work of either social observer. Three points need to be made. In the first place, the fact that their writings were not direct investigations of leisure is not a sufficient reason for assuming that the texts have nothing to say about leisure. On the contrary, it follows from the principle of 'decentring' (the structural contingencies of subjective meaning) that Barthes and Foucault would have been the last people to assert that their books are merely the sum of their cover-bound texts.[3] But there is no need to stake everything on the principle of decentring. The second point that I wish to make is that each of these writers touched upon methodological issues that are of central importance to leisure theory. Barthes's discussion of signification, and Foucault's ideas on power, point to deeply suggestive programmes of research for leisure study. By examining them in this book I hope to increase the number of workers in the field of leisure study who recognize these ideas as sources of insight and stimulation. The third point is that their work is widely believed to constitute the most serious challenge to neo-Marxism today.[4]

I shall divide the chapter into two sections. The first section discusses the development of Barthes's ideas on mythology and signification. The second attempts to explore Foucault's view of power and the government of the body.

Signification and Leisure

Barthes's key proposition for leisure theory is that leisure goods and services can be studied as sign systems. Stated minimally like this, the idea does not seem so very new. As Culler (1981: 21–2) has pointed out, philosophers have always shown an interest in signs. Long before Barthes turned to the subject, considerable contributions to semiotics (the study of signs) had been made by the American philosopher Charles Sanders Peirce and the Swiss linguist Ferdinand de Saussure. Indeed, for that matter, Adorno and Horkheimer in their thesis on the culture industry had observed that 'the product prescribes every reaction: not only by its natural structure (which collapses under reflection) but by signals' (1979: 137). This comes close to the pith of what Barthes argues in his early writings.

One of the central arguments that I shall put forward in this section is that it is appropriate to speak of a 'break' in the intellectual development of Barthes's writings.[5] The key work of the break is the book *S/Z*. Before this, Barthes's discussion of signs seemed to relate closely to the central themes of Marxism. After *S/Z*, this connection no longer exists. Barthes's work increasingly embraces conventions and preoccupations which Marxists regard as the hallmarks of idealism. This is a complex matter which cannot be discussed in detail here. However, I shall attempt to convey the contrast between the two periods of Barthes's thought in the following way. I shall argue that in his early writings, the concept of 'signification' is of central relevance to leisure theory. In his later work, the concept of *signifiance* assumes this position.

Before turning to an examination of the concept of signification in Barthes's early work, I want to situate his thought in the context of the development of semiotic thought. This is necessary if we are to appreciate the originality of Barthes's early methodological writings. I propose to do this by briefly examining Saussure's work. It is this intellectual system, above all others, which was the greatest influence upon the young Barthes's writings on sign systems.

SAUSSURE'S SEMIOLOGY

Saussure's semiology is based on the study of language. It hinges on the opposition between *langue* (language) and *parole* (speech). For an understanding of what each term means it is useful to think of *langue* as corresponding to a structural (synchronic) dimension; and *parole* as corresponding to a dynamic (diachronic) dimension. *Langue* refers to the total matrix of words, necessary conventions, and rules which make up the structure of language. *Parole* consists of the exercise of *langue*, i.e. acts of speech. The important point is that Saussure regards *langue* as the structure which is prior to, and determinant of, *parole*. Saussure's own analogy is actually quite appropriate for leisure theory. He draws on the distinction between the abstract set of rules and conventions in the game of chess, and the moves which people actually make in playing the game.

Saussure introduces another level of refinement into his analysis with the celebrated distinction between 'signifier' and 'signified'. Semiology, as we have noted, is the study of signs. But signs are not simple things. All signs consist of a compound between signifier and signified. The signifier refers to the medium of communication, e.g. sound. The signified is the conceptual representation of a thing. An example might be helpful to clarify the point. If we consider the word 'tennis' as a linguistic sign, the signifier is the sound made by the utterance of the word 'tennis'; the signified is the concept that we always associate with the sound. There is no law in nature or logic which requires the sound 'tennis' to bring to mind the concept of 'tennis'. Saussure insists that the relationship between signifier and signified is arbitrary. From a structuralist standpoint the importance of all this lies in the following idea: meaning is the effect of discrete signifying systems. To put it differently, a word has no intrinsic meaning. Rather, its meaning derives from its relation of difference to other words in the same language. For example, the word 'tennis' means 'tennis' not because of any intrinsic property which it has, but rather because it does not mean soccer, hockey, boxing, billiards, or golf. In each case the sign, and its relation to other signs, is arbitrary. The meaning of the subject derives from its place in the signifying system of which it is a part. We have, then, the concept of a subject which is 'de-centred'.

BARTHES AND SIGNIFICATION

Barthes's initial methodological achievement was to liberate Saussure's method from the specialized area of linguistics and apply it generally to the study of social signifying systems (fashion, advertising, film, food, etc.). He suggested (1967b: 87–94) that the power of Saussure's method could only be fully extended if a further conceptual refinement were added to it: the distinction between 'denotation' and 'connotation'. Denotation refers to the indicative information that derives from the relationship between signifier and signified. Connotation refers to what the sign *implies*, over and above the information supplied through denotation. Barthes therefore opened up an exciting possibility for the sociology of leisure. The study of the 'rhetoric' of the sign could act as a means for scientifically understanding how ideology is maintained and reproduced in capitalist society. The term 'rhetoric' recalls Marx's work on reification and Gramsci's ideas on hegemony. The rhetoric of signs means the natural, spontaneous appearance of the sign as a neutral representation of reality. For example, when we look at the Union Jack we see, automatically and in a highly condensed form, what it is to be British.[6] We see, *inter alia*, the distinctiveness of national life, the glory of Empire, the unity of the realm, etc. The way in which the sign works on consciousness is not natural. The individual's response to signs is socially constructed and reproduced. According to Barthes, the sign and its modalities are invested with historically specific meanings and messages.

In sum, Barthes's early work on 'signification' (the affixing of concrete meanings to the sign) suggests a radical programme of demystification in the semiotic analysis of everyday life under capitalism. The task of semiotics is to interrogate systematically the rhetoric of signs (the 'mythologies' of everyday life) in order to expose the social interests which lie behind them. It is very important to note that the foundation of this entire project is the assumption that a science of signs can be constructed which is objective and truthful. Barthes was well aware of the mythologies that Marxism had spawned. He produced a stinging attack on the deviations of Stalinism as a form of political writing and speech (1967a: 23–5). Even so, in his early writings Barthes suggests that Marxism might function as the basis for a truthful science of signs:

> 'There is . . . one language which is not mythical, it is the language of man as a producer: wherever man speaks in order to transform reality and no longer to present it as an image, wherever he links his language to the making of things, meta-language is referred to a language-object, and myth is impossible. . . . The bourgeoisie hides the fact that it is the bourgeoisie and thereby produces myth: revolution announces itself as revolution and therefore abolishes myth.'
>
> (Barthes 1973: 146)

Barthes applies these theoretical insights in a series of glittering essays on contemporary mythologies. Many of these relate to leisure activities. Thus, in *Mythologies*, he decodes wrestling, novels, cuisine, toys, film, and theatre. Later (1979) he published essays on the music hall, the 'bourgeois art of song', journalism, and cycling (the 'Tour de France'). The longer study on photography (1981) also deserves to be singled out for its acuity and the elegance of its argument.

These early works produce a simulacrum of convergence between Marxism, Freudianism, and semiotics. Barthes's discussion of signification seems to promise the realization of the dream that Freud nourished in the last years of his life, of founding a scientific theory of how the unconscious shapes society. Crucially, however, Barthes uses it in the context of a materialist understanding of history and power. We would see the mark of the unconscious in the sign; and in the sign also, we would see the tread-marks of history and the class struggle.

SIGNIFIANCE: THE 'PLAY OF SIGNIFIERS'

In fact, even in his initial excursions into understanding myth, Barthes's commitment to Marxism was always a makeshift arrangement. The position can be defined in this way. The logic of the semiotic calculus which Barthes set in motion demanded that he reject his own theory as a limiting case of the mythologies which it enumerated. As one author put it, the reason for this is that the language which semiotics uses to 'criticize or formulate alternatives works according to the principles being contested'.[7] After showing, at least to his own satisfaction, that the meaning of signs cannot be contained, that signs spark off into multiple chain reactions of signification, Barthes submits his own science of signs to the same law. From his path-breaking analysis of Balzac's story 'Sarrasine' in *S/Z* (1975a), until his death in 1980, Barthes worked on and around the theme that 'a text is not a line of words releasing a single "theological" meaning (the "message" of the Author-God) but a multi-dimensional space in which a variety of meanings, none of them original, blend and clash' (Barthes 1977: 146).

The main quarry of his analysis in the later years of his career was the literary text. Barthes sought to bury the idea of finite meaning. He defied the conventional wisdom of the day according to which a text is a self-sufficient piece of work with a definite beginning, middle, and end. Instead, he insisted that texts must be read as 'galaxies of signifiers'. The idea that an 'authoritarian' law of correspondence exists between what the author writes and what the reader reads, is explicitly rejected. With it go a number of orthodox working assumptions about the nature of literary communication. Thus, the usual distinction between author (as producer) and reader (as consumer) is rendered defunct. The reader 'elicits' the text by his own reading of it. The author is now regarded as simply a participant in the endlessly emerging play of signifiers. These ideas are important for the following reason. They indicate that the earlier idea of signification is now cast aside. Instead, Barthes embraces a concept which was originally postulated by Julia Kristeva: *signifiance*.[8] *Signifiance* refers to the endless productivity of the text: it is always conceiving. Barthes applied this concept to the study of social life in general. Now the whole world was to be read as text: the demythologizers themselves would become demythologized. As he explains:

> 'By refusing to assign a "secret", an ultimate meaning to the text (and to the world as text), [radical semiotics] liberates what may be called an anti-theological activity, an activity that is truly revolutionary since to refuse to fix meaning is, in the end, to refuse God and his hypostases – science, reason, law.'
>
> (Barthes 1977a: 147)

In this 'truly revolutionary activity', the centre does indeed not hold; things fall apart. The entire world, and all the knowledge in the world, are considered to be a flux of signifiers. It is a project which openly celebrates the chaos of systematic meaning. Yet, paradoxically, it is not, in itself, chaotic. Barthes's self-appointed task is to study 'the decomposition of bourgeois consciousness' (1977a: 63). This is not a mournful task. On the contrary, Barthes continually stresses that the practice of radical semiotics can be blissful. It is not the 'bliss' which derives from an earth-shattering discovery that makes the practitioner a better person or the world a better place. The term that Barthes uses is *jouissance*. There is no equivalent in English for this word. It means, *inter alia*, enjoyment, the rights of privilege, pleasure, sexual climax, delight, and loss. In Barthes's work it refers to the individual's sensuous and emotional attachment to a datum in the physical and social world. The idea has mystical overtones. In the momentary acceptance of things as they are, in merging with the world as it is, rather than in trying to change it, lies *jouissance*. This emerges as the main organizing principle behind research and thought in the radical semiotics of Barthes's later writings. He invites the semiotician to take his pleasure from the play of signifiers in the world, and, in the knowledge that these things are transitory, to move on once his pleasure is complete.

How does Barthes's later work relate to leisure theory? Frith (1983) suggests that the concept of *jouissance* can be studied empirically in leisure experience. He uses the example of rock music to illustrate his thesis. In musical performance the audience is not merely the passive recipient of the fixed meanings produced on stage. Rather, they participate in the play of meanings, and gain their pleasure from identifying intensely with the dynamics of performance. Frith describes the experience in the following way: *'jouissance*, like sexual pleasure, involves self-abandonment, as the terms we usually use to construct and hold ourselves together suddenly seem to float free' (1983: 164–65). The experience is by no means confined to crowd behaviour in the performing arts and sport. The feeling of self-abandonment is also associated with the appreciation of literature, poetry, painting, and the other fine arts; it is also induced by the consumption of alcohol and drugs. This argument should not be pushed too far. Music, art, drinking, and drug taking refer to institutionalized social practices. It is in the essence of the concept that *jouissance* cannot be institutionalized. At all events, there is nothing in Barthes to suggest that the concept can be nailed down to signify determinate properties of human experience. Indeed, the concept is itself a signifier whose meaning is always deferred. Barthes refused to aspire to the construction of any social system. From the point of view of the author of *The Pleasure of the Text*, the formalist quest to build a general theory on the basis of comprehensive surveys of personal testimonies of freedom, self-determination and spontaneity, flatters the imagination. It ignores the play of signifiers which all of these social indicators participate in. Formalism strives to impose an internally consistent scientific order upon leisure experience. It is precisely the validity of order which Barthes denies in his discussion of *signifiance*. Where does this place the attitude of the mature Barthes in relation to Marxism? Barthes himself demonstrated the distance between his youthful and mature work in his statement that 'the social struggle cannot be reduced to the struggle between rival ideologies: it is the subversion of all ideology which is the question' (1975b: 32–3). Barthes now sees historical materialism as falsely reductive and misleadingly prescriptive. He does not seriously propose to go beyond it, since one cannot go beyond history and the material world without walling oneself into an indefensible position. He does, however, reject his youthful view that Marxism can function as the basis for a true science of signs. Marxists may like to think that they are laying down demonstrable truths about social life under capitalism and also realistic policies for the construction of a qualitatively better society. In fact, what they treat as signifieds (e.g. the class struggle, reification, alienation, and damaged sociability) are merely signifiers which cannot be insulated from the process of *signifiance*.

CRITICAL ESTIMATE

Barthes's early work repays the attention of those interested in leisure theory for the potent way in which it links action to forms of signification. There are, however, difficulties with the analysis. For example, the jump from signifying systems to the maintenance and reproduction of capitalism is a big one. Barthes does not give an adequate account of how the so-called 'rhetoric' of the sign is historically constructed. Instead he treats it as an automatic property of the social system. Individuals are portrayed as immediately and fatefully attached to discrete signifying systems whose values they merely exemplify in their thoughts, actions, and feelings. Even in these early writings there is a tendency towards narcissism. Barthes ensures that the distance between author and subject is scrupulously maintained. Even so, this detachment leaves Barthes in the position of the perpetual wise outsider looking on at the thraldom of others. In his later works this tendency becomes oppressive. Silverman and Torode (1980: 271) submit that these works show Barthes moving towards an openly élitist position. Thus, he spurns political action on the grounds that all political struggles and goals are doomed to collapse under the weight of their own mythologies. The alternative is to elevate radical semiotics into an élite leisure form. Barthes himself refers to it as 'a kind of intellectual "sport"' (1977b: 162). The same tendency is intensified a hundredfold in the 'deconstructing philosophy' of Jacques Derrida.[9] Pleasure in decoding the world is the sole justification of the intellectual's activity.

   This position is open to quite fundamental objections. In the first place, as Eagleton has exclaimed, 'there is something a little disturbing about this self-indulgent avant garde hedonism in a

world where others lack not only books but food' (1983: 83).
Perhaps this is putting the point too bluntly. It is certainly the
case that Barthes recognizes 'the real world' in his writings. For
example, in a sly piece of self-criticism (and expiation?) he writes:

> 'It frequently seems that he [Barthes] regards sociality simplis-
> tically: as an enormous and perpetual friction of languages
> (discourses, fictions, image-systems, reasonings, systems,
> sciences) and desires (impulses, injuries, resentments etc.).
> Then what does "reality" become in such a philosophy? *It is not
> denied* (often, in fact, invoked, on progressive claims) but
> referred, actually, to a kind of "technique", of empirical ration-
> ality, the object of "formulae", of "remedies" of "solutions".'
> (Barthes 1977: 167; emphasis mine)

The 'real world' undeniably breaks through in this passage. Even
so, Barthes does not really counter Eagleton's point, for it is
noticeable that the tendency to reduce the real world to linguistic
referents is evident in the string of 'techniques' and 'formulae'
mentioned in the last sentence.

The work of the mature Barthes may also be criticized for its
misleading view of power. Barthes pits the individual against the
endless play of signifiers in society. On this basis, he concludes
that the celebration of this perpetual movement is preferable to
social intervention. This is because all intervention becomes
myth in the end. Yet the truth is that no individual faces society
alone. It is axiomatic that from the point of view of the isolated
individual the prospect of changing society by dint of his or her
own action is dim. However, if the problem is put in terms of
collective organization and action, the prospects for real change
are clearly enhanced. Barthes consistently underestimates the
demonstrable power of collectivities to change the course of
history. The struggles to shorten the working week, to create a
better system of health care, and to improve educational opportunity for the poor and underprivileged cannot finally be reduced
to the play of signifiers.

I have left the greatest paradox about Barthes's later writings to
the end. 'The death of the author' is a remark that he is famous
for. He meant by it that radical semiotics had destroyed the
privileged site that the author had traditionally occupied in the
production of texts and in communicative action in general.
Indeed, as we have seen, the 'decentring' of the subject is frequently referred to as Barthes's most important intellectual

achievement. Yet, conspicuously and undeniably, there *is* a central subject in his later works: it is Roland Barthes himself. These texts explore *his* experience, *his* biography and *his* desire.[10] It might even be said that the latent solipsism of his approach to social study becomes manifest in these pages. Barthes succeeds in normalizing the idea that his own self can be used as the central resource in his exploits in semiotic analysis and social commentary.

Foucault and Leisure

I shall argue that the relevance of Foucault's work to leisure theory rests upon two of his characteristic theoretical interests: (a) the concept of power, and (b) the government of the body. It is important to recognize that each is no more than a facet of an astonishingly rich and varied intellectual output. In a relatively brief intellectual career, he made major contributions to the sociology of knowledge, the history of madness, the history of sexuality, and the sociology of discipline.[11] Not since Weber has the *oeuvre* of a single social theorist been so difficult to assimilate into the history of ideas. To be sure, the comparison with Weber is appropriate for other reasons. Foucault, like Weber, was interested in questions of power and rationality. Both shared Nietzsche's pessimism that rational knowledge is an inherently progressive force in the development of human societies. Both wrote brilliantly on the transmutation of enlightenment into terrorism, and the use of repression in the name of emancipation.[12]

The comparison is indeed illuminating. However, Smart's (1983: 123–32) argument against making glib comparisons in this regard deserves to be taken seriously. As he points out, Weber studies rationalization as an all-encompassing process that leads inexorably to the disenchantment of the world. Foucault, by contrast, constantly emphasizes the micro-politics and relativity of rational conduct. Similarly, Weber treats rationalization as a one-sided process which stifles resistance. For his part, Foucault stresses that power can be used against itself to mitigate the deadening effects of rationalization.

I shall consider Foucault's ideas on power and the government of the body under separate subheadings. As before when I have used this device in this book, it is necessary to emphasize the interdependence of these ideas in Foucault's thought. But treating them separately has the distinct advantage of clearly showing their respective influence as sources of insight for contemporary leisure theory.

THE POWER OF LEISURE

Two themes recur in Foucault's discussion of power. First, he stresses the positive influence of power in human affairs. This concern with the enabling effects of power is self-consciously contrasted with 'dominant' (formalist/Marxist) models which, he says, tend to accentuate the repressive effects of power in collective life. Foucault argues that 'power would be a feeble thing if its only function were to repress, if it worked only through the mode of censorship, blockage, repression, in the manner of the great Superego, exercising itself only in a negative way' (1980: 59). Once it is stated, the point is obvious. In everyday life we tend to regard power as a restrictive influence on our freedom to act as we please. What Foucault's work tries to show is that freedom is a positive effect of the organization and exercise of power. For example, our civil liberties are not only restricted by the rule of law, they are also founded upon it.

This perspective has important implications for leisure theory which I shall come back to in the last chapter of the book. At this point in my argument I want to consider the second theme in Foucault's discussion of power. Marxists characteristically focus on power struggle at the level of social classes. Foucault regards this as a false abstraction. It implies that individuals, families, and institutions are caught up in the 'general matrix' of the class struggle. Individual action is therefore incorrectly conceptualized as emanating 'from above', i.e. from the abstract level of class relationships. Against this 'homogeneous' view, Foucault emphasizes the manifold, decentralized traverses of power which are expressed within and between individuals, families, and institutions. Thus, for Foucault, everyone, however lowly and relatively powerless has power. Power is thus regarded as an omnipresent property in society. It is not a possession, a thing which someone has; rather, it is a chain of relationships. In Foucault's own words:

'Power is everywhere; not because it embraces everything, but because it comes from everywhere. . . . One needs to be nominalistic, no doubt: power is not an institution, and not a structure; neither is it a certain strength we are endowed with; it is the name that one attributes to a complex strategical situation in a particular society.'

(Foucault 1981: 93)

In studying power, Foucault submits that certain ordinances need to be obeyed. He draws these together into a five-point plan through which to examine the phenomenon (1982: 223–24):

(1) Power should be examined as a *differentiated* phenomenon. As examples of differentiations, he mentions relations of privilege, status, material wealth, knowledge, and skill.
(2) Power should be studied in terms of its *objectives,* i.e. the manifest and latent goals which animate the individual subject in the deployment of, and response to, power.
(3) Power should be examined in terms of its *realization.* By this Foucault means the ideological, technological, economic, and political 'signs' in power relations that evoke authority and obedience.
(4) Power should be studied with regard to its degree of *institutionalization,* i.e. to the traditional, legal, military, economic, and political mechanisms of power that support the 'signs' of power.
(5) Power should be investigated in terms of its *rationalization,* i.e. of the degree to which power is governed by the individual's rational calculation of costs and benefits in a given situation.

Foucault's analysis of power bears on questions of leisure in a number of ways. Three points need to be distinguished here. First, his analysis indentifies leisure as a form of power. This may be critically contrasted with formalist views which equate leisure with freedom. In emphasizing the enabling and prescriptive attributes of power, Foucault demonstrates that leisure should be conceptualized as simultaneously freedom and control. Second, and following on from the last point, Foucault's discussion underlines the interdependence of leisure relations with other areas of social life. He does this without recourse to an over-arching model of class or the state. Instead his analysis suggests that leisure activity is bound up with a complex division of power and discipline which permeates society in many-sided ways. The prominence which he accords to the multiplicity of power

relationships and the plurality of values in society further serves
to distinguish him from neo-Marxist positions. Third, his discussion drives home the importance of a historical dimension in
leisure inquiry. His work defies any notion that the organization
of leisure is a God-given or natural part of society.

THE GOVERNMENT OF THE BODY

According to Foucault, the question of how power works is
approached most directly by studying the 'political economy of
the body'. As he observes, 'the body is . . . directly involved in a
political field; power relations have an immediate hold upon it;
they invest it; mark it; torture it; force it to carry out tasks, to
perform ceremonies, to emit signs' (1977: 25). Thus, the deport-
ment of the body, the question of how it is trained, and how
knowledge is extracted from it, emerge as major themes in his
writings.

All his work is based on a distinction between body and society.
His historical investigations are concerned with the effects
visited upon, and initiated by, bodies in given historical and
social contexts. His historical research probes into this general
question from four different angles: (a) the social organization of
vagrant, unemployed bodies; (b) the creation and supervision of
'docile' bodies; (c) the hospitalization and medical administration
of bodies; and (d) the expression of sexuality in the body.[13] In all
of these inquiries the body is treated as the object of social techniques of power. This way of considering the body is unfamiliar
to most of us. I shall argue that it has important implications for
leisure theory. But before I develop this proposition I want to
illustrate briefly, by his analysis of the 'docile body', how Foucault studies bodies.

Durkheim had argued that the shift from mechanical to organic
solidarity was expedited by the growth in 'moral density' associated with the development of urban-industrial society. As the
pressures on restricted space and other resources intensified new
techniques of social differentiation emerged in society. The most
important of these was the division of labour. Foucault's discussion of the proliferation of modern techniques of discipline
and control over the body starts from the same basic premiss. It is
the growth of populations in urban-industrial centres that produces the impetus for new forms of social administration and

discipline over the body. The institutional expressions of this process include the development of timetables, school rules, examinations, and drill, manuals of practice, census forms, diets, and new systems of incarceration. The aim of these multifarious processes is everywhere the same: to achieve the wholesale control of populations. According to Foucault (1977), four principles regulate this process:

(1) The *individuation* of private space. In schools, prisons, factories, and dwelling places, individuals are increasingly assigned their own space. Foucault explicitly identifies social segregation with the technique of rational administration. 'Its aim was to establish presences and absences, to know where and how to locate individuals, to set up useful communications, to interrupt others, to be able at each moment to supervise the conduct of each individual, to assess it, to judge it, to calculate its qualities and merits' (1977: 167).

(2) The *coding* of activities. This refers to the prescriptions on movements and manners in social conduct. A vision of the 'correct' use of the body emerges from this disciplinary strategy. Thus, Foucault (1977: 152–54) refers to training manuals which specify the proper bodily posture to deploy in performing certain activities. One is struck by La Salle's advice on the practice of correct handwriting, in his *Conduit des écoles chrétiennes* (1759). The prescriptions which he demands for the posture and bearing of the body seem to codify activity in a highly rigid fashion. Individuals are asked to 'hold their bodies erect'. The elbow must be placed on the table. The left leg must be situated slightly forward from the right under the table. The distance between the body and table must be at least two fingers in order to prevent contact between the stomach and the table which is 'harmful to health'. The right arm is required to be held in a certain way, with an apportioned distance continuously maintained between it and the body during writing. The teacher is to supervise the children's training to ensure that these specifications are obeyed. Foucault refers to this historical process as 'the instrumental coding of the body' (1977: 153). He means by this that certain principles of discipline are instilled into individuals regarding the use of their bodies in the codified performance of particular tasks. These principles 'code' actions by imposing a routine on gestures which

regulates conduct. Action is permitted in certain contexts and 'organized out' of others. Foucault singles out the timetable which is imprinted on individuals in schools, as a major influence in socializing individuals in the coding of activities.

(3) The *routinization* of activities. This refers to the practice of subjecting pupils in training institutions, such as schools, universities and military camps, to a training schedule consisting of a series of exercises and tasks of increasing difficulty. In order to pass from one stage to the next, students are required to undergo some form of examination to test their abilities and accomplishments. This practice is programmed to lead to a final 'trial', e.g. a final examination of master work. Foucault notes that the linear, continuously progressive organization of training has a pre-industrial origin in religious institutions. However, with industrialization and the growth of cities the training schedules become more routinized and universalized to correspond to national and, in some cases, international standards.

(4) The *synchronization* of activities. The collective body of individuals, whether constituted as an army, a labour force, or any other social group, is subjected to the strict division of labour. The tactical aim of the rational manager is 'to construct a machine whose effect will be maximized by the concerted articulation of the elementary parts of which it is composed' (Foucault 1977: 164). The whole system is based in a precise network of command. Each individual is trained to fulfil a function in concert with others. The dream of the rational manager is to create an efficient social machine in which individuals act predictably on the principle of 'automatic docility'.[14]

Individuation, coding, routinization and synchronization: these are the hallmarks of 'the disciplinary society'. Foucault recognizes that they are associated with the development of efficient new techniques of surveillance and observation by the state and monopoly capital. At the core of his argument, however, is the idea that contemporary populations participate in the regulation and control of their emotions and desires by voluntary actions. It is at the micro-level of relations, in the home, schools, factories, and other organizations, that Foucault regards the regulation and consent of individual bodies to be maintained and reproduced.

The general theme of the complexity and pervasiveness of disciplinary control in modern social life is exploited and developed in

The History of Sexuality. Here, Foucault defines sexuality as 'the set of effects produced in bodies, behaviours, and social relations by a certain deployment deriving from a complex political technology' (1981: 127). How does this analysis relate to leisure theory? Foucault argues that the tendency to conceptualize and treat the body as a machine is a corollary of industrialization, the proliferation of the division of labour, and the dissemination of disciplinary tactics. As we have seen, the 'machine-like' quality of contemporary mass leisure is remarked upon in the sociological literature. Marxists often argue that leisure-time behaviour is structured by the requirements of the capitalist occupational sphere, and therefore reproduces the value and strategies deployed therein (Rigauer 1981). From a reading of Foucault's work on madness, discipline, and sexuality one might postulate a substantial degree of agreement with the idea that leisure relations are certainly not relations of freedom. On the contrary, they are relations of discipline, training, coding, and control. At the same time his work points to a different set of interests and preoccupations. It should be pointed out that there are formidable barriers to extrapolating a 'position' on leisure from Foucault's publications. As Sheridan (1980: 225) has pointed out, Foucault's work does not assume the objective of building 'a new system'. Rather, it concerns itself with breaking encrusted mythologies and probing the defects in established systems. Even so, one would imagine that such a position might address itself, first and foremost, to the discourses that surround leisure. It might begin with an investigation into whether leisure is a 'healthy' or 'unhealthy' phenomenon in society, i.e. whether it is expression of social vitality or of *malaise*. On this basis the following questions might arise. What images of healthy and unhealthy leisure exist in society? How does the discourse on leisure relate to the practice of leisure? How does leisure conceal and reveal the operation of power in society? What techniques of individuation exist in leisure to differentiate and control separate bodies? Equally, all of Foucault's work raises the general question of how it is possible to know anything through social study (e.g. leisure study). Perhaps what would be finally distinctive about such a position is not the line of questions it suggests, but its level of analysis. It would gravitate automatically to the local handbooks and membership requirements of the various leisure clubs and associations; it would scan the files, records, and memoirs of leisure enthusiasts. To put it in a few words, it would immerse itself in the volume of publications that surround a specific leisure activity, and use these data to plumb deeper truths about the forms of power and control that prevail in its elected field of inquiry, i.e. it would decentre the subject.

CRITICAL ESTIMATE

Foucault's work gives a clear statement of the positive character of power. It also produces an important counter to Marxist and formalist views by defining the body as the main axis of power relations in modern society. Even so, his work has been the subject of considerable critical discussion. I shall bring this chapter to a close by briefly examining two major criticisms that are frequently made of his work. Firstly, as Dews (1979: 164–65) argues, his concept of power is protean, and therefore imprecise. In his analysis, all events in the world are finally reduced to the effects of power. If power is everywhere this statement is necessarily true. But as a *theory* of power, its informative and predictive content is virtually nil. The concept of power is therefore drained of both its historical specificity and its relationship to social interests. Instead it is theorized as a universal property of the social system which, in being everywhere, is paradoxically elusive. Secondly, as Giddens (1981: 171–72) notes, the proposition that history is the effect of the 'play' of power leads to real conceptual problems regarding the status of the human subject. Foucault gives the impression that social actors are merely the obedient servants of power. Hence, for example, his whole discussion of the production and reproduction of 'docile' bodies. Against this, Giddens emphasizes the capacity of the individual to reject the labels and constraints of history by acting to change existing conditions.

7 LEISURE AND FIGURATIONAL SOCIOLOGY

This chapter is divided into four sections. The first examines the characteristic features of figurational sociology. The second explores how this approach to social inquiry has addressed the question of leisure. The third places the specialized investigation of leisure into the indispensable general context of Elias's theory of 'the civilizing process'. The fourth consists of an evaluation of the strengths and weaknesses of the figurational approach for leisure theory. Let us consider each of these in turn.

Figurational Sociology

'Figurational sociology' is the term that refers to the approach to social inquiry which is associated with the writings of Norbert Elias and his followers.[1] The key feature of Elias's work is the concept of 'figuration'. A figuration, he explains, is a 'structure of mutually oriented and dependent people' (1978a: 261). I find the terms 'mutually oriented' and 'dependent' problematic, for reasons that I shall give in the final section of this chapter. Even when figuration is described in this minimalist form, however, one can immediately recognize the force of the concept in rebutting conventional models of society as either (a) a reality which is 'above', and separate from, individuals, or (b) the sum total of individuals, i.e. a mere abstraction. Against both of these views, figurations are explicitly conceptualized as historically produced and reproduced networks of interdependence. Prima facie, the

figurational approach is apt to seem rather prosaic. This is deceptive. In fact, it proposes a reorientation in sociological theory and
research which is both profound and radical. This reorientation is
founded on a critique of what Elias calls the *homo clausus* model
of human beings and the *zustandsreduktion* tendency in sociological analysis. Let us look at each of these criticisms in more detail.

The *homo clausus* model of human beings is closely associated
with the stock conceptual dichotomy between 'the individual
and society'. It refers to all of those 'closed' perspectives in social
science which take the isolated individual – a person in the singular – as the prime unit of analysis.[2] *Homo clausus* models assign a
false methodological and ontological priority to the individual in
social analysis. They imply that one can speak of individuals as
separate from groups; or individuals and groups as separate from
society. The truth is, writes Elias, that

> 'there is no-one who is not and never has been interwoven into
> a network of people . . . one's self conception as a separate
> person, one's sense of personal identity is closely connected
> with the "we" and "they" relationships of one's group, and
> one's position within those units of which one speaks as "we"
> and "they".'
>
> (Elias 1978b: 128)

'Interdependence' is the core concept in the figurational approach.
It is conceived of as both a constraining and an enabling influence
on the actions of individuals. The concept of interdependence is
akin to the concept of structure in that it emphasizes that the
social bonds between individuals shape development in un-
planned and unanticipated ways. But it is quite unlike the
concept of structure in that figurational sociologists claim to be
anti-reductionist.

Elias uses the term *zustandsreduktion* (process reduction) to
refer to the tendency in language and thought whereby everything that is experienced and observed as dynamic and interdependent is represented in static, isolated categories.[3] Thus,
sociologists speak of the economic 'base' or 'structure', as if base
and structure referred to either a 'pre-' or 'extra-' social category:
society is seen as 'built upon' or 'determined' by it. According to
figurational sociologists, this line of reasoning leads to futile and
meaningless searches for the 'origins' or 'first principles' of social
development. Elias argues that both Marx, in his quest for the
origins of capitalism, and Weber, in his discussion of the rise of

Protestantism, succumb to these errors. Against them, he suggests that figurations should be studied as interdependent relations which are continually in flux. This does not involve abandoning the concepts of change and development. On the contrary, one of the main objectives of figurational sociology is to encourage sociologists to 'think processually', i.e. to counter *zustandsreduktion* tendencies by consistently studying social relations as emerging and contingent processes. Axiomatic to this position is the idea that shifts and transformations in patterns of social bonding can be identified in all patterns of figurational development.

These shifts are discernible because interdependence is neither an arbitrary nor a random phenomenon. On the contrary, the individuals, groups, and nations that make up a specific figuration are interconnected by a multiplicity of dynamic and polyvalent bonds. Marxists have tended to emphasize the importance of economic relations in social bonding. Figurational sociologists argue that affective (emotional) and political bonds have equal significance. They emphasize that the concept of the social bond is designed to reinforce the two-edged character of figurational relations: they are both enabling and constraining. Thus, bonding makes for particular types of action; but it also limits the scope of action. We have then four key features of figurational sociology. These can be listed in summary form as follows:

(1) The prime unit of analysis is the figuration. Figurations are conceptualized as multiple networks of interdependence which both constrain and enable the actions of individuals.
(2) Figurations are studied as irreducible social units, i.e. units which are produced and reproduced by individuals; but their integration and dynamics cannot be explained in terms of the properties of their component parts.
(3) The development of figurations is regarded as a relatively open-ended process. Individuals may deliberately engage in planned social intervention, but the whole network of interdependencies which binds people together at each phase of development has not been planned or willed by the individuals who compose it.
(4) The aim of figurational sociology is to establish a new type of theory which studies social relations processually. This departs crucially from 'structuralist' models of society. As Elias explains, 'structure theories . . . embody the spatial dimensions. They have . . . the character of three dimensional

models. Process theories have the character of four dimensional models . . . they do not abstract from either the spatial or the time dimension' (1974a: 40).

Figurational Sociology and Leisure

Figurational sociology is distinctive both in the way that it studies leisure and in the functions which it attributes to leisure behaviour in modern industrial societies. Accordingly, I shall organize my discussion around a consideration of the methodological and substantive levels of inquiry in the figurational approach to leisure.

Methodologically, people who engage in specific forms of leisure are studied as particular types of figuration.[4] In a felicitous example, Elias and Dunning (1971) fasten upon the game of soccer. The example is felicitous because it illustrates in a clear and straightforward fashion exactly how the concept of figuration may be applied in leisure study. In soccer, as in other group sports, the moves of one team are interdependent with those of their opponents. The figuration on the field of play is fluid and relatively open-ended in its action. The movement of the game is beyond the control of either side, or of any single individual. Yet both sides, and all individuals, are bound by the dynamics of play. Equally, play involves a multiplicity of dynamic, polyvalent tension balances between the players. Indeed, the game is never static. Even when the ball is out of play, individuals in the figuration adjust and readjust their positions in relation to each other.

Elias and Dunning (1971: 74) make a direct parallel between observable figurational dynamics in a game of soccer, and the figurational dynamics of urban-industrial populations involved in other leisure activities. They also submit that the activities of political parties, nation states, and capital/labour can be usefully subjected to figurational analysis. In all of these cases, individuals are enmeshed in social networks of power which shape their actions. It is important to note that this is not a 'one-way' process. Indeed figurational sociology is at one with the so-called 'theory of structuration', which has become so fashionable and influential in recent years, in stressing the 'recursive character' of social life.[5] Individuals are born into figurations. They grow up, work, play, and die in figurations (Elias and Scotson 1975; Elias 1974b). They are not, however, turned into robots or idiots in the process.

On the contrary, figurational sociology regards socialization as a two-way process which continually imprints role patterns on individuals, and therefore equips individuals with meaningful social capacities to interpret roles and transform conditions through social interaction.

There are few institutions in social life where the figurations formed by individuals are as directly observable as team sports. Elias and Dunning submit that the reason for this is that the individual is usually attached to figurations as 'the involved participant of one side and is therefore not quite able to visualize the paramount dynamics of the figurations which different sides form with each other and which determine the moves of each side' (1971: 69).[6] The problem of 'involvement' is a formidable one. As I shall argue in the last section of this chapter, there is reason to doubt whether figurational sociology has solved it satisfactorily. In the present section, however, it remains to be noted that the way in which figurational sociologists have tried to surmount the problem is by the use of comparative and developmental methods of analysis. By comparing current social relations with those in other states and past times, they claim to have achieved a high measure of 'detachment' in their work.

I want to turn now to the question of the main substantive function which figurational sociology ascribes to leisure in modern societies. The essential point is simple enough. 'In a simple or complex form, on a low or high level leisure-time activities provide, for a short while, the upsurge of strong pleasurable feelings which is often lacking in the ordinary routines of life' (Elias and Dunning 1969: 81). Thus leisure appears to be assigned a compensatory function in modern society.

The designation has been seized upon by critics and used as the basis for the argument that figurational sociology is actually no more than a masked and weak form of functionalism (Stedman Jones 1977: 168; Hargreaves 1982: 35; Smith 1984). It is a charge which figurational sociologists have gone to some lengths to extricate themselves from (Elias 1978a: 266–69, 246–47; 1978b; Goudsblom 1977: 176–78). They have pointed out that functionalist theories conceive of society as a system of interdependent parts. The stock analogy is with the human body. Functionalists typically ask themselves what functions the individual parts or organs play in the adaptation and survival of the whole social system or organism. I have already noted that figurational sociologists reject the conventional dichotomies between the individual and society, part and system, in favour of the concept of the figuration. It follows that they would also reject the attempt to explain leisure forms in terms of the needs or functions they fulfil in the maintenance and reproduction of the social system. Rejecting functionalism is not the same as rejecting the concept of function. Thus figurational sociologists examine leisure forms in terms of the specific functions which they perform for individuals in figurations. The point is best illustrated by means of an example. Consider the case of the rise of television as a mass leisure form. It is associated with a basic change in the pattern of leisure conduct. The home emerges as a major site of family leisure experience. Established sites such as the cinema and the theatre receive gradually smaller audiences. A change occurs in the balance of power between the economic units in the leisure industry. At the same time, TV audiences become attached to certain programmes. They budget their spare-time activities to fit in with their favourite broadcasts. The organization of family life changes. Similarly, the success of a given series limits the autonomy of programme planners. They begin to organize their planning schedules around hit programmes in a bid to retain a captive audience. Advertisers battle among themselves to win coveted slots in the peak broadcasting time of the most popular programmes. The leading actors in hit programmes become national and, in some cases, international figures. Their agents bargain for higher fees, more prominent roles, script control, etc. In short, a figuration develops. It consists of multiple, polyvalent power dependencies. The new interdependencies between groups and individuals cannot be thought of as a merely 'functional' arrangement, i.e. one which creates harmony and integration. On the contrary, these interdependencies engender structural tensions, conflicts, and struggles. Even so, the figuration must be understood and studied as a function of television in that it did not exist before television and it is organized around the maintenance and reproduction of television. At the same time, the development of the figuration is not subject to the will or power of any single individual or group. The individuals who own and run the broadcasting stations cannot control the overall bonding in the figuration. Rather, they are bound up with competing interdependent social units such as technicians, producers, actors, advertisers, audiences, viewers' rights panels, etc. The development of the figuration is relatively open-ended. Its integration and dynamics cannot be treated as a 'closed system'. Nor can its interdependence and development be explained in terms of the actions and organization of any one of its constituent parts.

Enough has been said to show why figurational sociologists dismiss the label of functionalism as an accurate description of their work. But these remarks deal with the criticism of functionalism only at a meta-theoretical level. What of the precise nature of the function which Elias and Dunning attribute to leisure practice in modern society? As I noted earlier, they appear to regard leisure as performing a compensatory function in social life. In this, they follow a well-established convention in the sociology of leisure. For example, in Chapter 4, I mentioned a number of formalist positions which conceptualize leisure activity as a functional response to the mental, physical, and emotional deprivations of the work sphere (see pp. 89–90). The same functionalist cast of thought exists in many Marxist discussions of leisure, e.g. in the idea that the character of working-class leisure pursuits is a direct reflection of the class struggle in capitalist society. Figurational sociology rejects both views. In place of them, it submits that the compensatory function of modern leisure pursuits must be viewed from the perspective of the long-term figurational shifts in patterns of economic, political, and emotional bonding. The argument is complex and links up repeatedly with Elias's model of 'the civilizing process'. Nevertheless, the essential propositions can be distilled in three separate points:

(1) Modern leisure activity is not synonymous with freedom. Rather, it obeys a historically specific affect economy of balances and restraints.
(2) The discharge of spontaneous, violent, and intense emotions or bursts of excitement in modern society observes higher thresholds of 'civilized' restraint than in the Middle Ages.
(3) Modern leisure activity increasingly corresponds to 'mimetic' forms of behaviour.

The term 'mimetic' is open to misinterpretation. It is therefore important to spell out its precise meaning in the canon of figurational sociology. In the context of leisure theory, the term refers to play events in society where intense emotions are unleashed in a controlled form. Examples include sport, film, musical events, and combat games such as poker and chess. In these leisure activities, deep-rooted emotions are discharged and accumulated in a relatively pleasurable way. As Elias and Dunning put it, 'in advanced industrial societies, leisure activities form an enclave for the socially approved arousal of moderate excitement behaviour in public' (1969: 53). Of course, deep emotions imply danger as well as excitement. Elias and Dunning (1969: 71) fully recognize that mimetic leisure activities can get out of hand. They cite football rioting and crowd disorder at pop concerts as examples.

As we shall see more clearly in the next section, the full import of mimetic leisure activity can only be understood in the context of the long-term sequence of changes in figurational bonding which has resulted in increased human control over nature and society. No one is claiming that human beings have complete control over natural and social phenomena. The point is that the collective capacity to anticipate and manage crises such as floods, famines, and violent attacks by antagonistic social units, has grown immensely. This tendency is a universal feature of industrializing societies although it is, to be sure, more fully developed in the economically advanced societies. The higher standard of control is associated with a corresponding reduction in the distribution and incidence of seriously threatening situations in social life, i.e. situations in which the safety and survival of the whole community or large sections of the community are put at risk. It is, of course, true that personal life in modern society is not 'risk free'. Indeed, a whole battery of risks to the life and limb of individuals could be itemized which are specific to modern times. It is also true that some of the threats facing human societies today, notably the nuclear threat, are more lethal than anything that has been experienced by communities in the past. Nevertheless, for most people, these dangers are remote and sequestered by the state. According to figurational sociologists, our lives are led in societies where levels of violence have become relatively reduced. For most of us, outbursts of intense physical aggression which result in serious injury or death are experienced or witnessed second-hand. We read about them in the newspapers, we see footage on television, but the number of people who come into direct contact with them is quite small. Even so, impressionistically, many people feel that life today is more violent than it has ever been. As I argued earlier (see pp. 23–4), everything in the debate on violence hangs on the use of a meaningful time-scale.

If a long-term time-scale is used, the pacification of present-day relations is immediately evident. As Elias puts it:

> 'we are choir boys compared with our ancestors . . . we no longer stop to imagine what a violent society really is, a society, for example, based on slavery. Consider ancient Rome, where the main restrictions on violence against hundreds and thousands of individuals was simply fear of losing valuable property. Imagine the sadistic abuses.'
>
> (Elias 1978c: 249)

It is against this long-term time-scale of changes in the organization of affect that the compensatory character of mimetic leisure must be situated.

Leisure and 'The Civilizing Process'

Stated simply, the civilizing process refers to a specific set of changes in people's personality structure which began during the waning of the Middle Ages. These complex changes pointed in the general direction of greater self-control and rising standards of shame and embarrassment in interpersonal relations. For example, in the thirteenth century it was usual to eat at table from a common bowl. Solids, especially meat, were taken by hand. People frequently wiped their noses on the table-cloth. They belched and broke wind unselfconsciously and without regard for others. Similarly, they undressed and shared their beds with casual visitors. Their interpersonal relations exhibited none of the characteristic standards of reserve and decorum which we associate with interpersonal relations today. Indeed, there is ample evidence to show that they took a 'naïve' delight in bodily processes and especially in their power to give pleasure and pain to each other. As an example of the latter point, Elias mentions the discharge of aggression. He shows that in the Middle Ages enemies captured in war had no prisoners' rights. Those who were poor were mutilated and killed; those who were rich were held for ransom. Violence and aggression were more frequent and more openly tolerated than is the case today. This is to be explained by the social bonding that characterized the figuration of that time. In conditions of striking imbalance in power between the mighty and the weak, and of relatively low collective control over nature and social forces, the mighty took exaggerated pleasure in the power that they were able to demonstrate over life and death.

Books of courtesy, songs, poems, and treatises of *savoir-vivre* survive from the Middle Ages and record the gradual shift of conduct in a 'civilizing direction'. Thus, new prohibitions against bad table manners emerge. People are advised that it is 'not decent' to pick their noses while at the table. Those who clear their throats during meals or who blow their noses in the table-cloth are disparaged for their 'ill breeding'. People are warned against pointing their knives at others. They are asked to pass a knife to someone else by grasping the blade and offering the handle, 'for it would not be polite to do otherwise'. Similar standards of restraint and decorum begin to regulate control of bodily functions in public, conduct in the bedroom, and public displays of nudity.

Two things need to be emphasized. First, the new standards of acceptable public behaviour were initially set by the secular upper class. However, especially from the Renaissance on, they were increasingly absorbed and developed by the lower orders in society. Second, the diffusion of new standards of restraint and the growth of higher thresholds of repugnance were slow and uneven. For example, Elias (1978a: 203–04) reports that as late as the sixteenth century one or two dozen cats were still burnt alive for the entertainment of the crowd on Midsummer's Day in Paris. This was, he writes, a popular spectacle on a par with horse racing and boxing in the present day.

What brought about the far-reaching changes in personality structure which make us today look back on the standards of public behaviour which obtained at that time and denounce them as 'savage' and 'barbarous'? Elias traces a direct line of connection between the reorganization of the personality structure and the development of figurational bonding. As he puts it:

'In keeping with the transformations of society . . . the affective make-up oɪ the individual is also reconstructed: as the series of actions and the number of people on whom the individual and his actions constantly depend are increased, the habit of foresight over longer chains grows stronger. And as the behaviour and personality structure of the individual change, so does his manner of considering others. His image of them becomes richer in nuances, freer of spontaneous emotions: it is "psychologized".'

(Elias 1982a: 272–73)

Three keynote tendencies in the long-term pattern of figurational change can be extracted from Elias's detailed discussion:

(1) The *centralization* of power in the state apparatus. In particular, the establishment of the dual state monopoly over the right to use physical force and collect taxes is singled out as being of fundamental importance.

(2) *Chains of interdependence* between people lengthen and multiply. This has the consequence of enmeshing people more closely together. The increasing specialization and differentiation of the division of labour, which is one facet of this process, has the effect of improving living standards and, simultaneously, of imposing restrictions on the individual's freedom to manoeuvre.

(3) The growth of *functional democratization*. This refers to the gradual historical tendency towards a more equal balance of power between the classes and sexes. As regards social class, examples include the extension of the franchise, the development of citizenship rights, and the development of national working-class political parties. As regards the sexes, examples include the growth of the women's movement, and legislation against sex discrimination and for equal pay. It goes without saying that Elias is not suggesting that either class or sexual equality has been attained. Rather, he is stating that, viewed over a long-time scale, a clear *tendency* towards more equality in these areas can be perceived.

These tendencies tell a story of increasing restrictions on the freedom of the rich and powerful to act as they please. Restrictions come from the state which, in the recitations of figurational sociology, achieves 'relative autonomy'. But also, and crucially, they come 'from below', as the dependency of the upper class on the labour power of the subordinate classes grows. Of course, these tendencies do not approximate to a unilinear, unbroken line of development. On the contrary, Elias repeatedly insists that every move in a civilizing direction produces corresponding struggles and tensions which act to hinder its effectiveness. These resistances in the 'civilizing curve' may last for long periods and therefore appear to reverse the overall trend of the civilizing process. Even so, viewed from a long-term perspective, the enumerated keynote tendencies can be shown to persist.

In the first chapter of this book I argued that modern leisure practice displays at least four characteristic features which are historically specific: leisure relations today are more privatized, individuated, commercialized, and pacified than ever before. Elias's theory of the civilizing process draws all of these themes together. It also provides a powerful rationale for explaining why they have assumed their characteristic form in modern society. He invites us to consider them as effects of the more complex and extensive web of interdependence which has emerged in the development of modern urban-industrial societies. A superficial reading of his work might support the impression that he is arguing that conflict and violence have been progressively reduced in the development of human figurations. Nothing could be further from the truth. Elias uses at least two arguments against the simplistic notion that modern society is 'aggression-proof'. First, mock physical aggression is still played out in mimetic leisure forms such as adult cinema, drama, and various combat sports such as rugby, wrestling, soccer, and boxing. The tension balance in these activities is always contingent and can act as a catalyst for real acts of physical aggression among the crowds as well as the players (see Dunning and Sheard 1979; Williams, Dunning, and Murphy 1984). Second, although the incidence of physical violence has diminished, aggression is still expressed in a variety of displaced forms. For example, it is evident in the obeisance of the masses to the 'achievement ideology' and personal competition of advanced capitalism (see Dunning 1981: 21–2). There is a direct parallel to be drawn here with the work of Foucault. Like Foucault, Elias suggests that the centralization of power in the state apparatus and the growth of reciprocal dependencies in urban-industrial figurations is associated with new systems of surveillance and punishment. These systems leave their most penetrating marks on the body. Power is at its strongest when individuals take its historically produced and reproduced effects to be 'natural' expressions of being. For this reason the 'civilized' body may be said to be a priest to subjugation: it always acts in contrition.

The Scope and Limits of Figurational Sociology

The figurational approach forces sociologists to take critical stock of many of their erstwhile and most cherished beliefs and assumptions. In particular, it tests and shreds familiar conceptual dichotomies in the field, such as 'individual and society', 'base and superstructure', and 'work and leisure'. In place of them it suggests a new, unifying problematic for leisure study: the integration and dynamics of human figurations. It also explicitly identifies leisure experience with the historically constructed economy of affect drives in society, i.e. with a historically produced and reproduced system of power. Leisure is not viewed mundanely as a general release from tension. Rather it is examined and portrayed as a specific form of tension balance.

These are really important contributions to leisure theory. Their radical and far-reaching significance to the study of leisure in history and in the present only serves to underline the undeserved neglect which has been shown to Elias's work by mainstream Anglo-American sociologists – neglect which may partly be attributed to the unusual circumstances surrounding the first publication of *The Civilizing Process*.[7] The fact that this seminal work in figurational sociology was effectively submerged for thirty years undoubtedly prevented Elias's ideas from reaching a wide audience. But the failure to recognize the importance of Elias's thought also has a lot to do with fundamental misunderstandings of the methodology of figurational sociology. For example, the use of the concept of function has led to the baseless charge that figurational sociology wheels out the props and splints of functionalist thought and clothes them in modern dress. Such criticisms ignore the paramount importance Elias and his followers place on the need to study figurations *processually* and in terms of power struggles and tension balances between people. To make the point absolutely clear, there is no sense in which figurational sociology theorizes figurations as determining structures in social life. Social development is always conceived of as a contingent and relatively open-ended process. The capacity of individuals to act knowledgeably and skilfully in everyday life is integral to the concept of dynamic interdependence which is the basis of the whole figurational approach.

Nevertheless, despite its outstanding analytical value, figurational sociology is vulnerable to a number of objections. I want to focus on three of them here. To begin with, the figurational approach is open to the charge of empiricism. The figuration, let us remember, is defined as a structure of 'mutually oriented' and 'dependent' people. The Marxist objection to such positions is well known. Marxists take a realist stance on the production and reproduction of social relations in capitalist society. In addition, for them, leisure cannot be meaningfully studied in isolation from the total context of power relations in society. They are expressions of the general inequality in the ownership and control of productive forces. Figurational sociology, for its part, emphasizes the plurality of power relations and the dynamics of change. According to Buck-Morss (1978: 192), this leads to fundamental errors in the analysis of how change occurs and how meaning is constructed. For example, as regards Elias's theory of the civilizing process, these errors are apparent in the relative neglect of the important categories of bourgeois repression and the capitalist work ethic in the development of human figurations. Meanings under capitalism are not constructed by the individual's position in the dynamic web of interdependencies, but by the general power dialectics which give capitalism its distinctive shape and form. The figurational approach in general is therefore condemned for underestimating the significance of struggles of class, race, and sex, in the integration and dynamics of capitalist society.

The second point also concerns the place of meaning in the figurational approach. Elias's theory is a monument to open analysis and free discourse. Yet oddly, Elias, a scourge of reified oppositions and closed theoretical systems, sets up a basic conceptual dichotomy and places it at the centre of his sociological analysis. Theories, opinions, strategies, and values, he argues, can be placed on a continuum between 'involvement and detachment' (Elias 1956). I have already alluded to the problem of involvement in my discussion of the figurational approach to the study of leisure forms (see p. 162). However, because the issue shows more clearly why figurational sociology is vulnerable to the charge of empiricism it is necessary to go into it in more detail. The hallmark of scientific inquiry is an attitude of detachment. The concept of detachment occupies a central place in Elias's methodological writings. He describes it variously as a 'standing back' from 'reflected' objects of thought, a 'self-distancing', and a 'stepping back' from something in order to 'look at it again'. However, he provides no ground rules to use as a guide to achieving detachment. This is a serious omission. Those who bind themselves over to science would not need to strive for detachment unless they were already looking at society with an 'involved' worldview. 'Involvement', in this sense, refers to the partial perspectives on social life that we receive via the socialization process. The question is how, in the absence of clear guidelines, figurational sociologists are to ensure that the statements of detachment which they either profess to or encounter in research, are not graduated forms of involvement in reality? The question is of major importance. Doubtless the proponents of orthodox Marxism and social formalism hold fast to a professional self-image of detachment in their approach to the study of leisure. Yet, as figurational sociologists have argued persuasively, it is possible to interpret their theories and methods of research as highly 'involved' practices. Figurational sociologists have even provided an explanation for the mask of detachment in such cases. They argue that professional formalists and Marxists claim value neutrality in order to enhance the prestige and influence of their respective approaches (Elias 1971: 149–68, 355–70; 1978b). However, having established this cogent line of criticism, figurational sociologists seem to have no means of defence when the charge is turned back against them.

My third, and final, criticism is that figurational sociology is rather low in propositional content and predictive value. It is, above all else, a *pragmatic* theory of social relations. Like all pragmatic theories, it defies falsification. For example, many people believe that class warfare, violence on picket lines, sexual harassment, genocide, terrorism, and abortion signify the real ideological basis of western claims to be 'civilized'. But, for figurational sociologists, increases in rates of violence merely indicate 'downswings' in the civilizing curve. They do not negate the long-term pattern of bonding which points in 'a civilizing direction' (see Dunning 1981: 2–3). Bauman (1979: 124) has observed that this line of reasoning confines figurational sociology to an essentially 'retrospective wisdom'. Changes in the economy of affect drives and shifts in the civilizing curve may be visible in the long sweep of history. Current and future patterns of bonding are less self-evident. This tension between the historical 'trend-maintaining' tendencies towards more 'civilized' behaviour, and the persistence of aggression in present-day societies, pervades the whole of the figurational approach. The Frankfurt Marxists clearly understood that the modern age is one where the fruits of enlightenment can be pressed into the service of terrorism. Nuclear weaponry is all the evidence that we need to confirm that we live on the brink of unimaginable violence. It may be right to stress that the mechanization, concentration, and sequestration of violence which these weapons signify corroborates the central propositions of the civilizing process. At the same time, it is also in order to point out that a single act of nuclear aggression would render all these propositions null and void.

8 THE SOCIOLOGY OF PLEASURE

There is, in the literature on leisure, a striking tendency which I have not so far commented on: leisure relations are often associated with the experience of personal authenticity. For example, Mannheim (1951: 269) observes that leisure in democratic societies involves real 'self-expression' and is the true basis for 'personal development'. Haworth (1977: 49), for his part, identifies leisure as the major site for 'validating experience' in an increasingly routine-dominated and predictable world. It is perhaps left to Frith to put the point with greatest clarity. 'Leisure', he writes, 'has become the only setting for the experience of the self, for the exploration of one's own skills and capacities, for the development of creative relations with other people' (1983: 262).

This view of leisure as something which the self possesses to exploit and develop represents a distinctively modern approach to the theory of leisure. We are far from the time when the objective of constructing an authoritative, scientific taxonomy of leisure experience in all of its types and masks had any meaning. Only an eccentric would set out today, as the great German photographer August Sander did in 1911, to produce an exhaustive 'scientific' classification and record of the 'social types' in the nation. No one else would begin to photograph 'samples' of the lowliest class in society (the peasants, the vagabonds, the idiots), and then work steadily through all the rungs of the social ladder to the 'highest representatives of civilization'. No one would now have the temerity to assert that forty-five folios containing twelve 'archetype pictures' (Sanders's term) could 'scientifically' sum up anything about social life.

Nevertheless, something of the idea remains, in the view that leisure demands authenticity. It is evident in the quest to fix the quality of leisure in social life once and for all. There is, in all of the analytical divisions between leisure and work, property, gender, status, subculture, and race, a thinly veiled desire to penetrate to the essence of leisure. There is also a desire to pare and divide experiential data in order to classify, quantify, and hence, clarify them. Given the multi-paradigmatic rivalry in the field, the convergence of opinion in the sociology of leisure on this single matter is remarkable. Kaplan, writing from a formalist standpoint, actually defines leisure as 'relatively self-determined activity experience . . . that is psychologically pleasant in antici-pation and recollection' (1975: 26). Gorz, who belongs to a dia-metrically opposed tradition of thought, concurs that what matters to people in their lives today is leisure which supports the pleasurable and 'unobstructed realization of individual develop-ment' (1982: 73). There is clearly a bridge of consensus regarding the medium and the content of leisure experience which spans the divisions of multi-paradigmatic rivalry. The medium is the self; and the content is pleasure.

Self and Selflessness

The conjunction of the concept of self-realization with leisure is an adult view. Only adults have leisure; children merely play. Freud expresses the view that the peculiar quality of children's play is its prolific inventiveness. Children can find literally anything to play with, and they return to it afresh again and again. This inventiveness is the inventiveness of selflessness. Under it, the whole world can inspire dizzy pleasure one moment, and harbour hectic anxiety the next. Freud presents this form of subjectivity as unstable and transitory. The whole trend of socialization is to replace selflessness with the self.

Ferguson (1983: 175) suggests that the structural opposition between the adult world and the world of children is the key to understanding leisure forms in modern societies. The adult self is defined in opposition to the selflessness of childhood. This is evident in the agents and principles of the adult leisure world which are organized to exclude the distinctive features of the child's play world (formlessness, frankness, lack of seriousness, and irrationality) or, instead, to tolerate them only in their mimetic forms. The private self, which dominates modern leisure relations, engages in communal pursuits as a participant or spectator. He always acts as an individual body, who is separate and distinct from others, with a life outside the leisure life. In the development of the self, the play world, with its exaggerated emotional polarities and pervasive sense of boundless immediacy is left behind.

The opposition between self and selflessness is also palpable in the historical emergence, descent, and organization of leisure forms in the advanced societies. The trends of privatization, individuation, commercialization, and pacification represent the increasing emphasis on the self as the focal point of action and experience. There is no important place in modern leisure for the mass experience of selflessness. Bakhtin, whose work was evidently a major influence on the work of Foucault, illustrates this sea change in human relations by considering the deployment and action of the body. The body today acts as a closed and complete unit. It is separated from the rest of the world and pursues its appetites and functions privately. In contrast, the bodily element in carnival during the Middle Ages transcended individuals and families, to assume a pre-eminently public character. As Bakhtin observes:

> 'It is presented not in a private, egoistic form, severed from the other spheres of social life, but as something universal, representing all the people . . . the body and bodily life have here a cosmic and at the same time an all-people's character; this is not the body and its physiology in the modern sense of these words, *because it is not individualized*. The material bodily principle is contained not in the biological individual, not in the bourgeois ego, but in the people, a people who are continually growing and renewed.'
>
> (Bakhtin 1968: 19, emphasis mine)

The 'private, egoistic form', which Bakhtin alludes to, is the ideological shield of the rising bourgeoisie. Its doctrine of individual rights and possessive individualism arose as the historical counterpoint to traditional property ties. In mature capitalism, it is modified by various oppositional ideologies, notably forms of working-class collectivism and the women's movement. It is also undermined by the trend towards the joint ownership of the means of production (e.g. joint stock companies, share issues, etc.) which 'depersonalize' property (see Scott 1979). Even so, it remains the hegemonic force in contemporary economic and social relations.

Bourgeois cosmology defines the limits of permissible behaviour in modern leisure practice. The main contradiction in bourgeois cosmology is well known. As Lukács observes, 'the bourgeoisie endowed the individual with an unprecedented importance, but at the same time that individuality was annihilated by the economic conditions to which it was subjected' (1971: 62).[1] Bourgeois ideology defines man as an egoistic self who makes his way in the world by the strength of his own will and endeavour.[2] But the complex division of labour and stratification of power in capitalist society mean that the security and prosperity of each individual is ultimately interdependent with the security and prosperity of all. We have already described the errors involved in this situation several times: the individual is falsely represented as being outside, or opposed to, society; society is falsely represented as being above, or external to, the individual (see pp. 8, 95–7). This situation generates very important and unavoidable ambiguities and tensions in bourgeois consciousness. For example, the whole ideology of personal pleasure is at odds with the social organization and mediation of pleasure in capitalist society. Thus, the leisure industry bombards the individual with enticements to self-realization. Yet the paradox of self-realization is that it cannot be achieved alone.

At this point in the argument an obvious difficulty arises. Many people will be prepared to accept that bourgeois ideology is a major spur behind the processes of privatization, individuation, commercialization, and pacification in leisure practice. At the same time they may point out that team games and group leisure pursuits continue to thrive under advanced capitalism. The doctrine of individual rights and possessive individualism does not appear to suffice as an explanation for these forms of leisure practice. Here again, the heavy emphasis that figurational sociologists place on studying social relations processually is vindicated. Dunning (1967, 1971) has examined the rise of mass-entertainment sports such as rugby and soccer from their origins as undisciplined and rough folk games. He argues that discipline and regulation were introduced into these games largely by the industrial bourgeoisie. The main institutional mechanism in this process was the public schools where the game was codified and rule breaking was subjected to a systematic schedule of penalties. According to Dunning, team games were highly valued as 'an instrument of character training [imparting] such desirable traits as group loyalty, willingness to compete according to rules, co-operativeness, courage, leadership ability and the like' (1967: 885). The values that these games instil in individuals are therefore fully consistent with the achievement ideology of bourgeois society.

Leisure and Pleasure

A recurring theme of this book is that leisure relations should not be studied as relations of self-determination and freedom. Leisure relations are relations of permissible behaviour. What is considered legitimate and illegitimate in them is the socially produced effect of structural rules of pleasure and unpleasure. Earlier I argued that Freud and Weber each submitted that modern, rationally administered societies require a specific economy of pleasure. Their analysis does not deny the positive effects of this economy of pleasure in the development of industrial societies. For example, Freud explicitly states that industrial civilization has achieved relative affluence and security by accepting a portion of unhappiness in social life. Similarly, Weber, despite all his trenchant criticisms of rational administration, still concludes that it is the most superior form of rule known to humanity. Even so, both writers tend to give a higher profile to the repressive consequences of the economy of pleasure in social conduct.

Against this, I have tried to stress throughout the book that in the complex, highly individuated societies of the present day, these rules are the resources for regulation *and* innovation in leisure activity. The work of Foucault and Elias is particularly important in this regard. It may be the case, as Foucault suggests, that the original purpose and historical significance of this whole economy of pleasure were to facilitate the surveillance and control of large urban-industrial populations. It does not require a feat of imagination to understand that the proposition that pleasure can only be accumulated and developed through the self might act as a disincentive to an over-close, conscious identification of the individual with groups, mobs, and classes. It may also be the case, as Elias argues, that the new thresholds of restraint and affect controls associated with the civilizing process were an unintended corollary of the state monopoly over the legitimate use of physical force and the lengthening of inter-dependency chains. What is certain is that while 'the West has not been capable of inventing new pleasures, and it has doubtless not discovered any original vices . . . it has defined new rules for the game of power and pleasures' (Foucault 1981: 48).

It is therefore no cheap conclusion to remark that the sociology of leisure requires a sociology of pleasure. The rules of pleasure and unpleasure enable us to define leisure situations. For example, most of us can imagine that someone who has suffered needlessly at the hands of another might dream of exacting punishment on the aggressor in return. However, if this dream occupies every moment of time left over after essential labour, it is not described as leisure but neurosis. Normally the pleasure and life satisfaction that derive from such activity are not defined by society as legitimate leisure practice. Instead, they may be defined as a neurotic sickness, i.e. a condition which requires medical correction.

The example is not important; but the principle which it illus-trates is fundamental. Leisure experience is not an essence in human societies, but an effect of systems of legitimation. It must not be inferred from this statement that leisure practice is simply a dependent variable of received rules of legitimation. We all have the power to challenge and redefine the conditions and consciousness which define legitimate leisure behaviour. 'The Romantics', writes Sontag, 'invented invalidism as a pretext for leisure, and for diminishing bourgeois obligations in order to live only for one's art. It was a way of retreating from the world without having to take the responsibility for the decision' (1983: 37–8).[3] The ability to manipulate the rules of legitimate pleasure and unpleasure as resources for experiment and inno-vation is indeed a key attribute of selfhood. It is the main reason why people's experiences of leisure are certain to elude the limits of any theoretical classification system that we are capable of devising.

New Rules For The Sociology of Leisure

To live a life of leisure is to live a charmed existence. I have argued that the main sociological attempts to explain that charm can, for heuristic purposes, be polarized into two types.[4] On the one hand, there is the resolute bid to reduce composite relations of leisure to a finite sum of essences or particles. On the other, there is the bold attempt to penetrate beyond the apparent shapelessness of people's experience to hidden structures which explain the surface relations of everyday life. I have tried to show that each tendency is associated with fundamental errors in theory and research. The attempt to reduce leisure relations to their constituent parts produces the 'leisure without society' syndrome (see pp. 1–9). Equally, the attempt to impose logically consistent structures upon leisure practice seems to end in reification; everything that happens in society is explained as a consequence of the deep structures of social life.

The errors that we have explored here are deeply rooted in the main scientific establishments concerned with leisure. It is all too easy to conclude that sociology in general is fated to make the same mistakes for ever. I think that this view is reactionary and unduly pessimistic. There is no reason why sociologists should be doomed to neurotically repeat established defects in theory and research. What is required are new forms of theory which begin neither with the individual nor society, but rather with the multifaceted, dynamic relations that people have with each other. For, as Elias puts it, 'the manner of integration of component parts, in other words their functional interdependence, has an explanatory function' (1974a: 26). Elias's work on the science is important, because it shows that the problems of methodology and theory making that sociologists face are not new. Natural scientists also faced the task of explaining why events occur and how integration and development are produced, reproduced, and changed. To begin with, they too sought to explain physical relations in terms of immovable structures. In biology, palaeontologists and anatomists like Georges Cuvier and Richard Owen invoked theological pretexts for scientific knowledge and truth seeking. They were emotionally attached to an orientation to scientific study which placed the highest value upon discovering the eternal, ubiquitous laws and fixed principles of nature governing all plant and vertebrate forms. Richard Owen, for example, produced a theoretical blueprint of the vertebrate skeleton which he believed could be used as the universal model for all actual forms. We know, of course, that Darwin's theory of evolution, which regarded natural development as a *processual* phenomenon, eventually supplanted these 'lawlike' structure theories. But, as Elias points out, process theories only prevailed in the course of a power struggle which involved a rearrangement of scientific establishments and hierarchies (see Elias 1982b). Perhaps a similar rearrangement is required in the social sciences. At all events, there is already a palpable need in the sociology of leisure for approaches which avoid the snares of reification and the delusions of idealism.

From all that I have said in this book, it should be obvious that the attempt to solve the problems in leisure theory through the construction of 'alternative' systems and models is fundamentally misconceived. The most formidable problems are not defined by the inherent complexity of field data. On the contrary, they are the products of the prestigious and influential traditions in theory and research which place the utmost 'scientific' value upon the construction of exhaustive, fixed theories of leisure practice. My criticism of these traditions is by no means unqualified. I do indeed want to reject those aspects which I have identified as fallacious or misleading. At the same time, however, I want to retain the emphasis they place on the need for detailed, rigorous analysis in exploring leisure relations.

The most satisfactory way in which these objectives can be combined is by outlining some essential rules for the sociology of leisure. I shall list them in summary form, for this is the clearest way of expressing the points I want to make. The four rules which end this book are intended as a methodological contribution to theory and research. They also serve to bring together the shaping themes of my text.

(1) *Leisure activity is an adult phenomenon which is defined in opposition to the play world of children.*
The self is a construct of socialization: a datum of adulthood. The leisure relations of the self are structurally opposed to the selflessness of the child's play world. Selflessness is volatile and unpredictable. Where it occurs in adult leisure, it usually assumes a mimetic form which renders it amenable to discipline and control. However, these constraints bristle with contingencies: some of the most exciting and dangerous situations in adult leisure relations occur when social controls and disciplines break down.

(2) *Leisure practice is an accomplishment of skilled and knowledgeable actors.*[5]
One of the central errors of the conventional wisdom in the

sociology of leisure is the idea that socialization simply imprints values and beliefs regarding leisure behaviour on the individual self. Against this it is necessary to stress that the adult self is a skilled and knowledgeable actor who can manipulate social rules as resources for innovations and critical departures in leisure practice.

(3) *The structure and development of leisure relations is an effect of legitimating rules of pleasure and unpleasure.*

Leisure relations are not relations of freedom. On the contrary, they are relations of power whose dynamics and subjective meaning reflect the historically structured economy of pleasure in society. Pleasure is not an innate drive in the self. Rather, as is the case with the self, it is an aspect of social structures. Changes in its distribution and intensity can be examined historically. For example, it is possible to demonstrate that the rules of permissible conduct in the fifteenth century were qualitatively different from the rules that obtain in the present day. Furthermore, it is possible to be still more precise, and compare and contrast latitudes of pleasure and unpleasure for stratified classes and power factions in each period.

(4) *Leisure relations must be sociologically examined as dynamic, relatively open-ended processes.*

The use of an extended historical perspective reveals a number of trend-maintaining tendencies in the organization and dynamics of leisure practice. The key ones are privatization, individuation, commercialization, and pacification. I have argued that these tendencies combine to give modern leisure relations their distinctive form. They have projected the self, the individual body, to the forefront of leisure action and experience. At the same time, they must be studied as contingent processes which provide the basis for new initiatives and counter-developments. There is no reason to suppose that the enumerated tendencies are now so well established that the prospects for change in their individual structure or collective pattern of integration have been effectively arrested.

NOTES

Introduction: Leisure Without Society?

1 As an example of the first tendency, see Klapp (1969); Dumazedier (1974). For the second tendency, see Kaplan (1975) and Dower *et al.* (1981).
2 See, for example, Dower (1965); Dumazedier (1967); Kerr *et al.* (1973).
3 My general position here owes much to the work of Norbert Elias. See, in particular, Elias (1956), (1972), (1982b).
4 For example, in the UK the Leisure Studies Association was not formed until 1975. *Leisure Studies*, the journal of the LSA, did not commence publication until 1982.
5 See, for example, Roberts (1978), (1981); Parker (1983); Kaplan (1975); Neulinger (1981).
6 I have examined some of the distinctive features of capitalist organization elsewhere. See Rojek (1980), (1984).
7 For examples of 'structuration' theory, see Bourdieu (1977); Giddens (1976), (1979), (1981, especially pp. 26–9).
8 The key works are Freud (1939), (1961), (1979).

1 The Structural Characteristics of Modern Leisure Practice

1 *'Leisure* is defined by reference to the time left over after work and essential activities have been carried out; in addition to housework, shopping and basic child care, essential activities include sleeping, eating and personal hygiene. Leisure time is thus the free time people have available to allocate to all other pursuits, whether they be forms of entertainment, amusement and relaxation, or hobbies, voluntary or social activities and education. It includes the free time made available as a result of unemployment, though this

enforced leisure is naturally of a different quality to that now considered to be a normal part of everyday life.'

(Martin and Mason 1982: 18)

For a critique of the concept of 'enforced leisure', see pp. 134–35 of this book.

2 Vickerman (1980: 195) recognizes the importance of the informal economy in post-war changes in the organization of work–leisure time.

3 The term 'domestic capital goods' refers to labour-saving devices, e.g. dishwashers, washing machines, vacuum cleaners, food mixers, etc.

4 The ESRC/Sports Council Joint Panel Project (1984), entitled 'People's Own Conceptions of their Leisure', confirms this finding. See Stockdale (1984).

5 The information is given in Clayre (1974: 155). Rudé (1967) reports that there were 111 official holidays *per annum* recognized under the *ancien régime* in France.

6 Quoted in Bailey (1978: 180).

7 For details of the size and economic consequences of the bequests see Heers (1966); Lestocquoy (1952); Veyne (1976).

8 See in particular Alt (1976); Coalter (1980); Critcher (1982); Van Moorst (1982).

9 See the exchange between Critcher and Roberts, in Tomlinson (1981). For comments on the issues related to this debate see Parry (1983: 75–7).

10 Barrett and McIntosh (1982) single out the writings of Marx, Engels, Bebel, Lenin, Trotsky, Kollontai, and Zetkin.

11 Freud elaborates on his position thus: 'I have no concern with any economic criticisms of the communist systems; I cannot enquire into whether the abolition of private property is expedient or advantageous. But I am able to recognize that the psychological premisses on which the system is based are an *untenable illusion*' (emphasis mine) (1979: 50).

2 Leisure and Social Intervention: Marx and Durkheim

1 See Marx (1977(I): 496). Marx argued that the construction of communist society is bi-phasic, i.e. it occurs in two stages. The first stage, which is of unspecified duration, consists of the *dictatorship of the proletariat*. Under it the state assumes the directive role in constructing the social and economic conditions for fully developed communism. The second stage consists of *communism proper*. Under it, the socio-economic requirements of real communist relations have been met and the state 'withers away'. After this point, relations supporting the free and full development of individuals hold unimpeded sway.

2 See, for example, Althusser (1969); Godelier (1972).

3 'Pre-history' is Marx's term. History proper only begins with the commencement of communist relations.

4 Nuclear war would be one example of 'catastrophe'!
5 This is just as well. Engels's writing in this book teeters on the brink of bathos.
6 The formal subordination of labour is analysed by Braverman (1974); Brighton Labour Process Group (1977). The position is criticized by Friedman (1978); Littler and Salaman (1982); Rojek (1984).
7 The concept of the real subordination of labour is a heuristic device. Marx always argued that the organization of capitalism involved class contradictions.
8 For a Marxist analysis of the manipulation of monetary and fiscal policy in class exploitation, see Wright (1975); Jessop (1982).
9 It is necessary to emphasize that the class struggle is not a closed process. The working class may not accept the ideology of the dominant class that change is impossible or futile.
10 Harrington (1974) has recognized the importance of this insight.
11 One of the most imaginative attempts to extrapolate a systematic position from Marx's discussion of communism is made by Ollman (1979: 48–99). Ollman submits that there are six core characteristics of Marx's vision of social relations under communism: (a) the abolition of private property; (b) the allocation of resources by social need; (c) a self-regulating (automated) economy; (d) the abolition of divisions between families, communities, and nation states; (e) the end of alienated labour; (f) the collapse of the division between work and leisure.
12 This case has been powerfully made by Popper (1957), (1962).
13 Durkheim writes, 'the perfect spontaneity is never met with anywhere as a realized fact' (1933: 378).
14 The term 'total institution' was coined by Goffman (1961).
15 Dunning and Sheard (1979) are figurational sociologists. Dunning (1981: 3, 13–15) points out that there are important points of contact between Elias's theory of the civilizing process (notably the lengthening of interdependency chains) and Durkheim's discussion of the movement from 'mechanical' to 'organic' solidarity.
16 Dunning and Sheard (1979) claim that their analysis also confirms the main propositions of Elias's theory of the civilizing process.
17 See Giddens (1971); Lukes (1973, especially pp. 172–78); Garnsey (1981).

3 'Laissez-Faire' Leisure: Weber and Freud

1 See, for example, Marcuse (1965); Factor and Turner (1979); Turner (1981); Löwith (1982); Brubaker (1984).
2 Weber attributes these questions to Tolstoy; see Weber (1970: 152–53).
3 Discussed by Weber (1968). See especially the opening pages of Volume I.
4 Quoted by Thompson (1967: 90).
5 Weber's concept has obviously influenced the following works: Roberts (1978); Rapoport and Rapoport (1975); Glyptis (1981).

6 See, for example, Freud (1966), (1933).
7 The model is clearly outlined in his paper, 'The Ego and the Id', in Freud (1984: 339–407).
8 Freud seems to legitimate a pre-social basis for understanding social life. Compare this with Marx's theory of historical materialism.
9 See Freud (1984: 132). Freud follows this remark with the thought that the coupling 'is by no means so invariably complete and exclusive as we are inclined to assume'.
10 The key works are, Freud (1939), (1961), (1979).
11 Freud's position does not lend itself to straightforward summary. For example, later in *The Future of an Illusion* (1961: 12) he writes, 'It goes without saying that a civilization which leaves so large a number of its participants unsatisfied and drives them into revolt neither has, nor deserves the prospect of a lasting existence.'
12 In *Beyond the Pleasure Principle* (1984: 290–94), Freud discusses the relation between repetition compulsion and the pleasure principle.
13 Freud's theory was clearly a major influence on Elias's theory of the civilizing process. See pp. 161–69 of this book and Elias and Dunning (1969).

4 Social Formalism and Leisure

1 I have deliberately used Dumazedier's own words to give a flavour of his style. The word 'genus' is indicative of the tradition of social thought to which he is attached (positivist empiricism). For a discussion of the tradition and its influence in the sociology of leisure see Rojek (1983).
2 Griffin *et al.* (1982: 91) describe Stanley Parker's work as 'something of a backbone to the study of leisure in Britain'. The other leading formalist in the British sociology of leisure is Kenneth Roberts.
3 Parker (1983: 97–8) also mentions a third type: self-containment, which he identifies with a neutrality pattern of work and leisure.
4 Parker examined various occupational groups in the business and service sectors, e.g. banking, child-care, residential social work, youth employment, and manual work.
5 See Wilson (1980) for a critique of the survey method in social formalism.
6 Quoted by Parsons (1954: 222).
7 Parker's discussion is based upon the paper by Gross (1961).
8 For recent discussions of forms of resistance, see Mungham and Pearson (1976); Hall *et al.* (1978); Brake (1980).
9 Parker is entitled to complain that I am giving him a hard time in this book. This is not the first time I have subjected his work to criticism. My concentration on his work reflects both his eminence in the field and the clarity of his exposition.

5 Neo-Marxist Approaches to Leisure

1 For an analysis of social relations in state socialist societies, see Bahro (1978); Vajda (1981).

2 Anderson (1983: 21–3) suggests that in the last decade western Marxism has returned to classical themes in its new interest in the 'laws of motion of the capitalist mode of production as a whole'.

3 For a recent general discussion of the development gap, see Frank (1980).

4 See, for example, Skopcol (1977); Aronowitz (1981).

5 Other major figures associated with the Institute were Leo Lowenthal, Otto Kirscheimer, Erich Fromm, Carl Grunberg, Henryk Grossman, Bruno Bettelheim, Walter Benjamin, and Frederick Pollock. For comprehensive bibliographies of the publications of the Frankfurt Institute, see Arato and Gebhardt (1978: 530–41); Slater (1977); Held (1980: 483–95).

6 At the same time it would not be true to say that they are uncritical of the works of either Weber or Freud. For discussions of the Frankfurt School on these writers, see Held (1980: 64–6, 110–17); Jay (1984, especially pp. 102–04).

7 For example, Adorno (1975: 18) argues 'only their deep unconscious mistrust, the last residue of the difference between art and empirical reality in the spritual makeup of the masses explains why they have not, to a person, long since perceived and accepted the world as it is constructed for them by the culture industry.' See also his paper, 'Leisure' (1969: 655) where he observes, 'the integration of consciousness and leisure is obviously not yet successful. The real interests of individuals are still strong enough, at the margins, to resist total control' (quoted by Jay 1984: 128).

8 See especially, Jay (1973); Buck-Morss (1977); Held (1980).

9 Marcuse's later work endeavours to represent this contradiction and may therefore be exempted from this criticism.

10 This point is particularly well made by Turner (1981: 93–4). He specifically compares Marcuse's ideas with Parsons's, but his criticisms could be applied more widely: (a) Parsons and the Frankfurt School both argue that a common culture (ideology) integrates society; (b) socialization induces conformity in individuals; (c) concensus in society is achieved by ideological persuasion rather than physical force; (d) both stress that the institutionalization of conflict has diminished the possibility of open antagonism.

11 See, for example, Poulantzas (1973), (1978); Althusser (1969); Miliband (1983, especially pp. 26–63).

12 See Hindess and Hirst (1977); Thompson (1978); Mouffe (1979); Larrain (1979), especially pp. 79–83, 154–64, 167–70); Wolff (1981, especially pp. 80–3, 129–32).

13 For a discussion of the importance of the concept to the Centre's work, see Hall (1981, pp. 19–37).

14 Notably in connection with the rise of welfare capitalism and the alleged fragmentation of the working class.

15 Gorz (1982: 97) acknowledges a debt to Ivan Illich in the formation of his position on the 'autonomous sphere'. See Illich (1973).

16 See, for example, Beynon (1973); Hyman and Brough (1975); Gorz (1976); Salaman (1981).

6 Leisure, Signification, and Power: Barthes and Foucault

1 Foucault, quoted by Culler (1981: 33). I have used Culler's translation here rather than Alan Sheridan Smith's translation for Tavistock (*The Archaeology of Knowledge*, 1974). I shall use Sheridan Smith's translation in the rest of the book. But in this instance, Culler's translation fits in better with the meaning of 'decentring' that I want to draw out in this passage. Sheridan Smith's translation of the same passage reads: 'the laws of his desire, the form of his language, the rules of his action, or the games of his mythical or fabulous discourse' (1974: 13).
2 Other historians have grappled with the same problems. For a brilliant study of how *episteme* operated to suppress knowledge, see Yates (1964).
3 It is axiomatic to Barthes and Foucault that the reader participates in 'creating' the text by his or her personal reading and impression of it.
4 By the same token, their work is regarded as the major challenge to social formalism. See also the writings of Jacques Derrida, Jacques Lacan, and Julia Kristeva.
5 I do not claim any originality in making this point. See Eagleton (1983); Silverman and Torode (1980).
6 Barthes own celebrated example refers to the Negro soldier saluting the French flag (1957: 116–18).
7 Culler (1981: 41). Culler makes the remark with reference to Derrida's critique of 'logocentricism'. But it applies equally to Barthes's ideas in *S/Z*.
8 For a discussion of the concept, see the Translator's Note, in *Image-Music-Text* (Barthes 1977a: 10).
9 See, for example, Derrida (1973), (1977), (1978).
10 See, especially, Barthes (1975b), (1977b), (1978), (1981).
11 Foucault died in Paris on 25 June 1984 of septicaemia – a deadly form of blood poisoning. He had just published Volumes 2 and 3 of a projected six-volume study, *The History of Sexuality*. He was 57 years old.
12 There are also parallels here with the work of the Frankfurt School, especially Horkheimer, Adorno, and Marcuse.
13 Foucault investigates these matters in the following books respectively: (a) *Madness and Civilization* (1967); (b) *Discipline and Punish* (1977); (c) *The Birth of the Clinic* (1973); (d) *The History of Sexuality* (1981).
14 Foucault's discussion of synchronization bears a striking resemblance to F. W. Taylor's 'principles of scientific management'.

7 Leisure and Figurational Sociology

1 See Gleichmann, Goudsblom, and Korte (1977); Goudsblom (1977); Dunning (1967); Dunning and Sheard (1979); Mennell (1980); Swann (1981).

.

REFERENCES

Adorno, T. (1941) Veblen's Attack on Culture. *Studies in Philosophy and Social Sciences* 9: 389–413.
—— (1954) How to Look at Television. *The Quarterly of Film, Radio and Television* 8 (Spring): 213–35.
—— (1975 [1967]) Culture Industry Reconsidered. *New German Critique* 6 (Fall): 12–19.
—— (1978) Culture and Administration. *Telos* 37 (Fall) 97–111.
Adorno, T. and Horkheimer, M. (1979 [1944]) *Dialectic of Enlightenment* (trans. J. Cumming). London: Verso.
Alt, J. (1976) Beyond Class: The Decline of Industrial Labour and Leisure. *Telos* 28: 55–80.
Althusser, L. (1969) *For Marx.* Harmondsworth: Penguin.
—— (1971) *Lenin and Philosophy and Other Essays.* London: New Left Books.
—— (1976) *Essays in Self-Criticism.* London: New Left Books.
Althusser, L. and Balibar, E. (1970) *Reading Capital.* 2nd edn. London: New Left Books.
Alvater, E. and Kallscheuer, O. (1979) Socialist Politics and the 'Crisis of Marxism'. In R. Miliband and J. Savile (eds) *The Socialist Register 1979.* London: Merlin Press.
Anderson, P. (1976) *Considerations of Western Marxism.* London: New Left Books.
—— (1983) *In the Tracks of Historical Materialism.* London: Verso.
Arato, A. and Gebhardt, E. (eds) (1978) *The Essential Frankfurt School Reader.* Oxford: Basil Blackwell.
Ariès, P. (1962) *Centuries of Childhood.* London: Cape.
—— (1981 [1977]) *The Hour of Our Death* (trans. H. Weaver). London: Allen Lane.
Aron, R. (1962) On Leisure in Industrial Societies. In J. Brooks (ed.) *The One and the Many.* New York; Harper & Row.

Aronowitz, S. (1981) A Metatheoretical Critique of Immanuel Waller-stein's 'The Modern World System'. *Theory and Society* 10: 503–20.

Bacon, A. W. (1972) Leisure and Research: A Critical Review of the Main Concepts Employed in Contemporary Research. *Society and Leisure* 2: 83–92.

Bahro, R. (1978) *The Alternative in Eastern Europe*. London: Verso.

Bailey, P. (1978) *Leisure and Class in Victorian England*. London: Routledge & Kegan Paul.

Bakhtin, M. (1968) *Rabelais and His World* (trans. H. Iswolsky). Cambridge, Mass.: MIT Press.

Barrett, M. and McIntosh, M. (1982) *The Anti-Social Family*. London: Verso.

Barthes, R. (1967a [1953]) *Writing Degree Zero* (trans. A. Lavers and C. Smith). New York: Hill & Wang.

—— (1967b [1964]) *Elements of Semiology* (trans. A. Lavers and C. Smith). New York: Hill & Wang.

—— (1973 [1957]) *Mythologies* (trans. A. Lavers). St Albans: Paladin.

—— (1975a [1970]) *S/Z* (trans. R. Miller). London: Cape.

—— (1975b [1973]) *The Pleasure of the Text* (trans. R. Miller). New York: Hill & Wang.

—— (1977a) *Image-Music-Text* (essays selected and translated by S. Heath). Glasgow: Fontana.

—— (1977b [1975]) *Roland Barthes by Roland Barthes* (trans. R. Howard). London: Macmillan.

—— (1978 [1977]) *A Lover's Discourse*. New York: Hill & Wang.

—— (1979) *The Eiffel Tower and Other Mythologies* (trans. R. Howard). New York: Hill & Wang.

—— (1981 [1980]) *Camera Lucida: Reflections on Photography*. New York: Hill & Wang.

Bauman, Z. (1979) The Phenomenon of Norbert Elias. *Sociology* 13(1): 117–25.

Bellah, R. N. (1973) *Emile Durkheim on Morality and Society*. Chicago: Chicago University Press.

Bendix, R. (1966–67) Tradition and Modernity Reconsidered. *Comparative Studies in Society and History* 9: 292–346.

Benton, T. (1977) *Philosophical Foundations of the Three Sociologies*. London: Routledge & Kegan Paul.

Best, F. (1980) *Exchanging Earnings for Leisure*. Washington, DC: US Government Printing Office.

Beynon, H. (1973) *Working for Ford*. Harmondsworth: Penguin.

Bhaskar, R. (1979) *The Possibility of Naturalism*. Brighton: Harvester.

Bourdieu, P. (1977) *Outline of a Theory of Practice*. Cambridge: Cambridge University Press.

Bowles, S. and Gintis, H. (1976) *Schooling in Capitalist America*. New York: Basic Books.

Brake, M. (1980) *The Sociology of Youth Culture and Youth Subcultures*. London: Routledge & Kegan Paul.

Braverman, H. (1974) *Labor and Monopoly Capital*. New York: Monthly Review Press.

Brightbill, C. (1963) *The Challenge of Leisure*. Englewood Cliffs: Prentice Hall.

Brighton Labour Process Group (1977) The Capitalist Labour Process. *Capital and Class* 1: 3–42.

Brubaker, R. (1984) *The Limits of Rationality*. London: Allen & Unwin.

Buck-Morss, S. (1977) *The Origin of Negative Dialectics: Theodor W. Adorno, Walter Benjamin and the Frankfurt School*. Brighton: Harvester.

—— (1978) Review of 'The Civilizing Process'. *Telos* 37: 181–98.

Burch, W. R. (1971) Images of Future Leisure: Continuities in Changing Expectations. In W. Bell and J. A. Mau (eds) *The Sociology of the Future*. New York: Russell Sage.

Burgess, E. W. and Donald, J. B. (eds) (1964) *Contributions to Urban Sociology*. Chicago: University of Chicago Press.

Burns, T. (1973) Leisure in Industrial Society. In M. A. Smith, S. Parker, and C. Smith (eds) *Leisure and Society in Britain*. London: Allen Lane.

Callinicos, A. (1982) *Is There a Future for Marxism?* London: Macmillan.

Chambers, D. A. (1983) Symbolic Equipment and the Objects of Leisure Images. *Leisure Studies* 2: 301–15.

Champoux, J. E. (1978) Perceptions of Work and Non-Work. *Sociology of Work and Occupations* 5(4): 402–23.

Cheek, N. and Burch, W. R. (1976) *The Social Organization of Leisure in Human Society*. New York: Harper & Row.

Cheek, N., Field, D., and Burdge, R. (1976) *Leisure and Recreation Places*. Ann Arbor: Ann Arbor Science.

Clarke, J. (1976) Style. In S. Hall and T. Jefferson (eds) *Resistance through Rituals*. London: Hutchinson.

Clarke, J., Hall, S., Jefferson, T., and Roberts, B. (1976) Subcultures, Cultures and Class. In S. Hall and T. Jefferson (eds) *Resistance through Rituals*. London: Hutchinson.

Clayre, A. (1974) *Work and Play*. London: Weidenfeld & Nicolson.

Coalter, F. (1980) Leisure and Ideology: Notes toward a Context for the Study of the State and Leisure Policy. *Leisure Studies Association Quarterly* 2: 6–8.

Coalter, F. and Parry, N. C. A. (1982) *Leisure Sociology or the Sociology of Leisure?* London: North London Polytechnic.

Cohen, S. (1972) *Folk Devils and Moral Panics*. London: MacGibbon & Kee.

Collins, M. and Strelitz, Z. (1982) Families and Leisure. In R. N. Rapaport, M. P. Fogarty, and R. Rapaport (eds) *Families in Britain*. London: Routledge & Kegan Paul.

Connerton, P. (ed.) (1976) *Critical Sociology*. Harmondsworth: Penguin.

Critcher, C. (1982) The Politics of Leisure: Social Control and Social Development. In *Work and Leisure: The Implications of Technological Change*. Tourism and Recreation Research Unit Conference Proceedings, Edinburgh. TRRU 4: 45–53.

Culler, J. (1981) *The Pursuit of Signs*. London: Routledge & Kegan Paul.

Cunningham, H. (1980) *Leisure in The Industrial Revolution*. London: Croom Helm.

Derrida, J. (1973) *Speech and Phenomena*. Evanston: Northwestern University Press.

—— (1977) *Of Grammatology*. Baltimore: Johns Hopkins University Press.

—— (1978) *Writing and Difference*. London: Routledge & Kegan Paul.

Dews, P. (1979) The 'Nouvelle Philosophie' and Foucault. *Economy and Society* 8(2): 125–71.

Dower, M. (1965) *The Challenge of Leisure – The Fourth Wave*. London: Civil Trust.

Dower, M., Rapaport, R., Strelitz, Z., and Kew, S. (1981) *Leisure Provision and People's Needs*. London: HMSO.

Dumazedier, J. (1960) Current Problems of the Sociology of Leisure. *International Social Science Journal* 4: 522–31.

—— (1967) *Towards a Society of Leisure*. London: Collier Macmillan.

—— (1974) *The Sociology of Leisure* (trans. M. A. MacKenzie). Amsterdam: Elsevier.

Dunning, E. (1967) The Concept of Development: Two Illustrative Case Studies. In P. Rose (ed.) *The Study of Society*. New York: Random House.

—— (ed.) (1971) *The Sociology of Sport*. London: Frank Cass.

—— (1981) Social Bonding and the Socio-Genesis of Violence. In A. Tomlinson (ed.) *The Sociological Study of Sport: Configurational and Interpretive Studies*. Eastbourne: Brighton Polytechnic.

Dunning, E. and Sheard, K. (1979) *Barbarians, Gentlemen and Players*. Oxford: Martin Robertson.

Durkheim, E. (1933 [1902]) *The Division of Labour in Society* (trans. G. Simpson) (2nd edn). New York: Free Press.

—— (1952 [1897]) *Suicide: A Study in Sociology* (trans. J. A. Spaulding and G. Simpson). London: Routledge & Kegan Paul.

—— (1957 [1950]) *Professional Ethics and Civic Morals* (trans. C. Brookfield). London: Routledge & Kegan Paul.

—— (1959 [1928]) *Socialism and St Simon* (trans. C. A. Sattler). London: Routledge & Kegan Paul.

—— (1965 [1912]) *The Elementary Forms of Religious Life* (trans. J. W. Swain). New York: Free Press.

Eagleton, T. (1981) *Walter Benjamin, or Towards a Revolutionary Criticism*. London: New Left Books.

—— (1983) *Literary Theory*. Oxford: Basil Blackwell.

Elias, N. (1956) Problems of Involvement and Detachment. *British Journal of Sociology* 7: 226–52.

—— (1969) Sociology and Psychiatry. In S. H. Foulkes and G. Stewart-Price (eds) *Psychiatry in a Changing Society*. London: Tavistock.

—— (1971) Sociology of Knowledge: New Perspectives. *Sociology* 5.

—— (1972) Theory of Science and History of Science. *Economy and Society* 1: 117–33.

—— (1974a) The Sciences. Towards a Theory. In R. Whitley (ed.) *Social Processes of Scientific Development*. London: Routledge & Kegan Paul.

—— (1974b) Towards a Theory of Communities. In C. Bell and H. Newby (eds) *A Sociology of Community*. London: Frank Cass.

Elias, N. (1978a [1939]) *The Civilizing Process* vol. 1: *The History of Manners* (trans. E. Jephcott). Oxford: Basil Blackwell.

—— (1978b [1970]) *What Is Sociology?* (trans. S. Mennell and G. Morrissey). London: Hutchinson.

—— (1978c [1974]) Interview with Elias, conducted by Stanislas Fontaine (trans. A. Blok and R. Aya) *Theory and Society* 5: 243–53.

—— (1982a [1939]) *The Civilizing Process* vol. 2: *State Formation and Civilization* (trans. E. Jephcott). Oxford: Basil Blackwell.

—— (1982b) Scientific Establishments. In N. Elias, H. Martins, and R. Whitley (eds) *Scientific Establishments and Hierarchies*. Reidel: Dordrecht.

Elias, N. and Dunning, E. (1969) The Quest For Excitement in Leisure. *Society and Leisure* 2 (December): 50–85.

—— (1971) Dynamics of Sport Groups with Special Reference to Football. In E. Dunning (ed.) *The Sociology of Sport*. London: Cass.

Elias, N. and Scotson, J. (1965) *The Established and the Outsiders*. London: Frank Cass.

Engels, F. (1952 [1892]) *The Condition of the Working Class in England in 1844* (trans. F. Wischenewetzky). London: Allen & Unwin.

Factor, R. and Turner, S. (1979) The Limits of Reason and Some Limitations of Weber's Morality. *Human Studies* 2: 301–34.

Ferguson, H. (1983) *Essays in Experimental Psychology*. London: Macmillan.

Foucault, M. (1967 [1961]) *Madness and Civilization* (trans. R. Howard). London: Tavistock.

—— (1973 [1963]) *The Birth of the Clinic* (trans. A. Sheridan). London: Tavistock.

—— (1974 [1969]) *The Archaeology of Knowledge* (trans. A. Sheridan Smith). London: Tavistock.

—— 1977 [1975]) *Discipline and Punish* (trans. A. Sheridan Smith). Harmondsworth: Penguin.

—— (1980) *Power/Knowledge: Selected Interviews and Other Writings 1972–77* (ed. C. Gordon). Brighton: Harvester.

—— (1981 [1976]) *The History of Sexuality* vol. 1: *An Introduction* (trans. R. Hurley). Harmondsworth: Penguin.

—— (1982) The Subject and Power (trans. L. Sawyer). In H. C. Dreyfus and P. Rabinow *Michel Foucault: Beyond Structuralism and Hermeneutics*. Brighton: Harvester.

Frank, A. G. (1980) *Crisis in the World Economy*. London: Heinemann Educational Books.

Frankfurt Institute for Social Research (1973) *Aspects of Sociology* (trans. J. Viertel). London: Heinemann.

Freud, S. (1905) Three Essays on the Theory of Sexuality. In *The Standard Edition of the Complete Psychological Works of Sigmund Freud* vol. 7. London: Hogarth Press and the Institute of Psycho-analysis.

—— (1909) Analysis of a Phobia in a Five Year Old Boy. In Standard Works vol. 10. London: Hogarth Press and the Institute of Psycho-analysis.

—— (1933) *New Introductory Lectures on Psycho-Analysis*. In Standard Works vol. 22. London: Hogarth Press and the Institute of Psycho-analysis.

Freud, S. (1939) *Moses and Monotheism*. In Standard Works vol. 23. London: Hogarth Press and the Institute of Psycho-analysis.

—— (1961 [1927]) The Future of an Illusion (trans. J. Strachey). In Standard Works vol. 21. London: Hogarth Press and the Institute of Psycho-analysis.

—— (1966) *The Psychopathology of Everyday Life*. London: Ernest Benn.

—— (1976 [1900]) *The Interpretation of Dreams* (trans. J. Strachey). Harmondsworth: Penguin.

—— (1979) *Civilization and Its Discontents* (trans. J. Riviere). London: Hogarth Press.

—— (1984) *On Metapsychology: The Theory of Psychoanalysis* (including: The Instincts and Their Vicissitudes [1915], Beyond the Pleasure Principle [1920], The Ego and the Id [1923]) (compiled and ed. A. Richards). Harmondsworth: Penguin.

Friedman, A. (1978) *Worker Resistance and Marxian Analysis of the Capitalist Labour Process*. British Sociological Association conference paper, mimeo.

Friedmann, G. (1961) *The Anatomy of Work*. London: Heinemann.

Frith, S. (1983) *Sound Effects: Youth, Leisure and the Politics of Rock 'n' Roll*. London: Constable.

Gadamer, H. G. (1975) *Truth and Method*. London: Sheed & Ward.

Garnsey, E. (1981) The Rediscovery of the Division of Labour. *Theory and Society* 10: 325–36.

Geoghegan, V. (1981) *Reason and Eros: The Social Theory of Herbert Marcuse*. London: Pluto Press.

Geras, N. (1983) *Marx and Human Nature: Refutation of a Legend*. London: Verso.

Gershuny, J. (1978) *After Industrial Society? The Emerging Self-Service Economy*. London: Macmillan.

—— (1979) The Informal Economy: Its Role in Post-Industrial Society. *Futures* 11 (February): 3–15.

Giddens, A. (1971) The 'Individual' in the Writings of Emile Durkheim. *Archives européennes de sociologie* 12: 210–28.

—— (1976) *New Rules of Sociological Method*. London: Hutchinson.

—— (1977) Habermas's Social and Political Theory. *American Journal of Sociology* 83(1): 198–212.

—— (1979) *Central Problems in Social Theory*. London: Macmillan.

—— (1981) *A Contemporary Critique of Historical Materialism* vol. 1: *Power, Property and the State*. London: Macmillan.

Gleichmann, P., Goudsblom, J., and Korte, H. (eds) (1977) Human Figurations: Essays for Norbert Elias. Amsterdam: Amsterdams Sociologisch Tijdschrift.

Glyptis, S. (1981) Leisure Life-styles. *Regional Studies* 15(5): 311–26.

Godelier, M. (1972) Structure and Contradiction in *Capital*. In R. Blackburn (ed.) *Ideology in Social Science*. London: Fontana.

Goffman, E. (1961) *Asylums*. Harmondsworth: Penguin.

Goldthorpe, J. H. (1964) Social Stratification in Industrial Society. In

P. Halmos (ed.) The Development of Industrial Societies. *Sociological Review Monograph* 8: 97–122.

Gorz, A. (1965) Work and Consumption. In P. Anderson and R. Blackburn (eds) *Towards Socialism*. New York: Cornell University Press.

—— (ed.) (1976) *The Division of Labour*. Brighton: Harvester.

—— (1982 [1980]) *Farewell to the Working Class* (trans. M. Sonenscher). London: Pluto Press.

Goudsblom, J. (1977) *Sociology in the Balance*. Oxford: Basil Blackwell.

Gouldner, A. (1971) *The Coming Crisis of Western Sociology*. London: Heinemann.

Gramsci, A. (1971) *Selections from Prison Notebooks*. London: Lawrence & Wishart.

Griffin, S., Hobson, D., MacIntosh, S., and McCabe, T. (1982) Women and Leisure. In J. Hargreaves (ed.) *Sport, Culture and Ideology*. London: Routledge & Kegan Paul.

Gross, E. (1961) A Functional Approach to Leisure Analysis. *Social Problems* Summer: 2–8.

Guttman, A. (1978) *From Ritual to Record*. New York: Columbia University Press.

Habermas, J. (1971 [1968]) *Knowledge and Human Interests* (trans. J. Shapiro). London: Heinemann.

—— (1979 [1976]) *Communication and the Evolution of Society* (trans. T. McCarthy). London: Heinemann.

Hall, S. (1981) Cultural Studies: Two Paradigms. In T. Bennett, G. Martin, C. Mercer, and J. Woollacott (eds) *Culture, Ideology and Social Process*. London: Batsford, in association with the Open University Press.

Hall, S., Critcher, C., Jefferson, T., and Clarke, J. (1978) *Policing the Crisis – Mugging, the State and Law and Order*. London: Macmillan.

Hall, S. and Jefferson, T. (1976) (eds) *Resistance through Rituals*. London: Hutchinson.

Hargreaves, J. (1975) The Political Economy of Mass Sport. In S. Parker, M. Ventris, and J. Haworth (eds) *Sport and Leisure in Contemporary Society*. London: School of Environment, Polytechnic of Central London.

—— (1982) Sport, Culture and Ideology. In J. Hargreaves (ed.) *Sport, Culture and Ideology*. London: Routledge & Kegan Paul.

Harriman, A. (1982) *The Work/Leisure Trade Off*. New York: Praeger.

Harrington, M. (1974) Leisure as a Means of Production. In L. Kolakowski and S. Hampshire (eds) *The Socialist Idea: A Reappraisal*. London: Weidenfeld & Nicolson.

Hawkins, M. J. (1977) A Re-Examination of Durkheim's Theory of Human Nature. *Sociology* 25(2): 229–51.

Haworth, L. (1977) *Decadence and Objectivity*. Toronto: University of Toronto Press.

Hebdige, D. (1979) *Subculture: The Meaning of Style*. London: Methuen.

Heers, J. (1966) *L'Occident aux XIVe et XVe siècles*. Paris: Presses Universitaires de France.

Held, D. (1980) *Introduction to Critical Theory: Horkheimer to Habermas*. London: Hutchinson.

Hindess, B. and Hirst, P. Q. (1977) *Mode of Production and Social Formation*. London: Macmillan.

Hirst, P. and Woolley, P. (1982) *Social Relations and Human Attributes*. London: Tavistock.

Horkheimer, M. (1972) *Critical Theory: Selected Essays*. New York: Seabury Press.

—— (1973) The Authoritarian State. *Telos* 15 (3–20). (First published in 1940.)

Huizinga, J. (1955 [1924]) *The Waning of the Middle Ages* (trans. F. Hopman). Harmondsworth: Penguin.

Hyman, R. and Brough, I. (1975) *Social Values and Industrial Relations*. Oxford: Basil Blackwell.

Illich, I. (1973) *Tools for Conviviality*. London: Calder Boyars.

International Labour Office (1976) *Employment, Growth and Basic Needs: A One World Problem*. Geneva: International Labour Office.

Jay, M. (1973) *The Dialectical Imagination: A History of the Frankfurt School and the Institute of Social Research 1923–50*. London: Heinemann.

—— (1984) *Adorno*. Glasgow: Fontana.

Jessop, B. (1982) *The Capitalist State*. Oxford: Martin Robertson.

Johnson, R. (1981) Against Absolutism. In R. Samuel (ed.) *People's History and Socialist Theory*. London: Routledge & Kegan Paul.

Kaplan, M. (1975) *Leisure: Theory and Policy*. New York: Wiley.

Keat, R. (1981) *The Politics of Social Theory*. Oxford: Basil Blackwell.

Kellner, D. (1975) The Frankfurt School Revisited: A Critique of Martin Jay's 'The Dialectical Imagination'. *New German Critique* 5: 131–52.

Kelly, J. R. (1976) Leisure as Compensation for Work. *Society and Leisure* 8(3): 73–82.

—— (1978) A Revised Paradigm of Leisure Choices. *Leisure Sciences* 1: 345–63.

—— (1983) *Leisure Identities and Interactions*. London: Allen & Unwin.

Kerr, C., Dunlop, J. T., Harbison, F. H., and Myers, C. A. (1973) *Industrialism and Industrial Man* (2nd edn) Harmondsworth: Penguin in association with Heinemann Educational Books.

Klapp, O. E. (1969) *Collective Search for Identity*. New York: Holt, Rinehart & Winston.

Larrain, J. (1979) *The Concept of Ideology*. London: Hutchinson.

Lestocquoy, J. (1952) *Les Villes de Flandre et d'Italie*. Paris: Presses Universitaires de France.

Lévi-Strauss, C. (1962) La Pensée Sauvage. Paris: Plon.

Littler, C. R. and Salaman, G. (1982) Bravermania and Beyond: Recent Theories of the Labour Process. *Sociology* 16(2):: 251–69.

Löwith, K. (1982) *Max Weber and Karl Marx*. London: Allen & Unwin.

Lukács, G. (1971) *History and Class Consciousness*. London: Merlin Press.

Lukes, S. (1973) *Emile Durkheim: His Life and Work: A Historical and Critical Study*. Harmondsworth: Penguin.

Lynd, R. S. and Lynd, H. M. (1929) *Middletown: A Study in Contemporary American Culture*. New York: Harcourt Brace.

Lynd, R. S. and Lynd, H. M. (1937) *Middletown in Transition*. New York: Harcourt Brace.

MacIntyre, A. (1970) *Marcuse*. Glasgow: Fontana.

Malcolmson, R. (1973) *Popular Recreations in English Society 1700–1850*. Cambridge: Cambridge University Press.

Mannheim, K. (1951) *Freedom, Power and Democratic Planning*. London: Routledge & Kegan Paul.

Marcuse, H. (1955) *Eros and Civilization*. London: Abacus.

—— (1964a) *One Dimensional Man*. London: Abacus.

—— (1964b) *Soviet Marxism: A Critical Analysis*. Boston: Beacon Press.

—— (1965) Industrialization and Capitalism in the Work of Max Weber. *New Left Review* 30: 3–17.

—— (1978) *The Aesthetic Dimension*. London: Macmillan.

Marshall, G. (1982) *In Search of the Spirit of Capitalism: An Essay on Max Weber's Protestant Ethic Thesis*. London: Hutchinson.

Martin, B. and Mason, S. (1984) The Development of a Leisure Ethic: Some Practical Issues for the Future. Unpublished paper delivered at the Leisure Studies Association Conference, Sussex University, 1984.

Martin, W. H. and Mason, S. (1982) *Leisure and Work: Choices for 1991 and 2001*. Sudbury: Leisure Consultants Press.

Marx, K. (1973 [1857–58]) *Grundrisse* (trans. M. Nicolaus) New York: Random House.

—— (1976 [1859]) *Preface and Introduction to the Critique of Political Economy*. Peking: Foreign Languages Press.

—— (1977 [1867, 1878, 1894]) *Capital* vols. 1–3 (trans. S. Moore and E. Aveling, ed. F. Engels). London: Lawrence & Wishart.

Marx, K. and Engels, F. (1965 [1846]) *The German Ideology*. London: Lawrence & Wishart.

—— (1968) *Selected Works*. London: Lawrence & Wishart.

Meissner, M. (1971) The Long Arm of the Job: A Study of Work and Leisure. *Industrial Relations* 10: 239–60.

Mennell, S. (1980) *Sociological Theory: Uses and Unities* (2nd edn.). London: Nelson.

Mészáros, I. (1970) *Marx's Theory of Alienation*. London: Merlin Press.

Miliband, R. (1983) *Class Power and State Power*. London: Verso.

Mouffe, C. (ed.) (1979) *Gramsci and Marxist Theory*. London: Routledge & Kegan Paul.

Mungham, G. and Pearson, G. (1976) *Working Class Youth Culture*. London: Routledge & Kegan Paul.

Neulinger, J. (1981) *To Leisure: An Introduction*. Boston: Allyn & Bacon.

Oakley, A. (1974a) *The Sociology of Housework*. Oxford: Martin Robertson.

—— (1974b) *Housewife*. London: Allen Lane.

Ollman, B. (1979) *Social and Sexual Revolution*. London: Pluto Press.

Orthner, D. (1976) Patterns of Leisure and Marital Interaction. *Journal of Leisure Research* 8: 98–111.

Park, R. E. and Burgess, E. W. (1921) *Introduction to the Science of Sociology*. Chicago: University of Chicago Press.

Parker, S. (1981) Choice, Flexibility, Spontaneity and Self-Determination in Leisure. *Social Forces* 60(2): 323–31.
—— (1983) *Leisure and Work*. London: Allen & Unwin.
Parry, N. C. A. (1983) Sociological Contributions to the Study of Leisure. *Leisure Studies* 2(1): 57–81.
Parry, N. C. A. and Coalter, F. (1982) Sociology and Leisure: A Question of Root and Branch. *Sociology* 16(2): 220–31.
Parsons, T. (1954) *Essays in Sociological Theory*. New York: Free Press.
Pearson, G. (1983) *Hooligan: A History of Respectable Fears*. London: Macmillan.
Poggi, G. (1983) *Calvinism and the Capitalist Spirit: Max Weber's 'Protestant Ethic'*. London: Macmillan.
Popper, K. R. (1957) *The Poverty of Historicism*. London: Routledge & Kegan Paul.
—— (1962) *The Open Society and its Enemies*, vol. 2. London: Routledge & Kegan Paul.
Poulantzas, N. (1973) *Political Power and Social Classes*. London: New Left Books.
—— (1978) *State, Power, Socialism*. London: New Left Books.
Presvelou, C. (1971) Impact of Differential Leisure Activities in Intra-spousal Dynamics. *Human Relations* 24: 565–74.
Rapaport, R. and Rapaport, R. N. (1975) *Leisure and the Family Life Cycle*. London: Routledge & Kegan Paul.
Rattansi, A. (1982) *Marx and the Division of Labour*. London: Macmillan.
Riesman, D. (1954) *Individualism Reconsidered*. Glencoe. Free Press.
Rigauer, B. (1981) *Sport and Work* (trans. A. Guttman) New York: Columbia University Press.
Roberts, K. (1978) *Contemporary Society and the Growth of Leisure*. London: Longman.
—— (1981) *Leisure* (2nd edn.) London: Longman.
Rojek, C. (1980) Three Heresies against Modern Convergence Theory. In D. Dunkerley and G. Salaman (eds) *The International Yearbook of Organization Studies 1980*. London: Routledge & Kegan Paul.
—— (1983) Emancipation and Demoralization: Contrasting Approaches in the Sociology of Leisure. *Leisure Studies* 2(1): 83–96.
—— (1984) The Limits of 'The New Industrial Relations'. *Industrial Relations Journal* 15(2): 66–71.
Rudé, G. (1967) *The Crowd in the French Revolution*. Oxford: Oxford University Press.
Salaman, G. (1981) *Class and the Corporation*. Glasgow: Fontana.
Samuel, R., Hall, S., Johnson, R., and Thompson, E. P. (1981) Culturalism: Debates around *The Poverty of Theory*. In R. Samuel (ed.) *People's History and Socialist Theory*. London: Routledge & Kegan Paul.
Scott, J. (1979) *Corporations, Classes and Capitalism*. London: Hutchinson.
Sheridan, A. (1980) *Michel Foucault: The Will To Truth*. London: Tavistock.
Silverman, D. and Torode, B. (1980) *The Material Word*. London: Routledge & Kegan Paul.

Skopcol, T. (1977) Wallerstein's World Capitalist System: A Theoretical and Historical Critique. *American Journal of Sociology* 82(5): 1,075–090.

Slater, P. (1977) *Origin and Significance of the Frankfurt School: A Marxist Perspective.* London: Routledge & Kegan Paul.

Smart, B. (1983) *Foucault, Marxism and Critique.* London: Routledge & Kegan Paul.

Smith, D. (1984) Norbert Elias – Established or Outsider? *Sociological Review* 32(2): 367–89.

Smith, J. A. (1981) The Protestant Ethic Controversy. Unpublished PhD thesis, University of Cambridge.

Sontag, S. (1983) *Illness as Metaphor.* Harmondsworth: Penguin.

Staines, G. L. (1980) Spillover versus Compensation: A Review of the Literature on the Relationship between Work and Non-Work. *Human Relations* 33(2): 111–29.

Stedman Jones, G. (1971) The Marxism of the Early Lukacs: An Evaluation. *New Left Review* 70: 27–64.

—— (1977) Class Expression versus Social Control? A Critique of Recent Trends in the Social History of Leisure. *History Workshop Journal* 4 (August): 162–70.

Stockdale, J. (1984) Project Report, Leisure Studies Association Conference, Sussex University (unpublished).

Swann, A. de (1981) The Politics of Agoraphobia: On Changes in Emotional and Relational Management. *Theory and Society* 10: 337–58.

Thompson, E. P. (1967) Time, Work-Discipline and Industrial Capitalism. *Past and Present* 38: 56–97.

—— (1978) *The Poverty of Theory.* London: Merlin Press.

Thompson, G. (1983) Carnival and the Calculable. In *Formations of Pleasure.* London: Routledge & Kegan Paul.

Tomlinson, A. (ed.) (1981) *Leisure and Social Control.* Eastbourne: Brighton Polytechnic.

—— (ed.) (1981) *The Sociological Study of Sport.* Eastbourne: Brighton Polytechnic.

Turner, B. (1981) *For Weber.* London: Routledge & Kegan Paul.

—— (1983) *Religion and Social Theory.* London: Heinemann.

Vajda, M. (1981) *The State and Socialism.* London: Allison and Busby.

Van Moorst, H. (1982) Leisure and Social Theory. *Leisure Studies* 2: 157–69.

Veblen, T. (1925) *The Theory of the Leisure Class.* London: Allen & Unwin.

Veyne, P. (1976) *Le Pain et le cirque.* Paris: Seuil.

Vickerman, R. W. (1980) The New Leisure Society – An Economic Analysis. *Futures* 10(3): 191–200.

Wallerstein, I. (1982) Crisis as Transition. In S. Amin, A. Arrighi, A. G. Frank, and I. Wallerstein *Dynamics of Global Crisis.* London: Macmillan.

Walton, J. K. and Walvin, J. (1983) (eds) *Leisure in Britain 1780–1939.* Manchester: Manchester University Press.

Weber, Marianne (1975) *Max Weber: A Biography.* New York: Wiley.

Weber, Max (1968) *Economy and Society,* 3 vols. New York: Bedminster Press.

Weber, Max (1970) *From Max Weber* (trans. and ed. H. H. Gerth and C. Wright Mills). London: Routledge & Kegan Paul.
—— (1976) *The Protestant Ethic and the Spirit of Capitalism* (trans. T. Parsons). London: Allen & Unwin.
—— (1978) *Max Weber: Selections in Translation* (ed. W. G. Runciman and trans. D. Hytch). Cambridge: Cambridge University Press.
Wilensky, H. L. (1960) Work, Careers and Social Integration. *International Social Science Journal* 4: 543–60.
Williams, R. (1961) *Culture and Society*. Harmondsworth: Penguin.
—— (1981) *Culture*. London: Fontana.
Williams, J., Dunning, E., and Murphy, P. (1984) *Hooligans Abroad: The Behaviour and Control of English Fans in Continental Europe*. London: Routledge & Kegan Paul.
Willis, P. (1978) *Profane Culture*. London: Routledge & Kegan Paul.
Wilson, J. (1980) Sociology of Leisure. *Annual Review of Sociology* 6: 21–40.
Wolff, J. (1981) *The Social Production of Art*. London: Macmillan.
Wright, E. O. (1975) Alternative Perspectives in Marxist Theory of Accumulation of Crisis. *Insurgent Sociologist* 6(1): 5–39.
Wutnhow, R., Davison, J., Hunter, A. B., and Kurzwell, E. (1984) *Cultural Analysis*. London: Routledge & Kegan Paul.
Yates, F. (1964) *Giordano Bruno and the Hermetic Tradition*. London: Routledge & Kegan Paul.
Young, J. (1983) Striking Back against the Empire. *Critical Social Policy* 2(3): 130–40.
Young, M. and Willmott, P. (1973) *The Symmetrical Family*. London: Routledge & Kegan Paul.

NAME INDEX

SUBJECT INDEX